From

Mobtown

to

Charm City

From Mobtown to Charm City

New Perspectives on Baltimore's Past

Edited by

Jessica I. Elfenbein

John R. Breihan

Thomas L. Hollowak

BALTIMORE

MARYLAND HISTORICAL SOCIETY

Library of Congress Cataloging-in-Publication Data

From Mobtown to Charm City : new perspectives on Baltimore's past /
edited by Jessica I. Elfenbein, John R. Breihan, Thomas L. Hollowak.
    p. cm.
    Includes papers from two conferences held in Baltimore; the first,
Making Diversity Work: 250 Years of Baltimore History was held in
1996 and the second, People and Places in Time: Baltimore's
Changing Landscapes was held in 1999.
    Includes index.
    ISBN 0-938420-85-2 (alk. paper)
    1. Baltimore (Md.)—History—Congresses. 2. Baltimore (Md.)—
Social conditions—Congresses. I. Elfenbein, Jessica I. II. Breihan, John
R. III. Hollowak, Thomas L. IV. Maryland Historica Society.

F189.B157 F76 2002
975.2'6—dc21

                                                    2002070155

Contents

Preface

Participants in two public history conferences in 1996 and 1999 wrote the articles included in this anthology. The first conference, "Making Diversity Work: 250 Years of Baltimore History," was organized by the University of Baltimore and co-hosted by Coppin State College. Other sponsors included the Maryland Historical Society, the B&O Railroad Museum, the Baltimore Museum of Industry, Enoch Pratt Free Library, the Johns Hopkins University Press, and the Baltimore City Life Museums. The second, "People and Places in Time: Baltimore's Changing Landscapes," was organized by a committee that included the University of Baltimore, Baltimore Heritage, Inc., the Baltimore History Alliance, and Baltimore City's Commission for Historical and Architectural Preservation. Much of what was presented at those conferences is new and exciting scholarship that will surely shape future interpretations of Baltimore's past.

The articles in this anthology are arranged chronologically but easily could have been clustered thematically. Joe Arnold's Introduction is an overview of Baltimore's history centered on the important decisions made by Baltimore's governing elites. Other articles demonstrate that much of the current work on the city's history has more to do with lesser-known working-class or anonymous citizens and their collective actions. Mary Ellen Hayward examines the alley houses that were their traditional homes. Garrett Power discusses how neighborhoods came to be described as "slums" during the late nineteenth century. Deb Weiner explores the public housing projects of the mid-twentieth century that were meant to "clear" those very slums.

Another focus is civic engagement. Amy Greenberg describes how working-class and middle-class Baltimoreans worked together in volunteer fire companies. Besides protecting the alley houses and other structures of the town, the volunteer firemen staged elaborate public events, established neighborhoods, and even founded libraries. Frank Towers explains how Know-Nothings and reformers organized themselves in the era just before the Civil War. Jessica Elfenbein describes the challenge of organizing and fundraising among some of the poorest Baltimoreans in the effort to establish a black YMCA at the turn of the twentieth century. Ken Durr investigates late twentieth-century white working-class politics in his history of the South East Community Organization (SECO).

Race is perhaps the most common theme of recent historical work on Baltimore. African Americans' residence in alley houses, establishment of the Druid Hill Avenue YMCA, and the dominance of public housing projects are described here. Richard Fuke looks at white Baltimore's reactions to newly enfranchised black fellow citizens after the Civil War. Jack Breihan describes the influx of black workers into Baltimore during World War II. Race clearly plays a central role in Ed Berkowitz's exploration of the desegregation of Baltimore City's public schools.

Gender is another organizing theme of many of the works in this anthology. Amy Greenberg describes how male gender roles were mirrored among firemen. Seth Rockman reveals the unexpected appearance of female political activism in a nineteenth-century murder case. Jack Breihan discusses the distinctive record of African American women war workers.

Finally, the themes of our title recur again and again. The brutal murder of a postal employee by Morris Hull and Peregrine Hutton in 1820, the famous Baltimore riots that preceded (and to a certain degree began) the Civil War, the civil violence that threatened blacks long after that war, the more insipid brutality of racism in community organizations and housing and schools all combine to form an image of "Mobtown." Jack Breihan describes the threat of a race riot in 1943; Deb Weiner discusses the results of the actual riot of April 1968.

But the "Charm City" of the William Donald Schaefer era is here, too. Ken Durr describes its heyday in the 1970s, when Baltimoreans stopped a marauding superhighway and began to preserve their rich architectural heritage, including some (but by no means all) of the distinctive rowhouses studied by Mary Ellen Hayward. Does the sponsorship of this historic "charm" constitute another of the series of bold steps that Arnold asserts saved Baltimore from further decline? We look forward to papers at future Baltimore History Conferences to answer this question.

Jessica I. Elfenbein
John R. Breihan
Thomas L. Hollowak
Baltimore, May 30, 2002

From
Mobtown
to
Charm City

JOSEPH ARNOLD

Thinking Big About a Big City — Baltimore, 1729–1999

FOR THE PAST SEVERAL YEARS I have been engaged in writing a general history of Baltimore, and my purpose is to share some of my thoughts on the structure and underlying assumptions of the history I have written. This is, I realize, somewhat presumptuous of me. It is a bit like an artist telling you about a beautiful painting he is just now finishing but not actually showing you the painting itself. In thinking about the fundamental structure of such a history, and the approach I would take, I had to ask myself a number of questions.

Three of these questions seem to me to be of particular importance. What is my fundamental goal in writing this history? Second, how much attention should I give to the economic, political, social, and cultural aspects of the city's life over the past 270 years, and how should all this be related to the continuing transformation of its physical plant? Third, what is the scope of my history, or put another way, what is my working definition of that thing we call Baltimore?

First, what is my fundamental goal? It is to write an objective, analytical narrative of the city that will explain, as fully and as accurately as my talents will allow, the development of Baltimore as a society and a physical plant with a particular focus on how it came to be the sort of place it is today.

Joseph L. Arnold, Professor of History at the University of Maryland Baltimore County, is the author of *The New Deal in the Suburbs: A History of the Greenbelt Town Program; Maryland: Old Line to New Prosperity;* and *The Baltimore Corps of Engineers and the Chesapeake Bay, 1961–1987.* He has also written a number of articles dealing with the history of Baltimore and is currently working on a comprehensive history of Baltimore City from the eighteenth century to the present.

This is, I know, a bifurcated goal that seems to run out in two different directions. Can one write an objective history that is also overtly present-minded?

I had no real choice because my professional training as a historian, and perhaps also my basic temperament, is quite detached and "otherworldly," but another side of me is very much of this world. I cannot write a history of Baltimore without using such a work to provide the current generation of Baltimoreans and Marylanders the small benefit of my insights into what seems to me to be a remarkable paradox. How did a city that was Maryland's greatest engine of prosperity and progress from the 1760s to the 1950s turn into its greatest failure by the 1990s? In the face of what seems to have been the city's steady progress for two hundred years and then its dramatic decline during the past half-century there is a strong temptation to view this change as the inevitable outcome of deep-seated historical forces. This is a question of historical inevitability that each individual must decide for himself. Was Baltimore destined to travel the road that has led it to the present crisis? I think that to some degree it was, but only to a degree. The city's rise from the 1760s to 1819 was closely related to the fact that it was able to exploit a new and, as it turned out, uniquely rich agricultural hinterland that could produce unheard of amounts of wheat at a time when the demand for wheat and flour in Europe and the West Indies skyrocketed. The falling streams around the city made it a fabulous center for milling flour. Baltimore was of course established as a tobacco landing, not a milling center for wheat, so it was purely by accident that the little village was suddenly transformed into a large city and, by 1800, into the greatest exporter of wheat and flour in the world. For a time it became the fastest growing city in America. Some thought it might surpass Philadelphia and emerge as the nation's second city after New York.

Baltimore's failure to fulfill the promise of this golden age in the decades after 1819 was again due to vast economic, political and geographic changes far beyond its control. However, even though it ended up as the fourth city among the great Atlantic ports (behind New York, Philadelphia and Boston), it remained an important player in the national economy, altogether one of America's biggest cities until the middle years of the twentieth century. That success, I think, was not pre-destined. The city remained a major player by taking bold steps of its own that saved it from a decline that could have been almost as rapid as its rise. There was no inevitability about the decision to build, and complete, the B&O Railroad or to develop its strong economic ties up and down the Atlantic coast. This was done by individuals and groups who possessed the power, wisdom, and courage to invest in untried technologies and to develop new markets that allowed Baltimore to remain a major East Coast city in the face of the tremendous advantages that Philadelphia, New York and Boston all possessed by the 1840s and 1850s.

Once the international wheat and flour trade shifted away from Baltimore, and the industrial revolution gathered momentum, its position as a southern bordered city weakened it. The Northeast and Great Lakes regions became the nation's economic heartland, the lines between New York and Chicago its central axis. Unfortunately, Baltimore stood at the far southeastern periphery of this dynamic region. Yet even with this disadvantaged location, Baltimoreans did remarkably well with the hand they were dealt. For many decades they struggled to become an industrial city as well as a commercial center, only hitting their stride in the 1920s and again in the brief era from 1940 to the 1970s. That gave the city a major boost but not enough to put it into the big league of American business centers. Baltimore had too many branch plants and not enough large, home-grown industries. Of equal importance to the city's growth and prosperity was its ability to capture its suburban hinterland through hard-fought annexation battles in 1888 and again in 1918.

Then something happened. Not only did the city fail to find a new economic base to replace the dramatic loss of its heavy industry in the post-1970 era, it virtually gave away without a fight its option to annex the new post–World War II suburbs. Neither of these failures seem to me to have been inevitable. They occurred because the city's leaders, and to some degree its citizenry, either failed to grasp the magnitude of the changes occurring around them or were unwilling to take the bold steps necessary to meet new challenges such as the founders of the B&O had done 130 years earlier. To be sure, the world of 1970 was certainly more complex than the world of 1830, but one could have expected the city's leaders to be individuals of at least equal vision and determination. It now seems clear that they were not. A small number of people, perhaps the core group that led the Greater Baltimore Committee during its early years, were undoubtedly men of real vision and concern, but too many others acted conservatively, timidly, even uncaringly. It appears that many just lost faith in the future of the city or their ability to change its course. Unquestionably, post–World War II Baltimore was far more fragmented and constrained by outside forces than it had been in the nineteenth century; but regardless of whether it was more the leaders or "the changing times," the net result was a dramatic decline from which Baltimore has not yet recovered.

I have already tipped my hand to the way I will answer my second basic question, how much attention should one give to the various aspects of the city's life? Compared to Sherry Olson's book, *Baltimore: The Building of an American City*, I have given more attention to the economy, politics, and social life and relatively less to its development as a physical plant. The paramount aspects in my history are economic, social, and (in the larger sense of the term) political. This is based on my supposition that all American cities have been, first and foremost, arenas of economic activity and are therefore incomprehensible without some knowledge of their economic functions, especially those aspects that lead to job growth and increased wealth for all classes of residents. Likewise, the central question in the social and political sections of my work is how well the city has provided for the economic advancement, security, health, comfort, convenience, and education of its residents—responsibilities that from the 1840s onward fell increasingly to municipal government and large-scale private institutions.

The social aspect of my history—the story of Baltimore's residents—from rich to poor and all across the ethnic and racial spectrum, is an essential part of my narrative, and I have tried to cover the subject as best I can, but I will no doubt disappoint many readers by not mentioning this or that group in this or that era. While Baltimore does not have the broad range of ethnic groups that came to the cities of the North and Middle West, it is still a daunting task. My compromise has been to concentrate on just a few groups whose influence and/or numbers caused them to loom large on the urban landscape. Like most southern cities, the largest single group of in-migrants were native-born whites from the mid-Atlantic region. They constitute a shadowy and confusing target for analysis, since they come from both sides of the Mason-Dixon Line and thus bring a remarkably broad range of attitudes, behaviors, and skills with them. Among the various foreign ethnic groups that have come to the city, the Scots-Irish, the Germans (both Christian and Jewish), and the Polish-Russian Jews receive the lion's share of my attention since their respective contributions to the city have been quite out of proportion to their numbers.

The German immigrants were especially important to Baltimore between 1850 and 1920, decades when the city really struggled to maintain its role as a big-league player in the national economy. The large German migration into Baltimore constitutes one of those bits of good fortune onto which cities sometimes stumble. Germany's desire for Maryland tobacco stimulated a lively trade between Baltimore and Bremen, and as result thousands of Germans took advantage of the return voyage to emigrate to the Chesapeake metropolis. Once settled, they achieved remarkable success, enriching themselves as well as their adopted city. German manufacturers, department store owners, and skilled craftsmen gave Baltimore the edge that it needed to sustain its position as the South's leading manufacturing and commercial center. Unfortunately, with the notable exception of the unusually large Polish-Russian Jewish immigration to Baltimore (another happy spin-off of the Baltimore-Bremen connection), the so-called Second Migration of 1890–1920 did not bring many Europeans to Baltimore. In 1920 the city had a smaller percentage of foreign-born than any major city of the Northeast or Midwest, and its economy and culture suffered accordingly. The one bright spot was the unusually large Polish-Russian in-migration. This group, that seemed at first to be too poor and too "foreign," of course turned out to be the most dynamic and successful group of immigrants ever to set foot in the city. Without them and the German Jewish immigrants who arrived before them, Baltimore would be a far less wealthy and cultured city than it became in the twentieth century.

One other group I need mention are the city's Irish Catholics. I think this group has been an important element in the city for a very long time, but relatively little is known about them. Even the recent fine history of the Baltimore Archdiocese contains relatively little about this large and historic community. There are good histories of the local German and Jewish communities, but the Irish seem more reluctant to look back and chronicle their role in the city. Now that Baltimore has elected an Irish-American mayor, perhaps more light will be shed on this interesting and influential group of people.

The other major theme in the social part of my history is of course the evolution of Baltimore's African American community (or communities). The "race issue" has obviously been a fundamental factor throughout the city's history, although the city's black residents remained a relatively small minority until the post–World War II era. Baltimore's black population peaked at 23 percent in the 1820s, a number it did not exceed until the 1940s. This subject is so charged with strong feelings and so much given to such a wide range of mutual misunderstandings that no one in our time can discuss it without incurring criticism. Again, one must make his or her own decision on the race issue in Baltimore's past.

In telling this part of Baltimore's story, I come down clearly on the side of racial integration as the ultimate solution to the age-old "race question." Obviously I regard the entire era of white supremacy and racial segregation as harmful and wrong (hardly a startling view these days), but I also see the post-segregation era of black and white separatism as misguided and tragic. In a metropolitan region where African Americans comprise more than one-third of the population, I find the continuation of racial separatism personally very discouraging and in the long run dangerous. For this reason, my discussion of the growth of Baltimore's black institutions, and the development of a strong, independent and separate African American community, is presented with mixed feelings. The growth of African American institutions in Baltimore over the past two centuries is a triumph of initiative in the face of a demeaning and debilitating world of white supremacy, but at the same time I see the continuation of a separate city-within-a-city, really a society-within-a-society, as a great tragedy and a dangerous trend. Some day, perhaps, the nightmare will end, and Baltimoreans will no longer need to identify one another as black or white. That would finally bring to an end the grimmest chapter in the city's history.

Let me return to the political aspect of my story. I have attempted to give as much attention to political and administrative history as space will allow because, as I indicated above, I think it is of great importance and also because Sherry Olson's history of Baltimore, so admirable in many ways, does little with this subject. The history of the city's municipal government is often a tale of petty politics and small-scale corruption, but occasionally the city's middle and upper classes pushed the machine politicians aside for a time and tried to create a better urban environment for themselves and, to some degree at least, for the rest of the city's residents. Since these were the classes of people who have always possessed the power to create or destroy any urban community, they must be the central focus for those trying to explain the evolution of our cities and towns.

As is well-known, the city government did relatively little prior to the 1840s. Nearly everyone, rich and poor, was compelled to live close to the city center, and even the wealthy did not expect much in the way of public facilities or services. The rising expectations of the propertied classes during the 1850s did result in a number of substantial urban improvements during that decade, but progress was slow and uneven. The real drama began after the Civil War with the development of horse cars in the 1870s, the electric trolley in the 1890s, and finally motor vehicles in the years after 1910. These technological innovations, along with a host of others, finally began to make suburban life feasible for middle-income families. As increasing numbers of those families moved to areas outside the city boundaries, municipal leaders were compelled either to recapture them through annexation or hold them within the city by improving the quality and security of urban life.

Wrapped up in all of this is the issue of the lower-income classes, their increasing concentration in the older sections of the central city, and the increasing uneasiness that the middle and upper classes felt living near them. In the view of the more affluent, the working classes and the inner-city areas in which they had become concentrated were too noisy, dirty, unhealthy, immoral, and disorderly. In fact, the working classes of 1890–1930 were probably a good deal more orderly and healthy than they had been during the antebellum years, but once the quieter, safer, bucolic suburban alternative opened up beyond the city line, those who could afford the suburban alternative became increasingly critical of the shortcomings of the urban environment.

Between the 1890s and the 1920s Baltimore's political and economic leaders made major efforts to improve the city as a physical plant, encourage the growth of the local economy, and do at least something for the lower-income groups through expanded educational opportunities, public health, and social services. Unfortunately, these latter efforts on behalf of the city's most needy residents remained far too small. As the city expanded outward, with new middle- and upper-income housing rising on the periphery, the central city slums also grew outward. The slums grew because the city's employers did not pay a living wage to their least skilled workers, and neither the municipality nor private social service agencies stepped in to resolve the problem. Baltimore's reformers could not compel employers to hire all those who needed a regular job nor pay a living wage to those they did hire. The city's welfare and social service agencies did what they could to help the poor with their slender financial resources and limited staffs of social workers. Likewise, the criminal justice system attempted, again with limited resources, to deal with the increasing numbers of youthful and adult offenders. Some progress was made, but thousands remained in deep poverty or became troublesome subjects for the police and courts. As these poor, disorganized, and troublesome people expanded out from the old nineteenth-century alleys and courts into former middle-class neighborhoods, the suburban movement gathered momentum. The municipal government was at a loss over how to stop the trend. Seeing the problem essentially as a racial issue (poor black people "invading" middle-income white neighborhoods), the nearly all-white city council tried to prohibit black families from moving into all-white blocks. Aside from its gross unfairness, the legislation was nearly useless because the major "invasions" of 1910–1940 consisted of poor whites moving into middle-income areas. Only with the massive black migration of 1940–1980 did the majority of Baltimore's poor residents come to consist primarily of African Americans. However, when the racial housing covenants (that had replaced the segregation ordinances as the chief means of keeping blacks out of white neighborhoods) were struck down by the Supreme Court in 1948 and Baltimore's racially segregated school system was integrated six years later, the number of poor black people coming into the city had begun to grow at a very high rate. And truly vast white flight out of the city finally began. Initially, this white flight had at least one positive effect: it opened wonderful new housing opportunities for black residents, giving them good, solid houses in fine neighborhoods at bargain prices.

Unfortunately, Baltimore's white residents possessed the great majority of disposable income, and as they left the city they pulled with them the stores, shops, and other facilities that neighborhoods rely upon to remain convenient and attractive. The racial transition might have worked out better if white exodus had not been so swift and massive, but that is something over which no one had any control. The years from 1945 to 1980 saw the final great migration of rural black people from Virginia and the Carolinas into Baltimore, leading to the creation of an underclass of uneducated, untrained, and often bewildered people that overwhelmed the slender resources of the existing black community and sent tens of thousands of panicky whites flooding out into Baltimore and Anne Arundel Counties. The net result was the economic and social decline of whole neighborhoods, a swift and profound shift in school populations, and more white flight. The inability of low income black residents to buy or pay enough rent to maintain the housing in which they lived led to physical deterioration and widespread housing abandonment.

By the 1980s and 1990s the black middle classes began to flee the city, pulling their institutions out as well. The impending removal of the historic Bethel A.M.E. Church from Druid Hill Avenue in the central city out to a large tract of land in suburban Baltimore County marks a major turning point in the history of both the city and its black community. It is at once a great loss to the central city, but also the dawning of a new day for Bethel's current worshipers, who now live mostly in the suburbs. Needless to say, the decline of so many grand city neighborhoods, the destruction of so many priceless buildings, and the removal of so many of the city's best and most energetic white and black citizens casts a shadow over the last chapter of my history.

Nevertheless, I still hope to treat Baltimore's overall evolution, even its apparent devolution during the past fifty years, in a balanced and even a fairly positive way. I can do this because, to answer the third question I originally posed, I have adopted as the scope of my history not just the place we call Baltimore City but the entire metropolitan region. Why do this? First, it makes no sense at all to write only about the ninety-one square miles of territory contained within the 1918 city limits. To do so is to leave out the 400–500 square miles of now highly urbanized land around the municipality and the many thousands who have lived there during the past century or more—people who have thought of themselves as residents of a region-wide economy and society. Second, the story of the evolution of the surrounding counties from relatively remote rural hinterlands into parts of a single metropolitan region is both dramatic and inherently interesting. The development of Baltimore County from the 1860s to the present is really an amazing tale. Great battles over fire protection, the police, the school system, and highways have been fought out in Towson for well over a hundred years, and during the past two decades, the migration of thousands of African Americans into the Reisterstown and Liberty Road suburbs has begun a whole new chapter of the county's history. The great social and racial experiment in the new city of Columbia in Howard County is part of the history of metropolitan Baltimore as is the accelerating growth of Carroll and Harford Counties.

Finally, trying to explain the history of Baltimore City proper during the past hundred years (over one-third of its entire history) without reference to its surrounding suburbs, is simply impossible. For the past thirty years, the old municipality of Baltimore, while it is unquestionably the most important and special place within the region, has fewer residents and jobs than the suburbs. Not to chronicle this amazing change in the Baltimore region is to miss one of the major stories of twentieth-century America. Unfortunately, in spite of the best efforts of people like John McGrain and Neil Brooks in Baltimore County, and dedicated little groups in the other counties, little has been written about the history of the metropolitan region. I have therefore been compelled to make a number of (hopefully) informed guesses about the actual development of this vast territory and to paint its history with a very broad brush. Even so, the last part of this history ranges from Belair to Columbia and from Westminster to Glen Burnie—the current corners of the regional city of Baltimore.

In saying all this, I do not want to give the impression that I too have written off old Baltimore City. From a number of points of view, the ninety-one square mile territory at the center of the Baltimore region is by far its most important. The older section of the city, perhaps thirty or forty square miles, is the most valuable piece of property in Maryland. The physical plant sitting on this land, and the institutions collected there, are absolutely irreplaceable. They have already shown what a huge asset they can be if properly protected and recast. In places like the Inner Harbor, Fells Point, South Baltimore, Union Square, Mount Vernon Place, Roland Park, and Mount Washington, the city possesses assets that can never be replicated. Several dozen other areas within the old city hold the potential to become vibrant communities if their once splendid houses, stores, and other structures can be refurbished by a new generation of back-to-the-city people. In spite of the huge and depressing problems facing the city as a whole, the real estate I am speaking of seems well on the way to transforming itself into a series of gentrified residential areas, first-class entertainment and educational facilities, centers of new employment, and valuable, interesting tourist attractions. While perhaps one-third of the city's neighborhoods are in really desperate condition and many others appear to be in serious trouble, a number are currently doing quite well, given the great burdens under which they are forced to exist. The city government, which seemed to drift under the leadership of Mayor Kurt L. Schmoke, has a new mayor who exudes confidence and leadership. Mayor Martin O'Malley has inherited a municipal government struggling under extremely serious fiscal problems, but one can remain hopeful. He may be able to convince the state government to initiate some basic tax and/or administrative restructuring in the Baltimore region that will provide the city with the resources it needs to continue its reconstruction. The city subsidized the rural counties of Maryland for decades during the nineteenth and early twentieth centuries, so it seems only fair that some of these funds might come back to the city in its hour of need.

As an historian, I have always tried to avoid gazing into crystal balls and thus will make no attempt in my history to predict the future of the old city of Baltimore. My goal is to present an accurate, unsentimental, but appreciative look at the people who have walked the streets of this city for 270 years, explaining, as best I can, how their actions created both the magnificent things we still enjoy today in Baltimore, and also contributed to the huge problems that inevitably arise when large numbers of very different people come together in such a large and complex place.

AMY S. GREENBERG

Volunteer Fire Companies and Community Formation in Baltimore, 1780–1859

A S FOREIGN VISITORS TO THE United States frequently noted, nineteenth-century Americans were enamored with the power and possibility of their "associations." After his tour through America in the 1830s, Alexis de Tocqueville reported that "in the United States, Associations are established to promote the public safety, commerce, industry, morality and religion. There is no end which the human will despairs of attaining through the combined power of individuals united in a society."[1]

In an "era of associations," as one historian has termed the decades before the Civil War, the volunteer fire company stands out. Perhaps the most noble association, volunteer fire companies were free from obvious partisan or economic interest, and dedicated to the protection of all, regardless of occupation, ethnicity or religion.[2] Baltimoreans certainly viewed their firemen in this light. As the *Baltimore Sun* commented on the occasion of the firemen's anniversary parade in 1851, their firemen presented "a scene eminently and exclusively American." The volunteer fire department "leads the world as an exponent of practical energy and genuine ability" the paper proclaimed.

Amy S. Greenberg is Associate Professor of History at the Pennsylvania State University. She is author of *Cause for Alarm: the Volunteer Fire Department in the Nineteenth-Century City* (Princeton University Press: 1998) and has written articles on nineteenth-century expansionism, masculinity, and urbanization.

The material of the men and the means—their fitness one to the other, and to the purpose they profess—whether regarded as a grand demonstration of physical power and the efficiency of its application to public service—or as an exhibition of voluntary zeal for the common welfare—whether in the mass—in companies, or in the individual—it commends itself to universal admiration and respect.[3]

In the industrializing city of the early 1850s, self-interest and private gain may have appeared to Baltimoreans to have run rampant. Volunteer firefighting, dangerous work provided in the interest of the city, presented a reassuring contrast in a particularly American form. As the *Sun* pointed out, volunteer firemen were admirable for both their physical strength and their philanthropic outlook. They countered self-interest with their "voluntary zeal for the public welfare." Given this perspective, it shouldn't be surprising that Baltimore's volunteer firemen were recipients of praise, money, and respect in antebellum Baltimore.

This article will explore the volunteer fire companies lauded by the *Sun,* and will consider what role fire companies played in creating community in antebellum Baltimore. Between 1763, when concerned citizens formed Baltimore's first fire brigade, the Mechanical Company, and 1859, when the city of Baltimore instituted a paid municipal fire department, all firefighting in Baltimore was performed by volunteers. Volunteer firemen were crucial in helping the city of Baltimore grow from the late eighteenth century to the eve of the Civil War. For more than seventy years, Baltimore's volunteer fire department protected the city from fire, the foremost urban threat, provided members with a brotherhood of like-minded individuals, and fostered neighborhood community with otherwise unavailable services.

The most important contribution Baltimore's volunteer firemen made to their city was of course, in protecting it from fire. Fire was the premier threat to the health of cities in the eighteenth and nineteenth centuries. Mixed zoning, open hearths, and haphazard building techniques led to frequent urban conflagrations throughout America, and the high population density and insufficient water supply of cities like Baltimore insured that fires would cause extensive damage. Baltimore was more fortunate than most urban centers, and only lost $2 million worth of property and goods to large fires between 1832 and 1855, but the city still experienced a large fire almost every year. By contrast, St. Louis more typically sustained over $10 million worth of damage from large fires over a twenty-one-year period in the first half of the century. Some of the credit for Baltimore's record is not due to luck, of course, but to its firemen. After all, it was the firemen who prevented those yearly fires from consuming the entire city.[4]

As Baltimore expanded, so too did the number of men in the volunteer fire department. In 1790, Baltimore was served by three volunteer companies, by 1800 there were six companies, and in the following decade six more companies joined the department's roster. By 1843 there were seventeen fire companies in Baltimore, and by the time the volunteer department was replaced by a municipal force there were twenty-two volunteer fire companies in Baltimore, containing over one thousand active members, and two thousand honorary and contributing members.[5]

Volunteer firemen did not just physically protect the city, but provided Baltimore with some of its first urban services as well. Volunteer firemen were, by definition, philanthropic. They provided their services to the city without hope of financial reward. Many volunteer fire companies were also active in charitable causes in their cities. The Mechanical Fire Company was, according to its historian, "conspicuous for one especial phase. This was its charitable disposition. Outside of serving without pay, its members never failed to contribute its share to all contributions to any worthy cause."[6]

Some fire companies offered educational opportunities both for firemen and for residents of their neighborhood. Many of the first urban libraries were created by fire companies. In Baltimore, more than fifteen different library associations were created within the fire companies, several of which contained more than one thousand volumes. Although most Baltimore fire company library associations were intended for the self-improvement of the firemen, some were open to the public. The *Baltimore Clipper* reported that the Mechanical Fire Company library, whose rooms were "the handsomest in the city," contained more than four thousand volumes and was visited by an "astonishing number" of people from "every section of the country." The *Baltimore Sun* reported that in this elegant library, "the walls of the spacious saloon unoccupied by the shelving, are handsomely adorned with a large number of scenes of fires, &c, which give the interior a fine appearance." The Liberty Library Association, an adjunct to the company of the same name, allowed women access to their collection in 1850 and also set up an apprentices' library.[7]

Fire companies organized the first fire insurance in many cities. Baltimore's firemen created two insurance companies serving the city, and members of the Baltimore fire department elected the directors of the companies. The department also set up a mutual benefit insurance company for firemen and their families by mid-century. Any fireman who became a member of the association, by paying a small annual fee, was insured against injury while on duty. This association also paid for firemen's burials and offered payments to firemen's widows and orphans.[8]

Firemen also opened up their firehouses to use by the public, creating early civic centers within their buildings. Baltimore firehouses were used as schools and community groups. In 1856 the Women's Guild of the Fells Point Mission held a week-long festival in the engine house of the Columbian Company, and the upstairs room in the Independent Fire Company was rented out to a Female Sunday School for a period of time. As the *Sun* reported in 1843, the new building of the Watchman Fire Company in Baltimore, located on Federal Hill, contained "a public hall for that section of the city, the want of which has long been felt, and is now about to be supplied by this enterprising company." The Watchmen also placed an iron balcony in front of a second story window, so that the space in front of the engine house could be used for meetings of political and social groups.[9]

When the company remodeled five years later, their house became even more central to community life. As reported in the *Sun*, the addition featured rooms specifically designed for "the use of public assemblies, parties, balls, and for various other purposes required by the prosperous and increasing population residing in the southern section of the city." In the period before the evolution of the service-city, fire companies offered more than the extermination of fire. They not only protected cities from the threat of fire but also helped create community on the neighborhood level. In increasingly anonymous urban environments, the firehouse was a center for community and neighborhood cohesion.[10]

Firemen were openly lauded for their services, as praise-filled issues of the *Baltimore Sun* from the early decades of the nineteenth century make clear. The *Sun* described the anniversary of their fire department as "a day of public tribute on one side—the tribute of admiration from one class of citizens to another; and from bright eyes and smiling faces, to gallant hearts, manly forms and a daring and honorable vocation." But public tribute to the firemen was not limited to a particular day of the year—it was occasioned by any manner of event.[11]

Individual companies received ample praise in Baltimore's newspapers for their heroic efforts. A poem was composed to the Union Fire Company after an 1838 fire and appeared on the front page of the *Sun*. A short sample of the enthusiastic lyrics of this typical tribute to Baltimore's firefighting force will probably suffice to indicate the lavish extent of the tribute offered the firemen:

> Hail gallant sons of fire!
> Hail salamanders brave!
> Who dare the destroying angel's ire.
> Nor dread the grave.
> If ye can save,
> The helpless from a doom so dire.[12]

While the mythological salamander could withstand fire, the volunteer fireman, alas, could not. Volunteer firemen were praised for their heroism and bravery in Baltimore's papers of the first part of the nineteenth century, often in terms that compared them to classical warriors. "In our eyes," grateful Baltimoreans confessed to their fire department, "at each victory over the fiery vesta your chief becomes the Miltiades of another Marathon."[13]

Comparisons of these sorts, between firemen and classical heroes, were not simply a poetic convention, but held real political significance to Baltimore residents. As historians including Drew McCoy and Gordon Wood have shown, Americans in the Jeffersonian and Jacksonian period were schooled in romantic Republicanism.[14] They turned to ancient Athens and Rome for a model on which to construct society. Firemen, like classical warriors, fulfilled the definition of a model citizen by distinguishing themselves in the public realm and contributing to the welfare of civil society. By casting their firemen in classical terms, Baltimoreans were paying them the highest possible tribute, they were acknowledging that the sacrifice of the firemen made them full, honorable citizens, essential to the life of the city, and especially worthy as a result. Firemen were not beyond pursuing historical allusions

This artwork appeared on George Williamson's 1836 fire insurance policy. (Maryland Historical Society.)

themselves. The Independent Fire Company attempted to reproduce a famous Florentine marble tower built around 1300 in the middle of Baltimore in 1853. Renaissance Florentines, of course, were even more enamored with classical illusions than were antebellum Baltimoreans.[15]

In the glory days of the volunteer fire department, almost any notice of a fire, no matter how brief, was generally followed by a positive assessment of the firemen's performance. Typical reports of fires in Baltimore in the 1830s and 1840s included the following praise: "The firemen, as they always are, were prompt in attendance, and worked with their accustomed energy to subdue the flames." "It was only by the almost superhuman efforts of the firemen that the flames were confined to the square in which it originated." "The firemen were on the spot with their accustomed promptness, and succeeded in saving the surrounding property, though some of it is of a very combustible character."[16]

Reporters generally gave the volunteer firemen the benefit of the doubt in early nineteenth-century reports. Not only were firemen extensively praised in most reports, but they also appear to have been lauded even when they failed in their job. In one Baltimore fire, although the firemen made an "almost superhuman effort. . . . There was a rumor that a child was burnt in one of the houses." The reporter dismissed this rumor, apparently unwilling to entertain the possibility that the firemen would allow a child to die. "We could not learn that it was a fact, and are disposed to doubt it."[17]

Newspapers honored the firemen in other ways as well. In Baltimore the Volunteer Fire Department was always news. Descriptions of the details of the social life of firemen were considered legitimate stories and featured prominently in the columns of the *Sun*. No detail, about the elections of individual companies, visiting firemen, or other department business, appears to have been too small for note. When fire companies from Philadelphia arrived in Baltimore in 1851, readers of the *Sun* learned the intimate details of the visit in lengthy articles spread out over three days. Readers heard what train the firemen arrived on, where the firemen planned to stay, and what Baltimore firemen wore when they met the visitors. "The Deptford [Company members] were out in a new and beautiful uniform, the hats of New York pattern, and ornaments in front with a polished brass plate, bearing the name of the company, white wool shirts, with scarlet rolling collars." Gifts given to the Baltimore firemen were described in similar detail, as were the food and toasts given at the firemen's banquet.[18]

Any return of home of the Baltimore firemen was also news. In 1844, the *Sun* reported on

> *The Liberty Fire Company.*—This excellent company returned on Saturday evening from their visit to Philadelphia. They were escorted to their quarters by the Mechanical and New Market [fire companies]. They appear to be highly pleased with their visit and the attention bestowed upon them.[19]

In this example and in many others, Baltimore's press and its readers celebrated the return of the fire company as surely as did other firemen.

Fire companies received all manner of gifts from the municipality and from other Baltimoreans. The city subsidized new firehouses or fire engines, purchased fire hose, and otherwise financially supported the volunteers. The Deptford Company built a house in 1843 for six thousand dollars, four thousand of which was provided by the city. Firemen also received cash

This oil painting, entitled "Fire in the Warehouse of Henry Webb & Co.," by an unknown artist in the 1830s, is a romantic rendition of early fire-fighting. (Maryland Historical Society.)

donations, Bibles and other tokens of esteem from individuals or associations in Baltimore. The Liberty Fire Company was given a "wreath formed of hair, containing a lock of each of the members" created by "lady-friends" of the company. They proudly displayed the hair wreath in their firehouse.[20]

As I have outlined, volunteer firemen played a crucial role in creating community in Baltimore's neighborhoods. But no less important were the communities Baltimore's 1,000-plus volunteer firemen formed within their own department. Firemen were passionately committed to their organizations. They devoted extensive energy not only to fighting fires but to social activities as well. Company meeting minutes, for instance, are full of discussions not only about equipment and fires but also about teas, parties, and what uniform to wear during parades. The Liberty Fire Company of Baltimore chose to parade in 1851 in black pants and drab coats, white hats with gilt lettering, patent leather belts with brass plates, white comforts and gloves. Their motto on this occasion indicated their devotion to their company, "Where Liberty dwells there is my home."[21]

If the fire company was a fireman's home, then the firemen were also his family, and difficult to leave. A Baltimore fireman who moved to New York in 1856 kept up contact with his old fire company by publishing a monthly humorous paper for them. The *Pickwickian* provided news about life in New York in the form of cartoons, gossip about the Baltimore firemen, and "The Fireman: or the Ambitious Boot Jack, in any quantity of volumes," a farcical novel. Neither space nor time could sunder the tight bonds Baltimore's firemen formed. In 1890, 150 aged volunteers still met regularly to reminisce about their time spent firefighting.[22]

The communities created within the fire companies were significant not only to the firemen but also to the larger history of class and gender in the nineteenth century. Historians have identified the middle decades of the nineteenth century as a time of disorientation for urban men. Industrialization and the decline of the apprentice system increasingly forced working-class men to acknowledge the limits of their economic opportunity, while members of the emerging middle class were forced to balance discordant home and work environments. Masculinity itself had reached a point of transition for both groups, and specific class-related social activities emerged to fill the needs of these men. Members of the emerging middle class joined literary clubs and temperance and other reform organizations. Or, as one historian has shown, they joined fraternal orders with rituals that promoted "emotional transition from an identification from feminine domesticity to the relentlessly aggressive and competitive demands of the masculine work place."[23]

Working-class male culture, in contrast, was increasingly organized around drinking, gambling, theater-going, frequenting prostitutes, and, above all, physical violence. Urban workers repaired from their anonymous workplaces to saloons, where they found the camaraderie and respect missing from their jobs. They also found fist-fights, dogfights, and rat-baiting contests organized by saloon keepers as entertainment. One important way working-class men earned the respect of their peers was through their physical strength and ability to dominate others. Indeed, physical violence was central to urban working-class masculinity, which celebrated both bare-knuckle boxing, as well as less orchestrated exhibitions of virility. Personal acts of physical violence were common within saloon culture, and common also among working-class members of street gangs. By mid-century, both working men and members of the emerging middle class had developed masculine cultures that offered approval and respect distinct from any performance in the workplace. These two visions of masculinity were increasingly opposed to one another.[24]

Volunteer fire companies offered men of differing occupations and ethnicities a third option, a vigorous masculine culture that combined aspects of working and middle-class culture along with cultural forms singular to the fire department. Volunteer firefighting offered a cross-class vision of urban citizenship and masculine culture, one that at once celebrated physicality, and fighting in some instances, and also upheld a virtuous relationship to the public interest.

The manner in which fire companies crossed class boundaries is clearly evident in Baltimore. Temperance, the most significant antebellum reform movement in Baltimore and elsewhere, largely failed to catch on among the city's firemen. Minutes of meetings of Baltimore's fire companies document the copious consumption of wines and liquors after fires and at department picnics, as well as a short-lived attempt at forming a temperance league in one of the companies.[25] The editor of the *Pickwickian* regularly mocked both middle-class propriety and the manner in which Baltimore firemen flaunted standards of propriety in his humorous monthly sheet. Under a drawing of an intoxicated, unshaven individual, wearing what could be a fireman's hat, the editor composed a "letter" from the "Young Men's Un-Christian Association" to the Pioneer Hook and Ladder Company. The YM(un)CA explained to the firemen that they were hoping to expand their organization. "In casting about for a field in which to operate, its attention has been directed to that of the *Asso*[ciation] of *Firemen* as one peculiarly appropriate, composed as it is for the most part of '*Bummers*' like ourselves. We may proudly hail them as *Brethren* and co-labourers in endeavoring to get drinks when we have no '*Rocks*.'" The YM(un)CA also proposed to deliver lectures on Sunday on when to drink and where to drink.[26]

The real YMCA, an institution set up by white-collar men to help pro-

By Law

Creating a Standing Committee and defining its powers.

Article 6th. The Standing Committee shall be an executive body to the Baltimore United Fire Department, for the purpose of carrying into effect the rules and regulations for the government of the companies composing it; they shall have power to hear and determine disputes which may happen between its members at a fire, by process verbal: subject nevertheless, in all cases to an appeal to the Department. To do and transact in the recess of meetings such business as in their judgement may not require a meeting to be called. They shall have power to call special meetings of the Department, as herein before provided for; At fires they shall keep together as much as practicable, and be known only in their official capacity, by each member having an appropriate badge on his hat; to be provided by the Department for their use.

Rules and Regulations for the Government of the Fire Companies.

1st. Those Companies having Bells attached to their Engine Houses, are requested to place them under such regulation as will (as far as possible) prevent their being rung on false alarms of Fire.

2d. No Company, unless prepared with its apparatus to use the water of a pump, fire plug, or other water source, shall retain it, if demanded by a Company thus prepared.

3d. All Companies are requested to avoid passing with their apparatus on the pavement or footways, unless impelled so to do, by the condition of the streets.

4th. Each Company to be cautious in the admission of members, and prompt in the expulsion of the disorderly. The retention of one turbulent spirit, may bring discredit on the whole Fire Department.

Rules and Regulations of the Baltimore United Fire Department. (Maryland Historical Society.)

The Comet, owned by the Vigilant Fire Company, 1858. (Maryland Historical Society.)

mote self-control and to prevent vice among urban youth, is mocked in the *Pickwickian* for these very reasons. It would be difficult to imagine a more scathing indictment of the culture and values of the emerging middle class, but the Pioneer Hook and Ladder Company was not the bunch of laboring rowdies one might expect given the *Pickwickian's* rhetoric. The company's president at this time was the very proper Charles T. Holloway, who later became the chief engineer of Baltimore's paid department and fought for increased propriety and morality among the paid forces. The company kept a library, and a majority of members practiced white-collar occupations. In 1859, 55 percent of locatable members were listed in either the 1860 census or 1858 city directory as being engaged in white-collar occupations. What seems a contradiction between this language and its audience serves to highlight the fluid nature of the culture of the firehouse. These men could enjoy both a library and a drink (or two), and certainly enjoyed making fun of behavior they considered stiff.[27]

In a period when leisure activities were increasingly segregated by class, Baltimore's volunteer fire companies created communities across class and ethnic lines within companies. As late as 1858, the year before the volunteer department was replaced, 42 percent of active Baltimore firemen locatable in the city directory were listed as either owning shops or practicing white-collar occupations. Eight percent of the firemen were identified as high-white collar, including merchants, doctors, lawyers, and manufacturers. As one Baltimorean remembered years later, "the most prominent citizens affiliated with the Fire Companies, and it was in the engine houses that most of the town talk was heard."[28]

Likewise white men of all ethnic backgrounds found a place in some fire company, even if every fire company may not have been open to them. Because there is no surviving complete membership list for Baltimore's fire department, it is difficult to draw firm conclusions about the ethnic makeup of the department as a whole. But fragmentary evidence drawn from select company membership lists and the 1860 census indicates that most or all of Baltimore's fire companies contained some foreign-born firemen, and that foreign-born firemen were also more likely to join some companies than others. Irish and German firemen were more likely to join both the New Market and Deptford companies than the Pioneer Hook and Ladder or Mechanical companies, although both the New Market and Deptford companies contained a majority of Maryland-born firemen in the late 1850s. Fire company membership lists from earlier years support the conclusion that Baltimore's fire companies were not ethnically exclusive clubs; all include some German and Irish names.[29]

Fire companies also provided an arena where men of different generations could interact and form friendships. While a third of the firemen locatable in the 1860 census were still in their twenties, another third were in their thirties, 24 percent were in their forties, and 9 percent were in their fifties or sixties. These firemen were fairly evenly distributed among the four fire companies for which there are extant membership lists for the late 1850s. Although this sample is likely biased in favor of older firemen who were more stable, and thus more likely to appear in the 1860s census, the year after the department was municipalized, they indicate the inclusive nature of these organizations.[30]

It is significant to note that none of these figures include honorary mem-

The noble reputation earned by firemen in the first part of the nineteenth century suffered as they became ungulfed in the urban violence of the 1850s. (Maryland Historical Society.)

bers of the companies, those members who supported the department financially but were not required to fight fires themselves. Nor do these figures include veteran members, those members who had served seven years of active duty and now held emeritus status. Honorary and veteran members of Baltimore's department in many cases identified themselves with volunteer firefighting as vigorously as any young volunteer fireman and were even more likely to practice white-collar occupations than were the active members.

African Americans also appear to have participated in volunteer firefighting in Baltimore in a limited manner. The evidence is scanty on this point, but I have found two reports of African Americans fighting fires with volunteer companies. In 1846 the Mechanical Company discussed meeting with the mayor in order to "ascertain what method could be pursued to prevent the Coloured men in the habit of working our Fire apparatus at a Fire from being arrested" after the mayor passed a curfew for African Americans. In 1858 company minutes report that "a Colored Boy who was on the ropes" was shot while pulling the equipment of the Pioneer Hook and Ladder Company. The Pioneers took him to the doctor who extracted the bullet, after which point he recovered. It is difficult to conclude from these incidents if the African Americans involved were enslaved, were free-laborers in the service of the companies, or possibly were themselves volunteers of some sort, perhaps neighborhood occupants who chose to help with the firefighting. In any case, their efforts were sufficiently valued by the Mechanical Company that that company chose to lobby the mayor on their behalf. What is quite clear is that African Americans were not full members of these companies. All the firemen locatable in the 1860 census are listed as white. More significantly, social convention would have made membership by African Americans virtually unthinkable, although no laws officially limited company membership by race. The African Americans who fought fires were in a literal sense firemen, but they did not share in the firemen's culture; nor were these African American firemen respected and lauded by the press in the same manner as were white firemen. The fact that African Americans helped with the business of firefighting is never mentioned in any discussion of the companies in the Baltimore press. It seems clear that the brotherhood of firemen in Baltimore, as in most other antebellum cities, was an exclusively white brotherhood. Indeed, firemen may have been able to welcome members of different white ethnic groups, different generations, and different occupations only at the expense of African Americans.[31]

In sum, Baltimore's volunteer fire companies offered a heterogeneous white membership fine houses with libraries, lovely uniforms, and a full social calendar, along with the physicality and excitement of working-class culture. Urban volunteer fire departments developed a vision of masculinity that was accessible and appealing to men of different social strata. Firefighter masculinity lacked the constraints and hierarchies of middle-class cultural forms and celebrated physicality within narrower parameters than working class culture. Firemen in Baltimore and elsewhere held banquets and balls like members of the emerging middle class but had no elaborate rituals like those of middle-class fraternal organizations during this period. What the fire department offered men was an opportunity to race, parade, wear a uniform, and match strength with other like-minded men, regardless of occupation.

Unfortunately, this cross-class organization would not survive the antebellum period for a variety of reasons. Baltimore's firemen always enjoyed getting into fights at fires. As appropriate social behavior grew increasingly constrained over the course of the century, the violence and seeming disorder of the volunteers stood out and was condemned by the press and municipal government. Baltimore, once known as Mobtown, was looking for a more dignified title by the mid-nineteenth century.[32] As citizens strove for order in the city in the 1840s and 1850s, the culture of the firehouse was attacked and condemned. Baltimoreans were no longer willing to tolerate fighting among their firefighters, and other institutions emerged to provide neighborhoods with the services previously offered by the fire companies. At the same time, changes in firefighting technology and the spread of fire insurance worked to render urban volunteer firefighting obsolete on a national level. The emergence of a paid fire department in 1859 marked the end of volunteer firefighting in Baltimore, but it did not take away a history of good deeds, valiant efforts, and community formation in a young city.

Notes

[1] Alexis de Tocqueville, *Democracy in America: The Henry Reeve Text as Revised by Francis Bowen and Further Corrected by Phillips Bradley*. Abridged with an Introduction by Thomas Bender. (New York: Modern Library, 1981), 102.

[2] The phrase "era of associations" is drawn from Mary P. Ryan, *Cradle of the Middle Class: The Family in Oneida County, New York, 1790–1865* (New York: Cambridge University Press, 1981), 105–44; For more on volunteer fire companies in Baltimore and other American cities see Amy S. Greenberg, *Cause for Alarm: the Volunteer Fire Department in the Nineteenth-Century City* (Princeton: Princeton University Press, 1998).

[3] *Baltimore Sun*, November 20, 1851.

[4] David Dana, *The Fireman* (Boston, 1858), 65, 368–66; L. E. Frost, and E. L. Jones, "The Fire Gap and the Greater Durability of Nineteenth Century Cities," *Planning Perspectives*, 4 (1989): 338–41; Lawrence H. Larsen, *The Urban West at the End of the Frontier* (Lawrence: Regents Press of Kansas, 1978), 78–79

[5] *Baltimore Sun*, August 26, 1843; J. Albert Cassedy, *The Firemen's Record* (Baltimore, 1891), 53.

[6] George McCreary, *The Ancient and Honorable Mechanical Company of Baltimore* (Baltimore, 1901), 67.

[7] McCreary, *Ancient and Honorable Mechanical Company of Baltimore*, 80; John Colson, "Fire Company Library Associations of Baltimore," *Journal of Library History*, 21 (1986): 166–70; *Baltimore Sun*, August 24, 1848.

[8] Colson, "Fire Company Library Associations of Baltimore," 163.

[9] Clarence H. Forrest, *The Official History of the Fire Department of the City of Baltimore* (Baltimore, 1898), 49; *Baltimore Sun*, August 25, 1843.

[10] *Baltimore Sun*, December 7, 1848, December 2, 1856.

[11] Ibid., November 20, 1851.

[12] "To the Union Fire Company," *Baltimore Sun*, July 16, 1838.

[13] Ibid.

[14] Gordon S. Wood, *The Creation of the American Republic, 1776–1787* (New York: W. W. Norton & Co., 1972), 46–90; Drew R. McCoy, *The Elusive Republic: Political Economy in Jeffersonian America* (Chapel Hill: University of North Carolina Press, 1980); Philip Ethington, *The Public City: The Political Construction of Urban Life in San Francisco, 1850–1900* (New York: Cambridge University Press, 1994), 57.

[15] William A. Murray, *The Unheralded Heroes of Baltimore's Big Blazes* (Baltimore: Murray Books, 1977), 2.

[16] *Baltimore Sun*, April 1, September 11, 1844, November 21, 1846. See also the *Sun* on August 5, 1843, June 1, 1849, and September 4, 1849.

[17] Ibid., September 11, 1844.

[18] Ibid., November 18 and 19, and December 8, 1851.

[19] Ibid., September 23, 1844. See also October 12, 1846, September 14, 1849, March 12, 1850, October 20 and 21, 1858.

[20] Forrest, *Official History*, 46; *Baltimore Sun*, November 20, 1851.

[21] *Baltimore Sun*, November 20, 1851

[22] *The Pickwickian*, published by "Daughter, Julius and Pickwick," in New York, 1856. In the Pioneer Hook and Ladder Collection 662, of the Maryland Historical Society Documents Collection.

[23] Mark C. Carnes, "Middle Class Men and the Solace of Fraternal Ritual," in *Meanings for Manhood: Constructions of Masculinity in Victorian America*, edited by Mark C. Carnes and Clyde Griffen (Chicago: University of Chicago Press, 1990), 48; Don Doyle, "The Social Functions of Voluntary Associations in a Nineteenth-Century American Town," *Social Science History*, 1 (1977): 347.

[24] On the development of urban working-class culture see Elliott J. Gorn, *The Manly Art: Bare-Knuckle Prize Fighting in America* (Ithaca: Cornell University Press, 1986); Elliott J. Gorn, "'Good-Bye Boys, I Die a True American': Homicide, Nativism, and Working-Class Culture in Antebellum New York City," *Journal of American History*, 74 (1987): 388–410; Christine Stansell, *City of Women: Sex and Class in New York, 1789–1860* (Urbana: University of Illinois Press, 1987), chap. 5; Susan Hirsch, *Roots of the American Working Class: The Industrialization of Crafts in Newark, 1800–1860* (Philadelphia: University of Pennsylvania Press, 1987), chaps. 1, 2, and 5; Howard B. Rock, *Artisans of the New Republic: The Tradesmen of New York City in the Age of Jefferson* (New York: New York University Press, 1979), 295–319; Jon Kingsdale, "'The Poor-Man's Club': Social Functions of the Urban Saloon, Working Class," *American Quarterly*, 25

(1973): 472–89. On the crisis in masculinity in general during this period see Paul E. Johnson and Sean Wilentz, *The Kingdom of Matthias* (New York: Oxford University Press, 1994.)

[25] Mechanical Fire Company documents, November 29, 1856, February 11, 1840; Pioneer Hook and Ladder Collection, October 22, 1854, Manuscripts Department, Maryland Historical Society; record book of the Washington Hose Company of Baltimore, 1815, 1835, Enoch Pratt Free Library.

[26] The *Pickwickian*, March 2, 1856 (emphasis in the original).

[27] On the YMCA, see E. Anthony Rotundo, *American Manhood: Transformations in Masculinity from the Revolution to the Modern Era.* (New York: Basic Books, 1993), 72–73; Joseph F. Kett, *Rites of Passage: Adolescence in America, 1790 to the Present* (New York: Basic Books, 1977), 199–201. Thirty-three of forty-six members of this company in 1859 were locatable in either the 1860 census or 1858 city directory. Of these thirty-three members, 55 percent practiced white-collar occupations. Pioneer Hook and Ladder Company membership list of 1859, from the Peale Museum Collection, Maryland Historical Society, no contributing or honorary members included. List cross-referenced with William H. Boyd, *Baltimore City Directory: Containing the Names of the Citizens, a Subscriber's Business Directory, State and City Records, a Street Directory, "Never before Published," and an Appendix of much useful information* (Baltimore, 1858); Ronald Vern Jackson, *Baltimore Md., 1860 Census Index* (Salt Lake City, 1988) and the 1860 census returns for Baltimore. On the library see Forrest, *Official History*, 275–76; occupational scale in Greenberg, *Cause for Alarm*, 167–68.

[28] Forrest, *Official History*, 53; Statistics based on four fire company rosters. Of the 491 active firemen taken from these lists, 222 individuals were locatable and identifiable in Boyd, *The Baltimore City Directory*, 1858; 1858 Mechanical Company roster in McCreary, *The Ancient and Honorable Mechanical Company of Baltimore*; 1859 Pioneer Hook and Ladder company roster, 1857 New Market company roster, and 1858 Deptford company roster, all from the special collections at the Maryland Historical Society, Baltimore. Occupational scale in Greenberg, *Cause for Alarm*, 167–68. Even given the white-collar bias of city directories in this period, the occupational profile of these Baltimore firemen, the year before municipalization, presents a dramatically different vision of who belonged to a volunteer fire company than that previously presented by historians of firefighting. For examples of histories that argue that fire companies were largely working-class institutions, see Sean Wilentz, *Chants Democratic: New York City and the Rise of the American Working Class* (New York: Oxford University Press, 1984); Bruce Laurie, "Fire Companies and Gangs in Southwark: The 1840's" in *The Peoples of Philadelphia: A History of Ethnic Groups and Lower Class Life, 1790–1940*, Allen F. Davis and Mark H. Haller, eds. (Philadelphia: Temple University Press, 1973), 71–88.

[29] These conclusions are based on a small fraction of firemen from four companies and are only suggestive. Of ninety firemen identifiable in the census (out of a total sample of 427), twenty-two were foreign-born. Eleven firemen were born in Ireland, one was born in England, and ten were born in one of the German states. It seems clear that foreign-born firemen are underrepresented in

this sample, in part because Irish names were often too common to positively identify any one individual, and in part because foreign-born firemen may have had higher mobility rates than native-born firemen. I feel more comfortable basing my assertions about heterogeneous fire companies on the diversity of names in fire company lists than on this census work. 1858 Mechanical Company roster in McCreary, *The Ancient and Honorable Mechanical Company of Baltimore*; 1859 Pioneer Hook and Ladder company roster, 1857 New Market company roster, and 1858 Deptford company roster, all from the special collections at the Maryland Historical Society, Baltimore. No contributing member names used from any list. Names cross-referenced with Jackson, *Baltimore Md., 1860 Census Index* and the 1860 census returns for Baltimore.

[30] Statistics based on ninety firemen locatable in the 1860 census, from a total sample of 427. 1858 Mechanical Company roster in McCreary, *The Ancient and Honorable Mechanical Company of Baltimore*; 1859 Pioneer Hook and Ladder company roster, 1857 New Market company roster, and 1858 Deptford company roster, all from the special collections at the Baltimore City Life Museum Collection, Maryland Historical Society. No contributing member names used from any list. Names cross-referenced with Jackson, *Baltimore Md., 1860 Census Index* and the 1860 census returns for Baltimore.

[31] December 3, 1846, Minutes of the Proceeds of the Mechanical Fire Company, 1839–1863, 584 of the MdHS documents collection; March 17, 1858, in the Pioneer Hook and Ladder collection, 262 in the MdHS documents collection.

[32] For more on the violence of Baltimore's firefighters, see Amy Sophia Greenberg, "Mayhem in Mobtown: Firefighting in Antebellum Baltimore," the *Maryland Historical Magazine*, 90 (1995): 164–79

MARY ELLEN HAYWARD

Baltimore's Alley Houses: Homes for Working People Since the 1780s

A LLEY HOUSES—HOUSES BUILT on the narrow streets running down the centers of blocks—have been built in Baltimore since the 1780s. But they have for generations been associated in the public mind with "poor" housing and slum conditions—as the places where black domestics lived— behind the big house. In his autobiography, *Happy Days*, H. L. Mencken wrote patronizingly of the African American alley dwellers near Union Square:

> Murphy reserved all his Berserker fury for the Aframericans who lived in Vincent alley, two blocks away. Our own dark neighbors in Booth alley were of a peaceful disposition, and the few ructions back there were almost always caused by visitors, but in Vincent alley the wars continued round the calendar, and were especially bloody on Saturday nights. I mean bloody in its literal sense. There were not many ladies of the Vincent alley set who had not been slashed more than once by the bucks they adored and supported, and I can recall no buck who had not had an ear bitten off, or a nostril slit, or a nose mashed. The alley began to buzz at 6 p.m. on Saturday, when such of its male inhabitants as worked at all came home with their pay, and by 8 o'clock Murphy was hard at it dragging the wounded out of its tenements and clubbing the felonious into insensibility.[1]

Scholars of black Baltimore have consistently identified alley housing with

Mary Ellen Hayward is co-author with Charles Belfoure of *The Baltimore Rowhouse* (New York: Princeton Architectural Press, 1999) and is director of the Alley House Project in Baltimore.

black housing, and in his book *Alley Life in Washington* James Borchert states that the alleys of the District were 90 percent black.[2]

We now know that for Baltimore at least, this is simply not true. Alley houses in Baltimore were inhabited by every newly arrived ethnic group, and the majority of alley houses were owned by these first generation immigrants, not rented from absentee landlords. Furthermore, the smaller, two-story houses built along the mid-block "alley" streets were part of planned speculative building enterprises that aimed to provide housing for a wide range of income levels within a single block, thereby creating economically diverse neighborhoods.

In the 1500 block of Lemmon Street, for instance, just south of Mencken's Union Square, the builder Jacob Saum put up two-story Italianate-style houses in 1872 at the same time he was building three-story houses to the north facing the square and along the side streets. The main street houses sold to German business owners and professional men; the Lemmon Street houses sold to a variety of German craftsmen. A decade later Saum built the three-story row on the north side of Union Square into which the Mencken family moved.[3]

Here, then, is the typical Baltimore alley street scenario—a narrow "alley" street, between twenty and thirty feet wide, running down the center of the block and faced with small two-story brick houses—each about eleven or twelve feet wide and either two or three rooms deep. In some neighborhoods the main street houses would be three stories tall and cost two and a half to four times the cost of the small street houses. In other neighborhoods all the streets were built up with two-story houses, but the main street houses were a foot or two wider, had more stylistic features, and cost half again to twice as much as the "alley" houses. In this way, Baltimoreans of a wide range of income levels all lived within the same block in the same neighborhoods.

In Baltimore, the design of alley houses always followed closely the design of main street row houses, as such designs changed over the course of the nineteenth century. There are Federal-style alley houses, Greek Revival alley houses, Italianate alley houses, and even late nineteenth- and early twentieth-century Artistic period alley houses. There are few courts or blind alleys in Baltimore, the type of alley dwelling most frequently described in reformers' literature, and no frame alley "shanties," because a

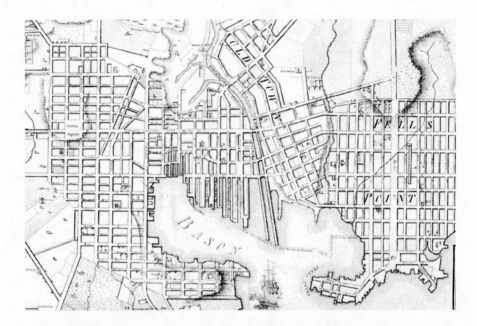

Detail from Warner & Hanna's *Plan of the City and Environs of Baltimore,* 1801. (Maryland Historical Society.)

1799 city ordinance mandated brick construction from that date on. Today, despite vast demolitions of blocks of the city in the name of urban renewal over the past six decades, some five hundred blocks of alley housing survive, ranging in date from circa 1785 to 1910. About two-thirds of surviving houses are three rooms deep; about a third only two rooms deep.[4]

Baltimore should be proud of its so-called alley housing. This development tool gave first generation, working-class Baltimoreans an opportunity to live in a home of their own, with their own front door, front stoop, and back yard—instead of being crowded into multi-story tenements as in many other cities. The alley streets of Baltimore and other cities are part of a long tradition of building small houses in close proximity to larger houses, so that better-off people could have a handy source of nearby labor in a walking city—a tradition that James Borchert traces to the days of ancient Egypt.[5] In Baltimore this practice was closely tied to speculative development—to maximizing the number of lots to be carved out of city blocks, therefore maximizing the number of ground rents created. (In Baltimore, land developers made their profits from ground rents—the annual income they received from "renting" the land the houses they built sat on to the house buyer.) When two large landowners, Edward Fell and John Eager Howard, laid out large tracts east and west of the original tract of Baltimore Town in 1762 and 1782, respectively, they both used a formal pattern of main street blocks bisected by narrow alley streets, with building lots laid out along both street faces.[6] One of the most useful early maps of Baltimore, published by Warner & Hanna in 1801, clearly shows the alley streets running down the center of main street blocks in Howard's addition to the west and Fells Point to the east. When the city hired a professional surveyor to create the first comprehensive plan of the city (published in 1823), he merely extended the existing street grid upward and outward to the new boundary lines. In so doing he gave the official stamp of approval to the main street-alley street grid first created in Fells Point and on Howard's land and set the pattern for all future development.[7]

Until 1850 the narrow alley streets were called "alleys," with colorful names such as Strawberry Alley, Apple Alley, Happy Alley, Petticoat Alley, and Starr Alley in Fells Point; and on the west side of town Cyder Alley, Whisky Alley, Bottle Alley, Brandy Alley, and Welcome Alley (what does this suggest?), leading to Busy Alley, Honey Alley, and Sugar Alley in Federal Hill; and Cowpen Alley, Dutch Alley, Waggon Alley, and Vulcan Alley. When the surveyor, Thomas Poppleton, published a revised plan of the city in 1851 showing the growth that had taken place since 1823, all the previous charmingly descriptive alley names had been changed to more decorous street names—a move that suggests city fathers felt that real street names were now appropriate for this booming port city. In Fells Point Petticoat Alley became Spring Street, Strawberry Alley became Dallas Street, Apple Alley, Bethel Street, Happy Alley, Durham Street, and Starr Alley, Chapel Street. In Federal Hill, Sugar Alley became Churchill Street and Honey Alley became Hughes Street. But the original street grid layout devised by Poppleton in 1823, with all blocks divided by a narrower, fifteen to twenty-foot-wide "alley" street, persisted.[8]

In this early period of Baltimore's history, alley street homes were not necessarily the homes of the city's poorest people. When one looks at pages of the 1804 city directory, each of the Fells Point alleys had a sea captain living there, as well as ship carpenters, riggers, and blacksmiths. The

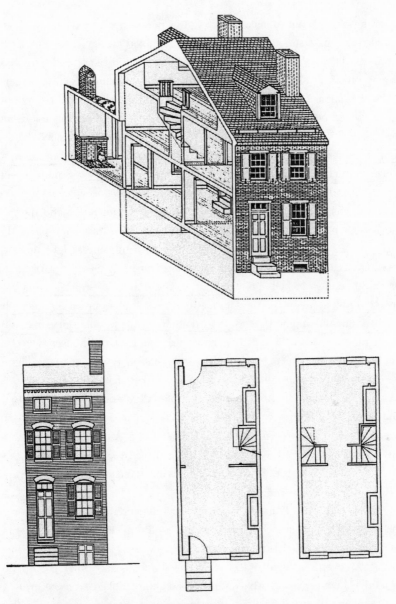

Typical of the early 1800s through the 1830s is the Federal style two-bay, two-and-a-half-story rowhouse at 29 East Hamburg Street (top), built in 1838 by John S. Gittings on a small street in Federal Hill. In the 1840s and early 1850s, Greek Revival two-story-and-attic houses like that at 920 Lemmon Street (bottom) acommodated Baltimore's growing working-class population. (Chester Design Associates, Gloria Mikolajczyk.)

other important point to make is that in this period not only the alley streets but also the main streets of Fells Point were mixed racially. The 1808 Baltimore city directory is the first to indicate "householders of color." In this year twenty-one free blacks lived on this maritime community's alley streets, with occupations like blacksmiths and riggers, but a black ship carpenter and a carter lived nearby on main streets. Since we know the persons compiling the directories were not thorough in their investigations, it can safely be assumed that the actual number of African Americans making their homes next to whites in the Fells Point alleys of the early nineteenth century was much larger.

What did these earliest alley houses look like? Many were frame, like surviving examples in the 700 block of South Regester Street and the 500 block of South Bethel Street in Fells Point, but even these houses of the 1780s were quite substantial when compared to the one-and-a-half story frame houses built earlier, like the surviving pair in the 300 block of South Wolfe Street, also in Fells Point. But after 1799 frame construction was outlawed in Baltimore and all new houses had to be built of brick. By the 1790s the Federal style reigned supreme in Baltimore. At the same time that substantial three-and-a-half story merchants' and sea captains' houses were being built on main streets, smaller, two-and-a-half story versions were lining the lesser streets, like this group on Shakespeare Street, built in 1796. Just around the corner on Bethel Street—Apple Alley—one-room deep, two-and-a-half story houses were going up, with very steeply pitched roofs set over the single main room, and a rear kitchen wing. A number of such early houses still exist on Fells Point's alleys and main streets, all built in the 1790s. The steepness of the roof pitch always gives away the small interior size and tells you the house is quite early.

Other early Fells Point alley houses, documented through the records of the city's oldest insurance company, the Baltimore Equitable Society, include one-and-a-half story, one-room deep houses, just twelve feet, nine inches wide and seventeen feet deep, tiny indeed, and other groups described as being two-and-a-half stories in height, with the one room measuring twelve or thirteen feet wide by fourteen or fifteen feet deep, with a one-story kitchen addition at the rear. All were insured in the first decade of the 1800s. Although these small houses documented in the insurance records no longer exist, another group built in 1812 does—on the west side of the 400 block of Dallas Street, formerly Strawberry Alley. Measuring twelve and one-half feet wide, the houses were acquired by the widow Sarah Jones in 1821, and she ran a boarding house there for years. These alley houses really are the economy model, with their low-pitched roof and no dormer windows—one room per floor, the cooking and heating fireplace in the small rear kitchen. Just to the north, four houses eleven feet wide and built in 1817 survive. Their description in the insurance records shows that they were clearly built as rental units. The owner, one George Bandell, proprietor of the Columbian Tavern facing the main street at the end of the block, insured his main street building and back building running along Strawberry Alley, and then also "a 2 story brick building adjoining to the south end thereof fronting on the west side of Strawberry Alley 44' x 14' deep, plain finished; having connecting roof and being equally divided into 4 tenements." While the main house was valued at $1,500, the four little houses were put at two hundred dollars each.[9] Federal-style two-and-a-half story row houses and alley houses continued to be built in Baltimore through the 1830s, with the pitch of the gable roof becoming less steep as the house expanded to two rooms deep, usually still with the kitchen in a one- or two-story back building. Thomas Poppleton's map of 1823 tells us exactly which of the alley blocks in Baltimore were built up at this time, and one can clearly see how far housing extended on the various streets. The housing represented by these shaded bands would have been a mix of older frame houses, built before 1799, and newer two-and-a-half story brick houses, much like ones surviving in Fells Point and in Federal Hill, south of the harbor basin.[10]

During this period working communities like Fells Point continued to be racially mixed, with both blacks and whites living on main and alley streets. An analysis of the 1822 city directory shows that all seven Fells Point alley streets in that year had both black and white householders, often following identical occupations. Strawberry Alley, for instance, had both black and white laundresses, sailors, and laborers; two black wood sawyers, a white cordwainer, and a white seamstress. Apple Alley was home to a black sailor and a white mariner, black laundresses, a white seamstress, and a white cooper. Register Street likewise was home to both black and white sailors and laborers. Many blacks lived on Fells Point's main streets as well—sailors lived on Caroline and Bond, a ship carpenter on Caroline, a cordwainer on Lancaster, a seamstress on Wolfe, and there was a black-owned boarding house on Bond and an African Methodist Meeting House on Dallas.[11]

By the late 1840s, however, Baltimore's working-class population had dramatically changed with the influx of waves of German and Irish immigrants seeking escape from political crises and the potato famine. They needed places to live as well as places to worship, go to school, and socialize. This era saw the creation of a new row house type and a new alley house type—the two-story-and-attic house, stylistically modeled after high style Greek Revival town mansions found in the fashionable Mount Vernon Place area. Now, instead of the steeply pitched gable roof with dormer windows of the Federal style, the houses had a more practical, lower pitched roof that allowed for two rooms in the upper story, each lit by the two narrow attic windows in the front and back of the house. Rows of these houses were built in Baltimore's working-class neighborhoods in the late 1840s—in west Baltimore near the B&O railroad yards to house the mostly Irish, but some German railroad workers; in Federal Hill for employees of the new steam engine factories as well as other maritime trades; and in Fells Point for the variety of laborers needed for an active maritime community.

A row of two-story-and-attic houses in the 900 block of the north side of Lemmon Street, across from the new car shops of the Baltimore & Ohio Railroad, were built by Charles Shipley, carpenter, in the summer and fall of 1848, on land leased to him by John Howard McHenry, a grandson of Revolutionary War hero General John Eager Howard. By September 1849 many of the houses had been sold to individuals of Irish descent, most of whom worked for the railroad—America's first—then in its twentieth year of operation. People like Thomas McNew, a watchman at the B&O depot; Thomas Medcalfe, a fireman; and Dennis McFaddon and Cornelius McLaughlin, laborers, paid six hundred dollars for their new six-room houses.[12]

The two-story-and-attic row house had a short life span in Baltimore. First seen in working-class housing built c. 1845, by 1855 builders had abandoned the form in favor of either a full three-story, gable-roofed house, or a smaller two-story house. This smaller form—a basic, two-story, gable-roofed house, two rooms deep with or without a kitchen back building—seemed a more economical housing type to meet the needs of the growing numbers of immigrants arriving in these years. In Fells Point, for example, John Ahern, the proprietor of the Cecelia Furnace in Canton, built tightly packed rows of eleven- and twelve-foot-wide houses on small streets east of Washington Street, which he sold for $200 to $250 to both Germans and Irish laborers,

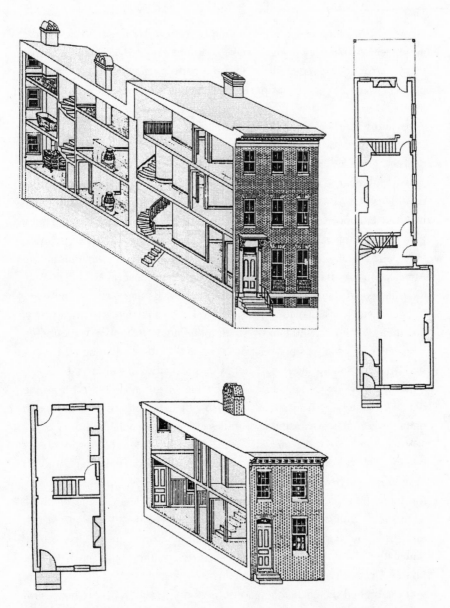

The three-story, three-bay rowhouse at 1412 Park Avenue in Bolton Hill (top) is typical of the elegant rows built around Harlem Park and Franklin, Madison, Union, and Lafayette Squares from the 1850s to the 1880s. The 12 North Amity street house (bottom), circa 1870, is typical of Baltimore's smallest alley houses—two rooms deep, four rooms total, and measuring 11 to 12 feet wide and 25 to 30 feet deep. (Chester Design Associates, Gloria Mikolajczyk.)

tailors, shoemakers, and porters among others. Today these houses give a good idea of what alley living was like when the houses were built. It is true, many narrow houses are packed into the narrow streets, and it is clear the builders were trying to maximize their profits. But these houses are still inhabited by people who own their homes, who take pride in their appearance, and who make use of the quiet alley street to socialize and interact.[13]

As the Germans and Irish prospered and moved out, these houses, as well as the many other small houses in Fells Point, became home to the growing number of Polish and Lithuanian immigrants moving into the area in the 1870s. By 1893 Fells Point housed 15,000 of the 23,000 Poles then living in Baltimore. Their presence can be keenly felt today through both their descendants still living there and the rich legacy of churches, schools, clubs, and building and loans they established to help make the transition to America. Just as the affordable rental of an alley house in west Baltimore today helps working African Americans make ends meet, so too the existence of cheap housing made it possible for the Polish workers to save money, buy their own home, and improve their lot in life. In Baltimore, gable-roofed vernacular housing was not built after the mid-1850s. Beginning in that period and continuing after the Civil War, speculative developers began to build new row house neighborhoods on higher ground removed from the old center of town. This was made possible by the existence of horse-drawn omnibuses and, later, horse-drawn trolleys. These new neighborhoods of the 1850s to the 1880s were created for the solidly middle, and upwardly mobile middle classes, who could now live in purely residential neighborhoods away from the growing industrial city. The builders donated land to the city for public parks to enhance the desirability of the new areas and filled the main streets with substantial Italianate three-story houses. These speculative builders followed Baltimore's 1823 street grid, laying out narrow "alley" streets down the center of their new blocks, on which they built much smaller houses for the people of modest means who would work in the area. Here was established the cliché alley house notion—large, three-story houses on the main streets, and small, two-story alley houses on the back streets to house the servants employed in the big houses. This is simply not true in Baltimore. As mentioned earlier, the "alley" houses just south of Union Square, built in the 1870s, were bought by Germans, and some Irish, with the help of the many ethnic building and loans becoming active in the city. Resi-

Alley houses in the 900 block of North Bradford Street, circa 1909. (John Dubas Collection, Maryland Historical Society.)

dents' occupations included a cooper and a machinist. In the next block the houses were sold to "investors," who in turn rented them to German workers who had not yet saved enough to purchase their own home. In this period many ads appear in the papers touting houses for sale as "good investments, with tenants already in place," and note the return on investment such a purchase would provide.[14]

In these same years, Baltimore's poorer black population, swelling in the years after the Civil War, tended to seek homes on the small alley streets of west and northwest Baltimore, and it is to this group that Mencken refers in the passage from his autobiography. By the late 1880s and 1890s, a newly prosperous black middle and upper-middle class had firmly established themselves in an area of northwest Baltimore centering on Druid Hill Avenue. These professional people lived in main street, three-story houses. But just as working-class German tradesmen and laborers made their homes in the small streets around well-to-do German neighborhoods like Union Square, so too did poorer blacks congregate in the small streets of their wealthier fellows' neighborhood. It was only when early twentieth-century Jim Crow laws kept the city's growing African American community concentrated in this small geographic area that the image of poor blacks and alley housing became fixed in the public mind. Images of overcrowded conditions were in no way limited to blacks, however. When reformer Janet Kemp published a searing investigation of some of Baltimore's most crowded, and therefore unhealthy blocks in 1907, most of the blocks surveyed were the homes of Eastern European immigrants.[15]

As a direct result of Kemp's study, in 1908 Baltimore's city council passed a zoning ordinance outlawing the construction of new housing on streets less than forty feet wide, facade to facade.[16] The enforcement of the new law did not keep Edward J. Gallagher, one of the city's largest row house builders from erecting two blocks of "alley" housing on Glover Street, just south of Patterson Park, in 1909, as part of his new "Park Side" development. All of the houses in Park Side were two stories high, built for Baltimore's burgeoning industrial workforce, but the main street houses had marble basements, lintels, steps, and a bay window, and the alley houses had no marble whatsoever. Whereas the six-room main street houses cost anywhere from $1,450 (facing the park) to $1,150 (on the side street), the four-room alley houses cost $750. The alley houses were bought overwhelmingly by recent

Polish immigrants, men like Bronislaw Wesolowski, a tailor, who borrowed money for the purchase from the local Kosciusko Savings and Loan Association. Mainly German skilled workers purchased the main street houses. Some years later Bronislaw Wesolowski bought a more expensive Gallagher-built row house, located on a wider street, but for now, only in Baltimore for a few years, he had already achieved the pride and stability of homeownership by being able to purchase his affordable alley street house.[17] Thus Baltimore's small, inexpensive alley houses provided, and provide today, the opportunity to buy or rent cheaply the equivalent of a "starter" home, an amenity important to the health of any city.

Notes

[1] Henry Louis Mencken, *Happy Days 1880–1892* (New York: Alfred A. Knopf, 1936; 1968 edition), 150–51).

[2] James F. Borchert, A*lley Life in Washington: Family, Community, Religion, and Folklore in the City, 1850–1920* (Urbana: University of Illinois Press, 1980). See Bettye Collier Thomas, "The Baltimore Black Community, 1865–1910" (Ph.D. diss., George Washington University, 1974; microfilm copy available at Enoch Pratt Free Library, Maryland Room), and Cynthia Neverdon-Morton, *"Black Housing Patterns in Baltimore City, 1885–1953," Maryland Historian*, 16 (1985): 25–31.

[3] Information regarding builders, dates of construction, and housing prices comes from Baltimore City Land Records, Clarence J. Mitchell Courthouse, Baltimore (hereafter referred to as BCLR) and Maryland State Archives, Annapolis. Information regarding occupations of homeowners comes from the Baltimore City Directories. The entire range of directories is available at the Enoch Pratt Free Library and the Maryland Historical Society. The titles and publishers vary from year to year; they will hereafter be cited as Directory. For more detailed information on building styles, builders, and homebuyers see Mary Ellen Hayward and Charles Belfoure, *The Baltimore Rowhouse* (New York: Princeton Architectural Press, 1999).

[4] For further, detailed information on the various blocks of alley housing still surviving in Baltimore City, see the Alley House Project Historic Site Survey forms, and accompanying photographs, on file in the library of the Maryland Historical Trust, Crownsville, Maryland. Survey forms exist for each developmental unit of alley housing in the city and give information regarding dates of construction, builders, early occupants, as well as detailed physical descriptions of the buildings, identifying style and surviving original features.

[5] Borchert, *Alley Life in Washington,* 224.

[6] Both the Maryland Historical Society and the Baltimore City Archives have copies of these plats.

[7] Warner and Hanna's map of 1801, as well as Thomas Poppleton's plan,

published in 1823, are available at the Maryland Historical Society and the Enoch Pratt Free Library's Maryland Room. For further information on the Poppleton plan, see Richard J. Cox, "Trouble on the Chain Gang: City Surveying, Maps, and the Absence of Urban Planning in Baltimore 1730–1823, With a Checklist of Maps of the Period," *Maryland Historical Magazine*, 81 (1986).

[8] Poppleton's revised plan of 1851 is available at the Maryland Historical Society and the Enoch Pratt Free Library.

[9] Baltimore Equitable Society, Policies, vol. D, 319, 332, 403, 409. Directory, 1818. the original policy books are housed on the second floor of the insurance company's main building at 21 N. Eutaw St., Baltimore. They are available to researchers by appointment. The policies are recorded chronologically from the Society's founding in 1794. Each volume is indexed by the names of policy holders.

[10] Spring Street between Fleet and Pratt; Dallas Street between Aliceanna and Lombard; Bethel Street between Shakespeare and Bank; Regester Street between Lancaster and Eastern Avenue; Durham Street between Lancaster and Gough; and Chapel Street between Fleet and Eastern.

[11] *The Baltimore Directory*, for 1822 and 1823, compiled by C. Keenan (Baltimore: Richard J. Matchett, 1822).

[12] BCLR, Directory.

[13] Ibid.

[14] For example, see *Baltimore Sun*, October 9, 1885 and September 16, 1897.

[15] Janet L. Kemp, *Housing Conditions in Baltimore* (Baltimore: Federated Charities, 1907).

[16] *Baltimore Sun*, September 12, 1907; June 20, 1908.

[17] Information on Edward J. Gallagher's real estate ventures comes both from the Baltimore City Land Records and the Gallagher Archives, Langsdale Library, University of Baltimore. The builder kept records of each house he sold, its price, and the name of the buyer. See also Hayward and Belfoure, *The Baltimore Rowhouse*, 106–28.

GARRETT POWER

Deconstructing the Slums of Baltimore

D URING THE NINETEENTH CENTURY, Baltimore and other American
port cities became centers of commerce and industry. Enterprise attracted workers from afar. Many of the newcomers were unable to demand
a living wage. They huddled on the edge of the marketplaces picking up
scraps.[1]

Close encounters with the poor left the comfortable majority with a
mixed sense of guilt and anxiety. Guilt sprang from the conflict between
charitable inclination and the desire to protect privilege. Disquiet came from
the concern that proximity to the poor might increase the incidence of
crime and contagion.[2]

Baltimore's nineteenth-century leaders responded by blaming the "un-
deserving poor" for their own social problems. In the 1820s, the historian
Thomas Griffith opined that "in this country, [the poor] cannot suffer for a
scarcity of bread or work" and that "inebriety" was a well-known cause of
pauperism.[3] In 1832, Dr. Jameson, the city's consulting physician, blamed
dirtiness, intemperance, and gluttony for the plight of the "lower class" residents.[4] Mayor Jerome, in his 1850 message, saw the city's foreign-born as
"beggars" and "filthy vagabonds" who were unproductive and violent.[5] The
board of health, in 1858, attributed the "miserable existence" of the "idle
and dissolute" to their "loss of ordinary sensibilities and humanity."[6]

Only when the poor posed a threat to the larger community need there
be a public response. On such occasions, pockets of disease and dens of

Garrett Power is a professor of law at the University of Maryland School of Law
with a special interest in property law and Baltimore history. He is a frequent
contributor to the *Maryland Historical Magazine*.

inequity would be cleared away to make room for a new street or market. The dispossessed could then again be overlooked, out of sight, out of mind.

It was not until the end of the century that photo-journalist Jacob Riis in his best-selling book *How the Other Half Lives* reminded the American public of the plight of the urban poor. His photographs of children in squalor and privation proved unforgettable.[7] Just two years later, the United States Congress responded by directing the Commissioner of Labor to make "a full investigation relative to what is known as the slums of the city."[8]

The term "slum" had been used on the back streets of Dickensian London in slang reference to the squalid sleeping quarters of the urban poor,[9] but Congress's directive represents the first known official occasion upon which city shacks and shanties had been referred to as "slums." Rather than directly dealing with the "problem of poverty," the focus on slums diverted attention to one its troublesome side effects—the substandard living conditions of the poor.[10]

Substandard housing seemed more susceptible of solution than the problem of poverty. Shacks and shanties could be cordoned off into segregated neighborhoods thereby buffering affluent communities from crime and contagion. Better yet, if poor houses were cleared away the locus of poverty could then be eliminated. Since slum dwellers had only themselves to blame, city leaders felt no moral imperative to improve the living conditions of the poor.[11]

The labor commissioner returned in 1894 with a report on *The Slums of Baltimore, Chicago, New York and Philadelphia.*[12] This essay takes a second look at the nineteenth-century housing conditions in one of those cities, the "slums of Baltimore." It argues that the characterization of these impoverished neighborhoods as "slums" served to justify the community's response to poverty and racial inequality.[13] Focus on these public choices may shed light and cast shadows on anti-poverty and racial policies yet today.

Baltimore was selected for study by the Commissioner of Labor as the "most typical business southern city in the Union . . . [with] all elements of a great metropolis."[14] The report reached two surprising conclusions. First, its statistics demonstrated "no greater sickness prevailing in the [slum] district than in other parts of the cities involved." And second , it determined that:

> White people . . . represent the great mass of people residing in the

slum districts. . . . [In] Baltimore . . . it is shown that 95.85 per cent of the residents of the slum district are white [and] 4.12 per cent black. The conclusion drawn . . . are briefly, that in Baltimore the proportion of blacks, mulattos, etc. in the slum district canvassed is much less than that found in the whole city.[15]

Both of these conclusions seem inaccurate.

Disease Rate

The first conclusion took the Commission investigators (and city authorities) by surprise. Since Baltimore's beginning, "crowds, poverty and filth, [were] everywhere regarded as among the most destructive combinations for the development of disease with all its dire attendants." For one hundred years, the conventional medical wisdom had been that the foul air associated with overcrowding was a primary cause of disease. Now the statistical evidence showed no greater sickness prevailing in the slums than elsewhere.[16]

Original Baltimore had encircled the tidal basin of the Patapsco River from Federal Hill on the southwest, past the docks to the north, and thence a mile and a half east along the edge of a swampy cove to Fells Point. It was cut in half by the Jones Falls, a freshwater stream flowing into the basin from the northwest. The first encampments of Baltimore's poor were at the water's edge. Small crude dwellings sprang up at the foot of Federal Hill, landward of the waterfront docks, on the sodden banks of the Jones Falls and, along the cove at Fells Point.[17]

Disease plagued nineteenth century Baltimore. Time and again, outbreaks of yellow fever, malaria, cholera, and typhoid fever swept the town. These epidemics seemed peculiarly associated with the low-lying encampments of the poor. The yellow fever epidemic of 1797, for example, was said to have begun in the stagnant waters of the Fells Point cove and to have been spread by a strong easterly wind to the huts and hovels on the banks of the Jones Falls, and thence on to the shacks and shanties at the foot of Federal Hill. Recurrent disease on Fells Point eventually convinced those residents who could afford to do so to relocate on the higher ground to the west of the Jones Falls.[18]

Nineteenth-century medical opinions differed as to whether blame for the "malignant effects of fever"[19] should be placed on "miasmatic poison,"[20] or on "stagnant water"[21] or on the "idle and wandering poor, who have . . . infested our City," themselves.[22] But in any case, the appropriate response seemed clear enough. The city fathers adopted measures designed to fill in the "low and sunken situations"[23] and to remove the "great hordes of . . . the depraved."[24]

Examples abound. In 1797 a "market-space canal" drained the marsh and displaced many of the huts and hovels along the west bank of the Jones Falls. The exceptionally high death rate from1818 to 1822 gave impetus to diking, filling and draining operations that gradually filled the shallow twenty-acre cove between the Jones Falls and Fells Point converting this "foul core in the heart of the city" into twenty new "city blocks."[25] After the cholera epidemic of 1832 decimated the gambling dens and whorehouses along the downtown waterfront, they were cleared away for an extension of Lombard Street.[26] During the cholera epidemic of 1866, one infected block was forcibly emptied and fumigated and, the Baltimore Health Department explained why:

> In Elbow Lane, in one square, 20 cases occurred in 2 days: the crowded conditions of the houses, the filth of the houses and the people (negroes) we thought justified extreme measures. Every person, both sick and well, was removed to the quarantine grounds, the sick in the hospital and the others in barracks.[27]

Now to the surprise of all, in 1894 the statistical evidence showed the rate of disease prevailing in the slum districts no greater than in other parts of the city.[28]

Looking back, the parity in sickness statistics can be in part explained. Nuisance diseases (those associated with environmental conditions) were for the most part either insect-borne (malaria, yellow fever, and typhus fever) or water-borne (cholera and typhoid fever). Historically, the high morbidity rate in poor neighborhoods was primarily attributable to their location on wet lands near the breeding grounds of mosquitoes. Public works draining and filling marsh land had reduced the mosquito habitat so that during the decades 1860–90 the rate of death from malaria and yellow fever was on the wane. By 1890 such insect-borne diseases accounted for a scant 1

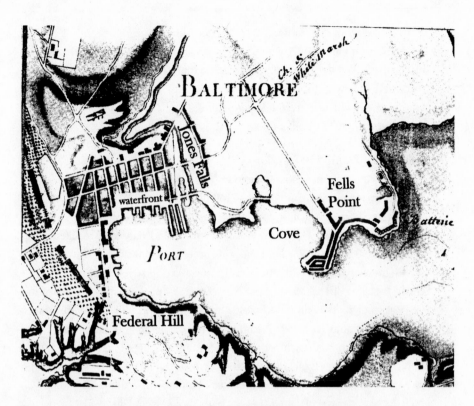

First Encampments of Baltimore's Poor. (Adapted from *Baltimore*, unsigned and undated map drawn in 1781, No., 13, Rochambeau Collection, Division of Geography and Maps, Library of Congress, Washington, D.C.)

percent of the total deaths in the city. Pathogen pollution, on the other hand, was no respecter of neighborhood. Rich and poor alike shared the risk of contracting cholera or typhoid fever from Baltimore's tainted water supply.[29]

With respect to the incidence of tuberculosis, however, the commission's conclusion seemed off the mark. Public health data compiled elsewhere showed that the death rate from tuberculosis among Negroes was much higher than for whites. In 1890, for example, the tuberculosis death rate among "colored inhabitants" was twice that of white inhabitants. The Commissioner of Labor statistics would not have reflected this, however, since the "slums of Baltimore" that he had selected as representative, categorically excluded poor black neighborhoods.[30]

For the whole of Baltimore's population the death rate from tuberculosis in the years after 1875 was undergoing a remarkable drop with the rate of decline for whites strikingly more acute than for Negroes. This left public health officials who associated tuberculosis with overcrowding and poverty unable to explain why declines were taking place "under sanitary conditions of the worst kind" in Polish and Russian Jewish neighborhoods.[31]

Racial and Ethnic Composition

By 1890 Baltimore inhabitants numbered 440,000. The black population, swollen by migration from the South following the Civil War, counted 67,000. The foreign-born population was almost as large. Successive waves of immigration from Ireland, Germany, Poland, Russia, and Italy had resulted in as many as 60,000 to 65,000 newcomers. The foreign newcomers found themselves in competition with the largely impoverished Negro population for cheap dwelling space. Most of the Negroes, and approximately 15,000 of the newest immigrants (primarily Poles, Russian Jews and Italians) lived in substandard dwellings clustered according to race, religion and nationality.[32]

Substandard houses in other great American cities (Chicago and New York, for example) typically took the form of tenement houses containing four or more families. Nineteenth-century Baltimore, on the other hand, was built in block rows of single family brick houses, and its leaders boasted "[t]here are no tenements in Baltimore."[33]

But this proposition proved too much. Baltimore landlords met the demand for low income housing by in-filling. Back buildings were constructed along the alleys and back-to-back at right angles to the street. Passageways through the front houses gave access to interior courts.[34] Profit-maximizing landlords filled every nook and cranny with living spaces. Baltimore had developed its own architecturally distinctive "haunts of misery" populated by the town "undesirables."[35]

The commissioner of labor had defined the "slums of the cities" as "dirty back streets, especially such streets as are inhabited by a squalid and criminal population; they are low and dangerous neighborhoods."[36] So defined, the term had a double meaning—physically "slums" consisted of defective dwellings, socially "slums" were the habitat of inferior residents. It was the foreign-born and the Negroes who bore the badge of social inferiority.

Using later data it is evident that in 1890 Baltimore had five neigh-

The Slums of Baltimore circa 1890. (Adapted from *Gray's New Map of Baltimore*, 1876, Joseph M. Coale III Collection, Maryland State Archives, G1213-147.)

borhoods which fit the commissioner's definition of "slums." On the east side of town, Poles inhabited Fells Point, while Russian Jews and a sprinkling of Italians lived along the east bank of the Jones Falls. On the west side of the harbor basin "rude and dilapidated tenements" housed Negroes at the foot of Federal Hill, and beyond Camden Station in Pigtown, and twenty-five blocks to the north in the Biddle Alley district.[37]

Fells Point

After losing its rivalry with the west side of town for economic and social dominance, Fells Point continued as the point of entry for immigrants. The Point's first poor residents had been Negroes who worked on the waterfront and lived along its alleys, but, by 1830, massive immigration found the Irish and Germans in competition with established African Americans for jobs and dwelling spaces.[38]

European newcomers displaced the Negroes in both the workplace and the homeplace. By the 1890s, Polish immigrants had supplanted the Irish and Germans, creating a ghetto of a new dimension. Single dwellings housed from six to eight families, one to a room. Water supply was from yard hydrants, and outdoor privies served as toilets.[39] Fells Point was described by a health official as "an augean stable . . . a mass of nuisance."[40]

East Bank of the Jones Falls

Early in the nineteenth century, city leaders filled in the marshy cove between Town and Point to create twenty new "city blocks" on the east bank of the Jones Falls. Projectors built 120 new houses along the newly created President, Albemarle, Eden, and Caroline Streets.[41] The first owners were native-born Americans, but, after a single generation the houses were repopulated by Russian Jews and Italians, who converted them into apartments housing three and more families. The area became the center of the city's garment district. Butchering of livestock sometimes took place on the premises, and water and sewerage were inadequate. Overcrowding left the living quarters ill-ventilated and unsanitary.[42]

Hughes Street District

Since Baltimore's beginning, Negroes had lived on interior lowlands to the west of the harbor basin and had worked in the nearby factories and brickyards. In 1852 the Baltimore & Ohio Railroad tore down the five blocks in the heart of this district to make way for its Camden Station. This clearance scattered Baltimore's black population. Some of the displaced persons crowded into the already established Hughes Street district at the foot of Federal Hill, a block to the east; others moved several blocks west of the station to establish a black presence nearby in Pigtown; and, some moved to the Biddle Alley neighborhood twenty-five blocks to the north.[43]

By 1890 most of the original wooden houses at the foot of Federal Hill had been replaced. Hughes Street [nee Honey Alley] lay at the center of a interconnected labyrinth of courtyards. Meyer Court, Brannan Court, Redmon Court, Butler Alley, Hess Court, and Hughes Court created a district consisting of 120 houses occupied exclusively by Negroes. Most of the dwellings were small, with four or five rooms, and many were built back-to-back with a house to the rear, so as to be without any ventilation. The occupants were forced to use a public privy on vacant land, and many had no water supply.[44]

Pigtown

Following the Civil War, rural blacks moving to Baltimore from the South joined Negroes displaced by the construction of Camden Station and clusters of white immigrants, to create a pocket of poverty to the west of the station.[45] The *Baltimore News* described the conditions there in 1892 as follows:

> Open drains, great lots filled with high weeds, ashes and garbage accumulated in the alleyways, cellars filled with filthy black water, houses that are total strangers to the touch of whitewash or scrubbing brush, human bodies that have been strangers for months to soap and water, villainous looking negroes who loiter and sleep around street corners and never work. . . . That's Pigtown.[46]

Biddle Alley District

On the northwest outskirts of the city there had been a black presence since the 1830s, when Negroes in domestic service to the wealthy families on the nearby hill had located there. Following the Civil War, the area became the preferred dwelling place of the black middle class. At the north end of the district, Baltimore's 250 Negro professionals acquired substantial three-story townhouses along the main streets, but on its southern edge lay a labyrinth of back streets. The so-called Biddle Alley district comprised over two hundred dwellings housing poor black families in damp and dilapidated alley houses with bad sanitation and insufficient water supply.[47]

"Representative" Slums

The commissioner of labor's conclusion that "white persons, . . . represent the great mass of persons residing in slum districts" seems to have been intentionally misleading. When he reported back to Congress in 1894, the commissioner made no effort to investigate Baltimore's entire slum population. He instead selected a "representative" district said to be the center of the slum population. Based upon his study of that district he concluded that white people represented 95 percent of the persons residing in Baltimore's slums.[48]

The report's conclusion was arrived at through the simple stratagem of omitting from the "representative" slum district any black neighborhoods. "In consultation with city authorities" the investigators denominated as the center of the slum population the all-white eastside neighborhoods and categorically excluded from their sample the westside Negro districts of Hughes Street, Pigtown and Biddle Alley.[49]

The facts point to the conclusion that the Negro slum population was larger than that of the white slum population. The black population of Baltimore, 67,000, was slightly more than the foreign-born population, and the poverty rate among the blacks was almost certainly higher.[50]

This sampling error was not likely one of oversight. The existence of black slums was in the news. A 1892 series of articles in the *Baltimore News* had described slum conditions among both immigrants and Negroes. Black Pigtown was characterized as the "worst slum in town."[51] Circumstances suggest that the city authorities purposefully prevailed upon the labor commissioner to draw district lines that would dramatically discount the Negro presence.

Authority in Baltimore City was then exercised by Boss Isaac Freeman Rasin. Under his leadership the Democratic Party had controlled the city for twenty years. He dominated the city council and retained the electoral support of the foreign-born through patronage. Negroes voted Republican, and the Democrat machine ignored them.[52] An 1884 editorial by the Democratic *Baltimore Sun* displayed the prevailing party attitude toward the Negro:

> The best thing that can be done for the colored people is to let them alone. If they are treated kindly, the fears that beset them will soon be dissipated and they will be put in the best condition for working out their own deliverance, politically and otherwise.[53]

Discounting the Negro slums supported the position of the Democratic Party. Perhaps, the poor Negro, if ignored, would go away.

The commissioner of labor statistically surveyed the race, nationality, literacy, occupations, income, and health of the inhabitants of the slums of Baltimore, Chicago, New York, and Philadelphia without making any recommendation as to corrective action. That he left to the city authorities.[54]

And authority in Baltimore City was changing. "Good government" Republicans ousted the entrenched Democrat machine in 1895. Thereafter, during the first decade of the twentieth century, Reform Democrats took over the administration of Baltimore. The city had fallen into the hands of Progressives.[55]

The reform city governments responded to the commissioner of labor's report on the slums of Baltimore not at all. Finally, in 1904 several private charitable organizations sponsored a study designed to improve housing conditions in Baltimore. The field inquiry (delayed by the fire of 1904) was conducted by Janet Kemp and completed in 1907. It was anecdotal rather than statistical. It focused its attention on both east side (foreign-born) and west side (Negro) slums. It assumed, without any additional quantitative evidence, that slum neighborhoods posed a significant health risk to the slum-dwellers and a threat to the larger community of contagion. It made recommendations for remedial legislation.[56]

Kemp's recommendations discriminated between immigrant tenements and the Negro alley houses. By 1900, Baltimore's leadership had come to recognize the inevitability of a large foreign-born population. Immigrants counted 70,000 of the city's 500,000 inhabitants and continued on the rapid rise. Kemp proposed a number of reforms intended to assimilate the Poles, Russian Jews and Italian newcomers into the mainstream of American society. To improve their living conditions she called for various building restrictions (e.g., height, light, ventilation, water, and sewer service, etc.) land-use regulations, licensing requirements, and frequent inspections.[57]

Kemp showed a less accommodating attitude towards Baltimore's Negro population, which by 1900 counted 77,000.[58] She observed that "low standards and the absence of ideals" were partly to blame for the conditions among the "negro race." and held "shiftless, irresponsible," Negro alley dwellers "in some degree accountable for the squalor and wretchedness" of their neighborhoods. She suggested that some of the defective black alley houses be condemned and destroyed by municipal authority and evidenced no concern as to where the dispossessed would relocate.[59]

Since the birth rate of Negroes in Baltimore had never approached the death rate,[60] Kemp may have thought that if in-migration could be discouraged, the colored population would shrink away. The historian George Frederickson described the nationwide acceptance of this viewpoint among the reformers:

> If blacks were a degenerating race with no future, the problem ceased to be one of how to prepare them for citizenship or even how to make them more productive and useful members of the community. The new prognosis pointed rather to the need to segregate or quarantine a race liable to be a source of contamination and social danger to the white community, as it sank even deeper into the slough of disease, vice and criminality.[61]

In order to protect the white community from invasion, crime, and contagion additional policies could be put in place to isolate the Negro neighborhoods. According to the credo of Social Darwinism, Negro slums, if left alone, would dwindle away.[62]

Deconstructing Slums

According to the political linguist David Bell "language shapes perception and thought." Words serve as a sort of perceptual lens through which decision-makers see their community and justify their policies. At the turn of the twentieth century, "slums" served city leaders as a useful linguistic category when they came to justify their choices as to what to do about the paupers in their midst.[63]

When urban poverty proved to be an endemic side effect of nineteenth-century capitalism, an obvious solution suggested itself. Philanthropists or governments might share their wealth so that everyone could afford adequate food, housing, clothing, and health care.[64] The plutocracy, however, dismissed this strategy as both too expensive, and too risky. Alms might be provided to impoverished widows and children, but a dole for the unworthy poor would only serve to "encourage idleness and extravagance" among the *lumpenproletariat*.[65]

Rather than dealing with poverty, the powers-that-be focused on one of its troublesome side effects—the substandard living conditions of the impoverished. The characterization of poor neighborhoods as slums "inhabited by a squalid and criminal population" relieved the better elements of humanitarian concern for the suffering of the poor, and re-enforced the notion that slums should be cordoned off, or cleared away.

Nineteenth-century truths proved false and trends did not continue, but policies persisted into the twentieth century. Modern medical science dismissed the fears that miasmas from poor houses were infecting the larger community. Baltimore's poor black population rather than dwindling away, doubled and re-doubled. But the ruling hegemony remained too cheap to provide relief from poverty, and the reform rhetoricians continued to blame the slums for the city's problems.

The twentieth-century discourse on slums presented several new turns of phrase. With tens of thousands of poor families unable to pay the rent on standard housing, Baltimore City kept its housing stock affordable by allowing defective dwellings to be rented to poor tenants at cheaper rents. Landlords of the units with severe problems were typically a disreputable lot of small-time entrepreneurs who bottom-fed on the capitalist food-chain. They came to be called "slumlords"[66] and shared the blame with "slumdwellers" for the privation among the city's poor.

"Blighted" housing conditions were also blamed for urban decay. The word "blight" played off on the historical association between poor houses and poor health, but here the blight affected not the human stock but the housing stock. A good example of this way of thinking (and talking) is found in the words of U.S. Supreme Court Justice William O. Douglas, in his 1953 opinion apologizing for the governmentally sponsored demolition of urban neighborhoods:

> Miserable and disreputable housing conditions may do more than spread disease and crime and immorality. They may also suffocate the spirit by reducing the people who live there to the status of cattle. They may indeed make living an almost insufferable burden. They may also be an ugly sore, a blight on the community which robs it of charm, which makes it a place from which men turn. The

misery of housing may despoil a community as an open sewer may ruin a river.[67]

To hear Justice Douglas talk one would think that slums cause poverty (rather than poverty causing slums).

There is a certain historical resonance in this mode of thinking and talking. Since substandard dwellings infect neighborhoods with crime and addiction, then the answer is to remove the source of the contagion. Just as filling the marshes eliminated yellow fever and malaria, the turning of poor houses and high-rise projects into rubble may be thought to cure the community's ills. The blight metaphor suggests a simple solution to the problem of urban poverty.

By talking about slums and blight community leaders have avoided talking about poverty. Embarrassing questions as to the redistribution of wealth in a market economy are left unaddressed and the slumdwellers and slumlords are blamed for the squalor. Moreover, since the slums are held responsible for sickness and crime, they deserve to be cordoned off or cleared away (without regard for what becomes of those segregated or dispossessed). Hence public policies respecting the "slums of Baltimore" have served to divert attention from the problems of poverty, to perpetuate racial segregation, and to make the "poorest of the poor" worse off, not better off.

Notes

[1] Lewis Mumford, *The City in History* (New York: Harcourt & Brace, 1961), 410–11; Blanche D. Coll, "The Baltimore Society for the Prevention of Pauperism, 1820–1822," *American Historical Review,* 61 (1955): 77–87.

[2] Jack Levin and William C. Levin, *The Functions of Discrimination and Prejudice,* 2d ed. (New York: Harper & Row, 1982), 50.

[3] Thomas Griffith, *History of the Baltimore Almshouse* (1821?), reprinted in Douglas G. Carroll, Jr. & Blanche D. Coll, "The Baltimore Almshouse an Early History," *Maryland Historical Magazine,* 66 (1971): 141, 145–46.

[4] Sherry H. Olson, *Baltimore: The Building of an American City,* rev. ed. (Baltimore: Johns Hopkins University Press, 1997), 92.

[5] Ibid., 139.

[6] Report of the Board of Health to the Mayor of Baltimore, December 31, 1858, 28–29; Coll, "The Baltimore Society for the Prevention of Pauperism, 1820–1822," 77–87.

[7] Jacob Riis, *How the Other Half Lives* (1890; repr. Dover Publications, 1971).

FROM MOBTOWN TO CHARM CITY

⁸ Carroll D. Wright, *The Slums of Baltimore, Chicago, New York and Philadelphia: Seventh Special Report of the Commissioner of Labor* (1894; repr. New York: Arno Press, 1970), 5, 13.

⁹ *Oxford English Dictionary*, 2d ed., 15:754–75

¹⁰ See, David V. J. Bell, *Power, Influence, and Authority: an Essay in Political Linguistic* (New York: Oxford University Press, 1975), 5–14.

¹¹ Levin and Levin, *The Functions of Discrimination and Prejudice*, 48–50.

¹² Wright, *The Slums of Baltimore*, 5, 13.

¹³ See Bell, *Power, Influence, and Authority*, ix–xii.

¹⁴ Wright, *The Slums of Baltimore*, 12.

¹⁵ Ibid., 19, 26–27.

¹⁶ Ibid., 19.

¹⁷ See A. P. Folie's *Plan of the Town of Baltimore* (1792) in Edward C. Papenfuse & Joseph M. Coale III, *Atlas of Historical Maps of Maryland, 1608–1908* (Baltimore: Johns Hopkins University Press, 1982), 96.

¹⁸ William T. Howard, *Public Health Administration and the Natural History of Disease in Baltimore, Maryland 1797–1920* (Washington: The Carnegie Institution of Washington, 1924), 87–88.

¹⁹ Baltimore Mayor's Message, February 14, 1803, Baltimore City Archives.

²⁰ Report from the Consulting Physician to the Mayor of Baltimore, December 31, 1829, Baltimore City Archives.

²¹ Baltimore Mayor's Message, February 14, 1803, Baltimore City Archives.

²² Ibid., February 11, 1811, Baltimore City Archives.

²³ Ibid., February 14, 1803, Baltimore City Archives.

²⁴ Report of the Board of Health to the Mayor of Baltimore, December 31, 1858, Baltimore City Archives.

²⁵ Olson, *Baltimore: The Building of an American City*, 53, 82.

²⁶ Ibid., 38, 83.

²⁷ Howard, *Public Health Administration*, 255.

²⁸ Wright, *The Slums of Baltimore*, 19.

²⁹ Howard, *Public Health Administration*, 19, 204–6, 230–31, 531–33.

³⁰ Ibid., 387–89.

³¹ Ibid., 386, 389, 404.

³² Wilbur Hunter, "Comparison of the Population of Baltimore in 1860 and 1900," unpublished manuscript, Baltimore City Life Collections, Maryland Historical Society; Population of Baltimore City 1790–1990, Maryland State Archives, *Documents for the Classroom*, MSA SC 2221-9-1; Howard, *Public Health Administration*, 179, 404; Wright, *The Slums of Baltimore*, 11–15, 26.

³³ Mary Ellen Hayward & Charles Belfoure, *The Baltimore Rowhouse* (New York: Princeton Architectural Press,1999); Janet E. Kemp, *Housing Conditions in Baltimore: A Report of a Special Committee of the Association for the Improvement of Conditions of the Poor and the Charity Organization Society* (1907; repr. New York: Arno Press, 1974), 8.

³⁴ Kemp, *Housing Conditions in Baltimore*, 20–36.

³⁵ Griffith, *History of the Baltimore Almshouse*, 146.

³⁶ Wright, *The Slums of Baltimore*, 13.

³⁷ Kemp, *Housing Conditions in Baltimore*, 20–36.

[38] M. Ray Della Jr., "The Problem of Negro Labor in the 1850's," *Maryland Historical Magazine,* 66 (1971): 20.

[39] Kemp, *Housing Conditions in Baltimore,* 36–42; Olson, *Baltimore,* 235–36.

[40] Olson, *Baltimore,* 131.

[41] Ibid., 53, 82.

[42] Kemp, *Housing Conditions in Baltimore,* 12–13, 36–44.

[43] Ibid., 20–36; Della, "The Problem of Negro Labor in the 1850's," 19–22.

[44] Kemp, *Housing Conditions in Baltimore,* 16.

[45] Olson, *Baltimore,* 233.

[46] *Baltimore News,* September 20, 1892 quoted in James B. Crooks, *Politics & Progress: the Rise of Urban Progressivism in Baltimore 1895–1911* (Baton Rouge: Louisiana State University Press, 1968), 19–20.

[47] Kemp, *Housing Conditions in Baltimore,* 19; Garrett Power, "Apartheid Baltimore Style: The Residential Segregation Ordinances of 1910–1913," *Maryland Law Review,* 42 (1982): 291–92.

[48] Wright, *The Slums of Baltimore,* 12, 26.

[49] Ibid., 23–24.

[50] Ibid., 26–27; Crooks, *Politics & Progress,* 6–9. A review of the census data indicates that in 1900 the Negro population of Baltimore was 77,000 while the foreign-born population numbered 70,000. See, Hunter, "Comparison of the Population of Baltimore in 1860 and 1900."

[51] *Baltimore News,* September 20, 1892 quoted in Crooks, *Politics & Progress,* 20.

[52] Crooks, *Politics & Progress,* 8-9.

[53] *Baltimore Sun,* November 18, 1884, quoted in Margaret Law Callcott, *The Negro in Maryland Politics 1870–1912* (Baltimore: Johns Hopkins University Press, 1969), 53,

[54] Wright, *The Slums of Baltimore,* 23–24.

[55] *Baltimore News,* September 20, 1892, quoted in Crooks, *Politics & Progress,* 19–20.

[56] Kemp, *Housing Conditions in Baltimore.*

[57] Hunter, "Comparison of the Population of Baltimore in 1860 and 1900"; Kemp, *Housing Conditions in Baltimore,* 86–90.

[58] Hunter, "Comparison of the Population of Baltimore in 1860 and 1900."

[59] Kemp, *Housing Conditions in Baltimore,* 18–19, 87–93.

[60] Howard, *Public Health Administration,* 184.

[61] George M. Frederickson, *The Black Image in the White Mind: The Debate on Afro-American Character and Destiny 1817–1914* (New York: Harper & Row, 1971), 255.

[62] Power, "Apartheid Baltimore Style," 289.

[63] Bell, *Power, Influence, and Authority,* 5.

[64] Richard A. Posner, *Economic Analysis of Law,* 4th ed. (Boston: Little, Brown, 1992), 455–66.

[65] Griffith, *History of the Baltimore Almshouse,* 141.

[66] In the year 2000 the Baltimore City housing authority estimated that renters occupy 49,000 substandard units. The American Housing Survey of 1991

showed Baltimore as having 26,100 units (21,400 rental units) with physical problems, with 19,500 being reported as moderate and with 6,600 as severe. Sixty thousand substandard units are owner-occupied. Lead paint renders many owner-occupied units problematic even though they are otherwise in good condition. Baltimore City Department of Housing and Community Development, *Consolidated Plan, July 2000–June 2005*, 10–15, 34–35.

[67] *Berman v. Parker*, 248 U.S. 26 (1954).

SETH ROCKMAN

Saving Morris Hull: Capital Punishment and Public Opinion in Early Republic Baltimore

BALTIMORE DESERVED ITS early-nineteenth-century reputation as Mobtown. Images abound: a burning effigy of Aaron Burr illuminating indignant Fells Point protesters in 1807; Revolutionary War generals James Lingan and Light Horse Harry Lee laying pummeled outside the city jail in 1812; expensive wines flowing in the streets as a crowd sacked the Monument Square mansions of the city's leading financiers in 1835; a year later, a young Frederick Douglass succumbing to an assemblage of white shipyard apprentices armed with sticks, stones, and handspikes. For each of these violent instances, there were numerous other moments when bored teen-agers pelted wealthy pedestrians with snowballs, disgruntled servants set fire to a master's shop, and enraged hucksters berated market clerks with oaths and imprecations. Some of Baltimore's most marginal inhabitants exerted political muscle in the city's streets and alleys. Lacking an outlet within the institutionalized electoral system, this vital plebeian impulse created an alternative political space for common people to address issues of public policy and social justice.[1]

Yet, the democratic mob did not rule post-Revolutionary Baltimore. Indeed, one historian has called Baltimore "perhaps the most conservative of cities" for its virtual exclusion of working-class men from elective poli-

Seth Rockman is an assistant professor of history at Occidental College in Los Angeles. He is currently writing a book investigating the survival strategies of working families at the intersection of slavery and capitalism.

tics. *Viva-voce* voting allowed wealthy creditors and employers to keep a watchful eye on the electorate until 1805. Continuing for another decade, property requirements barred renters and journeymen artisans from voting and office-holding. A small cohort of men monopolized city government and represented Baltimore on the state and national levels. Across party lines, these merchants, bankers, and entrepreneurs linked the right to participate in public affairs to wealth and standing. They gathered much of their authority outside government by serving as militia and fire company captains, benevolent association trustees, and church vestrymen. Blurring the lines between public and private, these men created a potent bourgeois public sphere defined by voluntary organizations, rational discourse, and the printed word. They could more readily shape city life from this realm than through the municipal government's miniscule infrastructure.[2]

Whether viewed from above or below, political life in early republic Baltimore materialized in a space distinct from the government itself. The bourgeois public sphere and the plebeian practice of politics out-of-doors both sought to speak for the broader population of Baltimore. Both claimed to represent *public opinion,* a relatively new construct that flourished in the political culture of post-Revolutionary America. The contest over public opinion—both to speak for it and to sway it—synthesized both plebeian and elite modes of political expression in the first decades of the nineteenth century. Like the bourgeois public sphere, public opinion was constructed discursively and hinged on the creative promulgation and exchange of the printed word. But like crowd actions, public opinion gave a political voice to segments of the community lacking the racial, gender, and class prerequisites of citizenship. Public opinion became central to American political life during the partisan conflicts of the late-1790s. The Sedition Act begged the question of whether the public might comment on governmental policy through non-elective means. The effort to rescind that law witnessed appeals to public opinion, just as the law's supporters asserted that the public had no opinion of consequence.[3]

Following the Jeffersonian triumph of 1800, the multiplication of printed materials expanded the purview of public opinion and included an ever-widening percentage of the population in its creation. As the historian Joyce Appleby has recently explained, this "cultural upheaval" saw political issues of every sort put before the public. Even "the most cloistered disputants took their causes to the public, usually through the press, allowing ordinary readers to become knowledgeable about what had once been confidential proceedings." Although elites continued to identify themselves as the only legitimate public and derided others' ability to comment on weighty matters, they were fighting a losing battle. The astounding power of public opinion attested to the democratization of nineteenth-century political life.[4]

Such broad historical developments are best examined through an illustrative case-study.[5] The 1820 trial and execution of Morris Norton Bartholomew Hull and Peregrine Hutton connect a *cause célèbre* in Baltimore to the largest questions in the political history of the early republic. Their cases provoked an extensive public conversation on the condemned men's lives and the nature of penal justice in a republican society. Advocates and detractors alike publicized every aspect of Hull and Hutton's past and present, and appealed to the court of public opinion. Revivalist clergymen, the editors of competing newspapers, and out-of-towners addressed the public as readily as they implored the governor—the only person with the power to commute the condemned men's sentences. No unitary public voice emerged, but instead multiple publics asserted their right to guide the events of early summer 1820. This democratization of the political arena prefigured the broader changes in political culture associated with the Age of Jackson. Yet, the legacy of Hull and Hutton also revealed the halting nature of those changes in the face of strong resistance. The voices claiming to speak to and for the public had multiplied around this one case, but the episode closed with a loud denunciation of the public's legitimacy in commenting on substantive issues. The struggle for the lives of Hull and Hutton reflected a broader contest over the democratic implications of public opinion.

The best entry into the Hull and Hutton case is to join the story in April 1820, after the men had been arrested in Baltimore for a murderous mail robbery outside the city. The public had become aware of their case in the short time between the crime and their confessions. Still, details remained uncertain and the piecemeal flow of information caused public sentiment to shift several times. This fickleness, said critics, disqualified the public from participating in a debate of this magnitude.

Peregrine Hutton and Morris Hull came to trial almost certain to receive the death penalty. Maryland's criminal code, thoroughly overhauled in 1809, demanded the lives of those convicted of premeditated murder. And had the two defendants eluded death under Maryland law, they would still have faced federal capital charges for mail robbery. In fact just two years earlier, Baltimore had witnessed the hangings of another pair of mail robbers, John Alexander and Joseph Thompson Hare. Those two had not killed anyone but nonetheless paid with their lives. Aware that both federal and state law spoke in no uncertain terms in regard to their crimes, Hull and Hutton cooperated with authorities, offered confessions, and pleaded guilt when brought before the Maryland Criminal Court on April 17. Their lawyer John N. Tyson, however, did request a delay in the trial so that Hull and Hutton might "die amid the commiseration instead of the vengeance of the people, which was now justly alive against them." Although the court denied Tyson's request for more time, it had no power to stem the transformation of public opinion that ultimately made Hull and Hutton the recipients of more sympathy than scorn.[6]

At the time of the trial, Morris Hull had little reason to expect public sympathy. Newspaper accounts depicted the gruesome murder of an innocent man, mail coach driver John Heaps. The coverage of Heaps's death was illustrative of what historian Karen Halttunen has called "the pornography of pain" in early-nineteenth-century crime reportage. *Niles' Weekly Register* depicted Heaps "with his arms extended and fastened to trees" by the reins of his coach. Readers learned that "the pistol was put so near to his breast that his clothes were singed." Sadly, Hull's shot did not kill Heaps instantaneously, and the murderers then administered several stabs to put him out of his misery. It did not help that Heaps was himself a sympathetic character, a recent immigrant who in the space of two years had established "a fair character and found the means of subsistence" in the United States. In fact, Heaps had only recently collected enough money for his wife and several children to join him in America. The gunman Hull had provided an abrupt ending to an early republic success story and propelled Mrs. Heaps and her children into a precarious dependence upon charity and the scant wages of their own labor.[7]

Initial newspaper accounts featured Hull and Hutton as sketchy characters within a much larger criminal underworld. The twenty-year-old Hull had originally met the twenty-eight-year-old Hutton in New York City in early March at John Whelpley's Greenwich Street boardinghouse. During the first two weeks of their acquaintance, Hull and Hutton spoke frequently with a Mr. Davis, who would soon face charges for his own attempt to rob the mails. When Davis testified in his own defense, he implicated Hull and Hutton in "a combination of fifty persons" whose assault on the mail would make the Baltimore heist appear "but trifling." Boardinghouse-keeper Whelpley linked Hull and Hutton back to Davis's expansive conspiracy and recollected Hull as no naïve youth. For example, Hull had used a total of five aliases (beyond his rather lengthy given name), and when asked why, replied that "he had several wives and assumed their names when it pleased him." Besides being a wise-acre, Hull toted a menacing "Spanish knife" with a ten-inch blade. According to Whelpley, another boarder "remarked to Hull that such an instrument was suitable only for a robber, at which [Hull] smiled." And although to Whelpley's knowledge Hull had not committed any robberies, the young man did skip town still owing sixteen dollars for room and board. Hull and Hutton had combined their belongings, departed together, and fooled Whelpley by leaving behind a rag-filled trunk as a guarantee on their debt.[8]

Such stories cast Hull as a common criminal, an image that the newspaper publication of his confession complicated but did not significantly contradict. Deposed by Judge Theodore Bland, the youthful Hull narrated his own tremendous fall from aspiring pharmacist to condemned criminal. The desire for work brought Hull from Utica to New York City in early 1820. There he met Hutton, who was also out of work but brimming with "great confidence" that money would come easy in Baltimore. Not until they had reached Wilmington, Delaware, did Hutton propose a mail robbery, and as they traveled southward by foot, the topic "was frequently spoken of." They had made up their mind before reaching Baltimore, although Hull left the specific plans to Hutton, who "knew the country." From this point onward in his confession, Hull cast himself as little more than Hutton's accomplice. After two abortive attempts to find a solitary mail coach driver on the roads outside Baltimore, they apprehended Heaps about eight miles north on the Philadelphia Road. It was a Friday evening close to midnight. Hull assisted Hutton in guiding the wagon into the woods and then in tying the cooperative driver to two saplings. After they pilfered the mail and prepared to ride away on Heaps's horses, Hutton "told Hull in a low voice 'now you must go up and shoot him.'" Hull protested, but Hutton was adamant that the driver had recognized him despite his mask and must not be left alive to testify. With great foresight, Hull predicted "we shall surely be hung." Despite further pleas for Heaps's life, Hutton stood steadfast and sent Hull forth, gun in hand. Hull did not confess to a particular state of mind at this point, saying only that he had shot the driver and that when it was discovered that the man still had a pulse, Hutton finished him off with a knife. Hutton and Hull then rode off with their loot, ditched the horses outside the city, changed their clothes, and entertained the strikingly bourgeois notion of opening a joint apothecary-grocery in Petersburg, Virginia.[9]

Peregrine Hutton offered a confession that corroborated Hull's, save for one crucial difference. As Hutton recollected, it had been Hull who insisted on shooting Heaps. In fact, Hutton had instructed Hull to free the driver, not to kill him. Hutton recalled assuring his younger associate that their disguises were sufficient. But no sooner had Hull gone over ostensibly to untie Heaps than a shot rang out. Hull then nonchalantly informed Hutton that the driver had given him a kick, and so he shot the man. Hutton immediately rebuked Hull and lamented that the murder would "lead to their detection."[10] Actually, their arrests were more fortuitous. Baltimore magistrates had known Hutton from several years earlier when he was himself a mail coach driver. They were surprised to see him in Baltimore in March 1820 because he was supposed to be serving prison time in Richmond for a kidnapping. Astute officers arrested Hutton on suspicion that he had participated in a recent jailbreak. They also arrested the nervous stranger with him, Morris Hull. A search of the two men's pockets revealed over $6,000 in banknotes and quickly established Hull and Hutton as the primary suspects in the robbery. Another $10,000 turned up in the room they were renting in Old Town.[11] After an initial silence, both Hutton and Hull confessed and the court did not concern itself with reconciling their accounts—both had confessed to the murder of Heaps, rendering further inquiry moot. Only the court of public opinion would seek to differentiate the degrees of guilt between Hull and Hutton. In fact, no sooner had the death sentence been announced than observers began probing the exact chain of events leading up to Heaps's murder. The law saw the men as equally culpable, but the public would soon argue otherwise.

The transformation began on the day of their sentencing, a mere two days after Hull and Hutton offered their guilty pleas. "There never was on any occasion so great a concourse of people at the Court House," reported the *Baltimore American*. Before handing down the sentence, Judge Dorsey gave the men an opportunity to speak. Hutton declined, but Hull declared himself resigned to his fate. "Aware of the enormity of the crime I have committed," Hull harbored "no hope of pardon" and expected mercy only "in the redeeming blood of Jesus." Hull expressed only one wish: "to make restitution to the woman I have widowed, the children I have made fatherless." Concerned less with his own earthly fate than with that of Heaps's family, Hull made a deep impression on both the audience and Judge Dorsey. Indeed, reported the *American*, "the manly tears which trickled down [Dorsey's] cheeks were responded by those of a majority of the bar and audience." Dorsey reiterated that neither man could expect forgiveness on earth, but only "beyond the grave." He added that their fate should "be a warning to the rising generation." Finally, claiming that "in cases of this kind the judges have no discretion," Dorsey read the fateful sentence: "The Court do therefore order and adjudge that you and each of you be taken hence to the prison, thence to the place of execution, and that you there be hanged by the neck until you are dead, and may God in his infinite goodness have mercy on your souls."[12]

The sentence set into motion three separate dramas. First, Morris Hull's father made a torturous trip from Utica, New York, to Maryland in order to plead for his son's life. In doing so, Dr. Amos Hull directed the nation's eyes toward Baltimore and put Maryland's penal statutes at the center of a debate on capital punishment. Second, public opinion embraced Morris Hull as a kind-hearted young man who had been led astray by bad company. The outpouring of petitions and letters on Hull's behalf gave the young man a reasonable expectation that his sentence would be commuted. Third, Peregrine Hutton, not content to be known only as Hull's corrupter, proclaimed a religious conversion and sought a baptism in the Jones Falls, the waterway running by the prison yard and through the center of the city. By the time of their scheduled execution in July, Hull and Hutton's respective plights had generated widespread public sympathy.

Amos Hull received word of his son's predicament during the first weeks of April. Morris had written home from prison sometime before the trial. As the anguished father readied himself to travel from upstate New York to Maryland, he surely recalled the carnival atmosphere three years earlier when a young man of Morris's age died on the scaffold outside Utica. Convicted of murder in nearby Whitesborough, seventeen-year-old John Tuhi had been carted through the center of Utica as a military band played "the dead march to the gallows." A pamphlet commemorating the event estimated that more than fifteen thousand New Yorkers braved the July heat for "the opportunity (shall we say, pleasure and gratification) of seeing a wretched malefactor sent, with violence and ignominy, into eternity."[13] With such a shameful ending perhaps awaiting the son of their friend, three Utica neighbors armed Doctor Hull with letters of introduction to some of the nation's leading politicians: Secretary of State John Quincy Adams, Secretary of War John C. Calhoun, and Secretary of the Navy Smith Thompson. Adams was asked to help "the unhappy father of the still more unhappy young man." Calhoun would learn that Amos Hull was "a respectable physician and surgeon" who faced a "most awful calamity." Unfortunately, these solicitations assumed that Morris faced federal charges for mail robbery rather than state charges for murder. Although these distinguished cabinet officials might be acquainted with Maryland officials, they had no ability to intervene in the administration of state justice. Nor did any of the three Washington figures correspond with Maryland's governor, Samuel Sprigg, about the matter.[14]

As Amos made the journey to Maryland, Morris wrote a second letter that disclosed his "awful sentence." Baltimore newspapers obtained and reprinted the April 23 letter, giving the public the chance to share in Dr. Hull's agony and Morris's repentance.[15] Both of these experiences caused readers to question the justice of the sentence. "Little did I expect when I left our happy home and an affectionate father," wrote Morris, "that before I could see you again I should have incurred such guilt and be a tenant of this doleful cell." Morris seemed unable to explain his failure in judgment at the crucial moment: "When the poor man [Heaps] begged for his life, I told him we would spare him and I meant it. Indeed I pleaded for him, but Hutton insisted we would be known, and told me it was no time for pleading, and at last told me either to shoot him or the driver, and then—O! my God forgive me." By making Hutton's ultimatum central to the murder and by linking his own fall to "bad company," Morris reduced his own culpability. Still, he did not question the justice of his sentence. Morris devoted the bulk of the letter to his religious penitence. "The Bible is now worth to me all you used to say it was worth," declared Morris in embracing the Christian teachings he had rejected for so many years. Morris quoted scripture to express his belief that "my guilty soul may be saved because Jesus Christ died for sinners." Morris concluded by reiterating his courtroom plea that something be done for John Heaps's widow and children. Perhaps his father could offer them a salary or pension, suggested Morris before signing off as "your guilty, afflicted, undutiful and imprisoned son."[16]

Morris Hull's April 23 letter to his father aroused the public to come to his defense, first in Baltimore and then elsewhere. Citing the letter, Baltimore's *Morning Chronicle* published the first editorial on Hull's behalf on April 27. It characterized the young man as "sincerely penitent" and reminded readers who would condemn Hull that "our Savior himself pardoned the dying and repentant criminal." More importantly, the *Chronicle* echoed the claim of Hull's letter by describing him as "seduced and betrayed into temptation." Although Hull and Hutton were both involved in the murder and robbery, the editorial pointed to "the difference in the degrees of their guilt." It contrasted Hutton ("nearly thirty years old, wholly devoid of any principle, moral or religious, prepared for the perpetration of any atrocity") and the youthful Hull ("prone to temptation"). The *Chronicle* also added a new piece to the story of the murder: after Hull's cowardice had botched their first attempt to stop a mail coach, Hutton alluded to another criminal who had killed a flinching accomplice. Accordingly, when Hutton demanded Heaps's life, Hull recalled the "threat which was given the night before." It had been Hutton who had planned the robbery, had reason to fear being recognized, desired the driver's death, coerced Hull into firing the shot, had stabbed Heaps to death when the bullet failed, then "spoke in exalting terms of its accomplishment" and ultimately concocted a false confession shifting the blame to Hull. The *Chronicle* did not explicitly ask for the commutation of Hull's sentence, but it offered ammunition for those who would.[17]

Such letters began arriving on the desk of Governor Samuel Sprigg the following week. Pleas for clemency, the commutation of sentences, abatement of fines, and squelching of prosecutions regularly flowed into Annapolis. Indeed, one of the governor's main responsibilities was to dispense justice in consultation with the state's executive council. During the 1810s, the governor and council issued such pardons to between twenty and forty petitioners each year. The process generally favored petitioners who were white, male, young, penitent, and perhaps most importantly, who had influential advocates.[18] All of those factors were working in Hull's favor. During the first week of May, two letters from Baltimore clergymen opened the official campaign to garner Governor Sprigg's mercy. "His age and respectable father and all his friends overwhelmed with sorrow, desire that his present [sentence] may be commuted for that of solitary confinement for life," wrote J. P. K. Henshaw, rector of St. Peter's Church, an Episcopal congregation at Sharp and German streets. Similarly, W. E. Wyatt, the associate minister of St. Paul's Episcopal church on Charles Street, assured the governor that sparing Hull's life was "scarcely a mitigation of punishment." All anyone desired for Hull was "the privilege of continuing to breathe in chains in a dungeon and in solitude—the privilege of passing from a guilty and deluded youth into a premature but penitent and sanctified old age." Such a favor would not strip penal justice of its power to deter future wrongdoers because Hull would "be made a lasting and living monument of the consequence of crime."[19]

One of Morris Hull's best advantages was having Peregrine Hutton as a foil. Recall that Hull and Hutton were initially apprehended because Baltimore authorities recognized Hutton as an accused kidnapper. Just a few months earlier, Hutton had faced charges in Virginia for transporting two free African American children from Philadelphia to Richmond for sale as slaves. Although acquitted of this crime, Hutton still reeked of criminality to those arguing on Morris Hull's behalf. The clergymen initiating Hull's pardon plea had visited the two convicts in prison and concluded that Hutton had been the instigator and that Hull had been coerced into the murder. It was fairly easy to contrast Hull the penitent with Hutton the reprobate, especially as Hutton seemed eager to ruin Hull a second time from within the prison walls. Now, reported Reverend Wyatt, Hutton was attempting "to throw upon his victim all the odium of the transaction." Hutton had initially offered a false confession in "an attempt to become state's evidence." Although Hutton would come to acknowledge "every point upon which the vast difference in the degree of their guilt is presumed to rest," he was still "endeavoring to destroy public sympathy for Hull." Remarkably, Hull never expressed any vindictiveness toward the man who had ruined his life. Moreover, as the condemned Hull immersed himself in Bible study, Hutton received in his jail cell "a woman of notoriously infamous character." These differences—clear both before and after the commission of the crime—suggested the need to reconsider Hull's punishment.[20]

In his plea, Reverend Wyatt spoke for what he described as "the feelings of a large and most respectable portion of our community." Indeed, a letter followed apace from Baltimore's mayor Edward Johnson and such other luminaries as Lyde Goodwin, William Winder, and Thomas Kell. This group of prominent merchants, lawyers, and politicians assured Governor Sprigg that he could "make a just and every way important discrimination between the different grades of criminality and endear yourself to the best feelings of the community by an act of grace." Showing mercy, these politically astute petitioners advised, was "always amiable, when it can be exercised in conformity with the obligations which the laws and interests of civil society imposes." Thomas Stansbury, member of one of Baltimore's most prominent families, attacked the efficacy of the death penalty in deterring crime, claimed that solitary confinement for life was "equal if not worse than Death," and pleaded that Doctor Hull should be spared "the ignominy attached to his Son's being hung."[21]

Pressure on Governor Sprigg mounted with the arrival of two powerful letters. The first was a bombshell from a local pharmacist named Jesse Talbot. A few days before committing the mail robbery, Morris Hull had applied for a position in Talbot's store. As Talbot recalled, the young New Yorker had described himself as "very desirable to get into business" and offered "very respectable references in that state as to his character or that of his connections." Sadly, Talbot had just dismissed one of his employees because "things were very distressingly gloomy among commercial men" and thus could ill-afford to hire someone else. In this light, Morris Hull was a notorious casualty of the Panic of 1819. For his part, Talbot felt terrible insofar as "if I could have given him employment when he solicited it, it might under the blessing of Providence have been the means of preventing him from committing the desperate act." The most important aspect of Talbot's testimony was that it commented on Hull's state of mind at the time of the murder. Rather than arriving in Baltimore a hardened criminal intent on robbery, Hull still hoped to free himself from Hutton's grasp. In fact, when told that Talbot had no employment to offer, Hull left the store "very much agitated in the mind" and "in a state of depression bordering on desperation." For advocates of clemency, Hull's participation in the robbery was a horrible twist of fate, easily averted if only he had found a legitimate job. Hull himself was well aware of the bind he was in. Unsuccessful at Talbot's, Hull left the store with a sense of impending doom. In corroborating Talbot's account, Dr. David Reese explained that Hull's "tears flowed in consequence of his despairing of his escaping from the hands of his abandoned companion and from the commission of an awful crime at which his heart revolted."[22]

Soon after learning of this persuasive new evidence, Governor Sprigg read the heart-wrenching words of Amos Hull, the father pleading for the life of his son. "May God deliver you even from an apprehension of that sorrow with which my bosom is wrung," began the distraught man. Amos Hull then launched a two-pronged attack, making a case for Morris's lesser criminality and for the great religious imperatives of mercy. "But oh! punish him not as a voluntary, unconstrained abandoned agent," implored Amos Hull, implicitly contrasting his son's character to that of Hutton's. Both God and Justice, he continued, recognized differences in the guilt of a man who plans a crime and "a boy seduced, reluctant, opposing the commission of it, and at last consenting only under the influence of a ferocious and threatening leader." The father then offered several Biblical injunctions calling on those who intend to receive mercy to first show it. Should the governor commute the sentence, "forever will many a devout Christian bless and thank you." From the Baltimore penitentiary, the spared Morris "will send up daily petitions to our common judge and Savior for him who spared his life," and from Utica the rest of the Hulls will "ceaselessly invoke blessings" on the governor's behalf. Perhaps no part of the letter was more evocative than Amos Hull's impassioned plea: "Oh! Save me from the deep and bitter anguish of beholding him die."[23]

There is no evidence as to how Governor Sprigg reacted to the barrage of petitions and letters he received in May and June of 1820. The case may have been an annoyance that interfered with his other work. It may have caused him discomfort and sleepless nights. Certainly, the advocates of clemency sought to put the governor into the shoes of Amos Hull, asking whether the governor could imagine himself in such a situation. "Every father who has sons young and inexperienced," admonished Thomas Stansbury, ". . . must sincerely sympathize with Doctor Hull." Socially and culturally, bourgeois fathers like Sprigg, Stansbury, and Hull actually had a fair amount in common. They shared in the loss of paternal authority during the decades following the American Revolution. As their professions removed them from domestic life, fathers ceded responsibility for the moral upbringing of their sons. Occupying a position as secondary parent, fathers struggled to play a role in their sons' lives. A father's key responsibility became the establishment of his son in a middle-class occupation. Amos Hull had overseen Morris's acquisition of some pharmacological training but had failed to guide his son into a productive life. Amos Hull's shame and frustration surely resonated with other fathers facing the same difficult task. To complicate matters further, early-nineteenth-century proscriptive literature stressed the affective relationship between fathers and sons. With only a fairly mechanical economic obligation toward them, bourgeois fathers nonetheless expressed a new sentimental love for their boys. This emotional bond made Morris's imminent death an unthinkably painful prospect for Amos Hull. All men of feeling—Governor Sprigg included—would be expected to empathize with the despairing father.[24]

Governor Sprigg also received advice on the political expedience of executing Morris Hull. David Reese assured the governor that by "extending mercy to this penitent youth, you will thereby obtain the support and prayers of this great community." It is not clear whether Baltimore's electoral backing was of concern to Sprigg, who was something of a conservative, rural Jeffersonian. Political leaders elsewhere also offered their two-cents to Sprigg. From New York, Governor Daniel Tompkins advised that "the execution of one of the murderers will answer the object of the laws, whilst the execution of two at the same time may perhaps excite public sympathy and defeat the object." Tompkins knew first-hand the relationship between clemency, public outrage, and political fortune. When he first won the New York governorship in 1807, Tompkins defeated the incumbent Morgan Lewis, who had incurred the wrath of the electorate for sparing the life of a child murderer in Otsego County. Tompkins seemed to suggest that Sprigg should sway with public opinion on such matters, especially when it could be done without jeopardizing the legitimacy of the laws. Executing Hutton and saving Hull would satisfy lust for retribution, demonstrate the futility of crime to potential violators, but not overwhelm the public with too much cruelty.[25]

For executives like Sprigg and Tompkins, such decisions were made all the more difficult by conflicting theories of criminal justice. The 1810s witnessed a heated debate over the efficacy of penitentiaries. In the early republic period, states such as Maryland and New York rewrote their penal statutes, reducing the number of crimes punishable by death and instituting fearfully long periods of confinement as the best means of both rehabilitating the offender and deterring others from committing crime. But after a decade or more of the new penitential regime, crime rates did not decline, nor did prisoners return to society as reformed citizens. In response to such failures, state officials tinkered with the system, sometimes adding hard labor to the convict's punishment, and other times isolating the convict in solitary confinement. In particular, advocates of solitary confinement touted the terror of isolation as more powerful than public executions in deterring future crime and as a greater punishment than instant death for the condemned.[26]

Such notions informed much of the debate over Morris Hull's pending execution. Many of those who wrote Governor Sprigg decried the death penalty as a barbaric relic. But lest the governor fear that commuting the sentence would appear a capitulation to rampant criminality, his petitioners insisted that a life of solitary confinement was as harsh as the death penalty. Baltimore resident William Williams reprinted his sentiments in a broadside that proclaimed life imprisonment "tenfold more lingering, terrifying, and painful than any species of death ever inflicted." With Hull laden down with irons and never to see the sun again, Williams intoned, "is not this enough for the lad? Is not this enough for EXAMPLE? Is this not enough for justice?" Of course, the other point of view had its advocates as well. A correspondent to the *American* under the name "Justitia" called efforts to spare Hull "exertions of mistaken and misapplied humanity" and demanded his execution "in the name of that divine law as well as human, which declares that 'blood shall be the sacrifice of bloodshed' and above all, in the name of the innocent widows and orphans." Interestingly, however, this pro-death penalty letter was the only one to appear in Baltimore newspapers during the period of Hull's incarceration.[27]

Baltimore residents were no strangers to the larger issues of criminal justice and penal reform. In fact, four days before Hull and Hutton's trial, two pirates were hanged in Baltimore. The *American* noted that "the terrible and ignominious end of the unfortunate men who have thus expired

on the scaffold must serve as a striking example to prevent the commission of similar offences." Although there was no outcry on the behalf of
Israel Denny and John Ferguson, the public must have juxtaposed these
two men with Hull and Hutton.[28] Baltimore residents might also have had in
mind the lengthy contest to prosecute James Buchanan, George Williams,
and James McCulloh, three directors of the Baltimore branch of the Bank of
United States. Their shady lending practices (read: embezzlement) precipitated a major financial crisis when exposed in 1819. Appropriate scape-
goats for the ensuing panic, Buchanan, Williams, and McCulloh faced serious criminal charges for conspiracy to defraud the bank and its sharehold-
ers. Their lawyers, however, petitioned to move the trial to rural Harford
County, where they were less likely to face a hostile jury. Over significant
protest, they escaped trial in Baltimore. Although the crimes were of a very
different nature from those of Hull and Hutton, the lawyerly machinations
of the Baltimore bankers raised troubling questions of legal equity.[29] Finally,
Baltimore residents were ideally situated to contemplate the effectiveness
of penitential rehabilitation because their city was home to the only such
institution in the state. Not only did most of the inmates hail from Baltimore, but they remained in the city once paroled. The walls of the penitentiary were not as permeable as had been those of the old gaols, but
nonetheless, city and prison existed in constant dialogue with one another.
Sadly, that conversation was largely muted by a decision of the *American*
to publish no more letters about Hull's case after May 8—just a few days
after the official proceedings for a pardon began. Other newspapers seemed
to share the sentiment of the *American*'s editors that the subject was "extremely disagreeable to us, and in our opinion, not proper to have its merits
discussed in a public newspaper."[30]

The inhabitants of Baltimore did rally to Morris Hull's cause by signing
numerous petitions. Signers might have included middle-class parents sympathizing with Amos Hull's heartbreak, or struggling artisans identifying
with Morris Hull's frustration at not finding a job.[31] Unfortunately, no Baltimore petitions survive, making it impossible to analyze the particular demographic groups, occupational segments, or neighborhoods invested in
his defense. What surely surprised Governor Sprigg, however, was not the
outcry he heard from Baltimore, but rather that which originated out of
state. These petitions were striking in their size. One from New York City

unfurled to over thirty feet in length and bore signatures that numbered well into the thousands.[32] Similar petitions arrived from Philadelphia, reiterating the standard arguments in favor of commuting Hull's sentence to life imprisonment. Hull's youth, as well as the distinction between him and Hutton, demanded something be done to "save this man from the ignominious death which awaits him." The three Philadelphia petitions carried several thousand names. Indeed, Philadelphia newspapers listed places where concerned citizens could join "a number of the most leading characters" in signing. S. Tyndale, one of the Philadelphia organizers, informed Governor Sprigg that the Hull case had excited "sympathy of feeling and prayers for commutation" with "no parallel." Tyndale added that the Philadelphia signers included "some of the most enlightened part of our Citizens," including the mayor, city treasurer, most aldermen, and "a great many" physicians, clergymen, and lawyers. Without question, Morris Hull had become a *cause célèbre* for urban humanitarians and an alluring scandal for public consumption. A fraudulent pamphlet entitled *The Confessions and History of the whole life of Morris. N. B. Hull, the wretched young mail robber, written by himself* circulated in cities up and down the Atlantic coast.[33]

By the time the national mobilization gained full momentum, two months had passed since Hull's and Hutton's convictions. It was now mid-June. The case was building to a climax, especially because the governor and council generally met at the end of June to consider pardons. If they denied clemency and instead signed the death warrant, an execution would follow soon after. Things appeared promising for Morris Hull. Among those signing a clemency petition was Mrs. Heaps, the widow of the murdered mail carrier. Additionally, Dr. David Reese offered new medical evidence that Heaps would have survived the shot from Hull's gun. It followed that Hutton should bear the brunt of the guilt because his stabs had been fatal. During the last week of June, rumors circulated in Baltimore that clemency was forthcoming. On July 1, the editors of the *American* reprinted a letter from a Philadelphia paper that declared that the governor and council had adjourned without making a decision, thus sparing Hull's life until the following December (notably, until after the fall's gubernatorial election). The *American* did not vouch for the accuracy of the report, but the *Federal Gazette*, a rival paper, quickly dismissed the news as a "false hope." Its editors had sources who could confirm that "the solemn determination has already been made by the Executive" and that an execution was imminent. But for Hull in his jail cell and for the public at large, the decision still hung in the balance.[34]

Things looked less promising for Peregrine Hutton. Indeed, the public's main argument on Hull's behalf necessarily lessened sympathy for Hutton: Hutton was the "bad company" responsible for Hull's seduction. With little reason to expect mercy in this world, Hutton perhaps turned his full attention to spiritual salvation. His resulting pursuit of a baptism added another sensational dimension to the case. On June 30, the *Morning Chronicle* published a letter from Hutton to Reverend James Osborne of the Third Baptist Church. Raised in total ignorance of Scripture, Hutton now placed all his hopes with Christ. But, wrote Hutton, "I conceive it my duty to be baptised." This request presented certain logistical problems for the clergymen who had been meeting with Hutton in jail. The nearest water in which one might be immersed was the Jones Falls, outside the prison walls. It seemed unlikely that the sheriff would permit such a ceremony. On the other hand, this baptism had the potential to galvanize believers and non-believers alike—always important in Baltimore's competitive religious marketplace. There is no reason to impugn the purity of religious sincerity on the part of Hutton and Osborne. But there is also no reason to expect that they did not envision the tremendous public impact of such a baptism. A ceremony was planned for Sunday, July 9, with the Baptist brethren forming a procession from the prison to the water. Late Saturday night, prison officials changed their mind and cancelled the event. Instead, Hutton received a more subdued baptism in the presence of four clergymen. Baptist leaders apologized "that such a respectable concourse of people should have been disappointed on Lord's Day morning." The private ceremony did seem to satisfy Hutton, who was received in Baptist fellowship a few days later by fifty-four members of Reverend Osborne's flock. They attended a Lord's Supper at the jail and extended to their "new brother the right hand of fellowship . . . and a final farewell for this world." Osborne later commented that Hutton's conversion "far exceeded any thing I have ever before seen in a person in the same space of time."[35]

When no pardon arrived from Annapolis, the *Morning Chronicle* warned readers that "we shall shortly be called on to witness a painful and an awful spectacle." Neither the *Chronicle* nor the *American* published anything resembling a clemency plea or a protest in the week leading up to Friday, July 14. Instead, the papers changed the entire tenor of the debate by admonishing the public against misplaced sympathy. "The execution of a legal sentence is not murder," one *Chronicle* editorial reminded those "who forget the crime when they witness the death." The day before the execution, the paper lamented anything "that converts criminals into saints and apostles to soothe the wounded feelings of their relatives and friends." If Dr. Hull remained in town for the execution, such harsh words must have added insult to injury. When Friday finally arrived, the *American* offered the following benediction: "May the ignominious and just punishment of these misguided men be a warning to all who are tempted by the hope of unlawful gain to swerve from the path of rectitude." The newspapers tried to put an abrupt stop to two months of vigorous debate over the validity of the death penalty. The plunging of a trap door on the gallows did put an abrupt stop to the lives of Hull and Hutton at 11:30 A.M. According to witnesses, both men died with devotion and dignity.[36]

Perhaps most surprisingly, the executions did not provoke public outrage. The citizens of Mobtown were known for their willingness to express outrage in the streets. Yet there was no riot outside the prison. No effigies of Governor Sprigg were paraded through town. Indeed, at the moment of truth, the public seemed to accept the sentence with little interference. The plight of Morris and Amos Hull—cast as a bourgeois melodrama— might have been unlikely to galvanize the segment of the community most likely to riot. Alternatively, the execution itself may have offered so compelling a display of state power that it made resistance appear futile. Of course, the newspapers' last-minute denunciation of public sympathy helped to reassert state (and thereby, elite) authority and initiated a more intensive effort to de-legitimize public participation in matters of criminal justice. Commentators did continue to debate the executions, but turned their attention away from issues of criminal justice and toward the validity of public opinion itself. The tremendous outpouring on Hull's behalf sparked a backlash that deserves further examination insofar as it touches on the larger issue of political democratization in the early republic.

No one offered a more cynical take on the preceding months than Hezekiah Niles, editor of the national paper of record, *Niles' Weekly Register*. As Niles recounted, "when the horror excited by their misdeeds had a little subsided, and the mangled body of poor Heaps no longer presented itself to the agonized imagination, a strong effort was made upon the public sensibility in favor of Hull." As Hull's stock rose, Hutton's fell, until "suddenly, Hutton came into repute—he too wrote letters, or had them written, like a saint, which were extensively published." After the sensational baptism, "the fashion had changed—it was now Hutton and not Hull that was offered to the public tenderness." Most absurd to Niles was that *Mister* Hutton received a church burial, replete with a procession and a sermon in his honor. Niles implied that two criminals had duped the public, and he hoped "such scenes shall never be repeated." Particularly blameworthy were the newspapers that "teemed with many imprudent articles."[37]

Niles also complained that Governor Sprigg's petitioners included "many women and others of a neighboring state." That Pennsylvania and New York residents imposed on Maryland's affairs might indeed prove irksome in an era of state sovereignty. Such a complaint, however, would seem odd coming from Niles, whose journalistic mission was nationalist through and through. Rather, female petitioners garnered Niles's disapproval. The first decades of the nineteenth century witnessed a contest over women's place in American politics. On the one hand, male politicians designated women as anti-citizens and excluded them from the realm of rational political discourse—which is to say, the public that might comment on Hull and Hutton's fate. On the other hand, women increasingly voiced opinions on political issues, especially those doubling as moral questions; women defined themselves as the most appropriate public for this particular debate. For Niles, female petitioners had intruded upon a fundamentally male matter of state. Public opinion could help shape issues of criminal justice, but not when illegitimate voices polluted the discussion.[38]

For other commentators, public opinion threatened the efficacy of capital punishment by glorifying criminals and undermining the certainty of the sentence. On the eve of the execution, the editors of the *Morning Chronicle* excoriated their readers for undermining the deterrent power of the death penalty. Executions could "inspire horror for the crime" only if the convicted were denied public sympathy. But when "the hail stones of descending justice are melted down into the soft dews of compassion," then executions actually promoted greater criminality. Hull's execution provided an interesting case in point. Among the crowd watching the execution was a pickpocket, a man apprehended soon after the sentence was carried out. Had that man been considering a greater crime, would he have been deterred by what he saw "within a few feet of the gallows"? No, the editors argued, such a criminal would envision "popular sensibility in his last moments greater than he had ever experienced before." Indeed, any daring criminal would soon find a way to be "transformed by the mysterious agency of popular sensibility from a criminal into a saint." With great vehemence, the editors declared "outlaws and ruffians, murderers and thieves are not the legitimate objects for the exercise of public sensibility."[39]

During the early 1800s, critics of capital punishment often seized on its failure as a didactic ritual. Executions regularly turned into disorderly festivals that fed the basest passions of human nature. With their drama and display, public executions might serve to reinforce state authority; but a capricious crowd and a provocative criminal combined in a volatile mix. Just as executions seemingly failed to deter criminality, so too did they lose their power to solidify public authority. Although the lack of protest following Hull's execution was telling, the punishment hardly served to strengthen public reverence for and obedience to the Annapolis government. That would have required the state to impose its own fixed and unitary meaning on to the execution. Yet when Hull ascended the scaffold, there were already so many competing narratives about the crime and the punishment that the state had no ability to control the execution's message. As one historian of penal law has recently suggested, once states recognized their tenuous grip on the meaning of public punishments, they began to move the mechanisms of discipline out of the public's sight.[40] That process was underway in Maryland at the time of Hull and Hutton's hangings. Although the public witnessed their executions, the gallows stood in the prison yard. It would not be difficult to keep the gates closed in the future, thereby eliminating public participation at the crucial and final moment. Despite broad-based opposition to capital punishment in the early republic, the most significant reform was not its abolition, but rather its removal from the public eye.[41]

Removing capital punishment from view marked one way to reduce the power of public opinion. But reformers proposed a far more effective means of making public opinion irrelevant to matters of criminal justice— removing the pardoning power from the governor. In the wake of Hull and

Hutton's execution, the *Morning Chronicle* argued that it was better to abolish the power of the governor to pardon than to witness again such misguided concern on the part of the public.[42] Effective punishment depended on its certainty. The death penalty lost its deterrent power if would-be criminals could hope for a sympathetic public to come to their defense. Executions could not reinforce state power if the state appeared too easily swayed by its subjects. The pardoning power was relic of monarchical rule, when a benevolent ruler might dispense grace to supplicants. However, pardons appeared inappropriate in a republic where the executive governed in accordance with precise laws. Pardons smacked of arbitrary and whimsical rule, especially when issued by a governor responsive to public opinion. There was no way to silence the public's right to petition, but those pleas might fall upon ears not so much deaf as impotent.

Daniel Raymond, a Baltimore lawyer and one of the first American political economists, echoed this opinion. Raymond had received a letter of inquiry from a New York State committee investigating the efficacy of its penitentiary in 1821. They asked Raymond to evaluate penal justice in Maryland and to offer suggestions for reform. After praising long-standing beliefs that certainty of punishment was central to effective deterrence, Raymond decried penitentiaries as "mere workshops and schools of vice." He advocated "rebuild[ing] the whipping post and pillory" for the poor, and subjecting more refined criminals to other forms of public humiliation. The key to such punishments was to deny the criminal any hope of escaping them. To that end, the pardoning power was counterproductive. Raymond's primary exhibit was the Hull and Hutton debacle. "There were thousands of persons, of both sexes," Raymond recalled, who had been "insensibly led first to palliate and then to defend the guilty murderer Hull by having their feelings enlisted in his favour, with a hope of saving his life." Raymond was incredulous "to see with what ingenuity and earnestness, respectable people . . . defended the crime of that monster, which ought never to have been mentioned but with execration and horror." His advice to the New York committee was to remove the pardoning power from the governor.[43]

Indeed, the Morris Hull case figured prominently in the New York State debate over capital punishment. In 1821, Utica publisher William Williams issued *Remarks on Capital Punishment*, a pamphlet containing a collection of Morris Hull's letters, a statement from Amos Hull, and anti-death penalty arguments drawn from the writings of Benjamin Rush, Sir William Blackstone, and Cesare Beccaria. The following year, Sylvanus Haynes published a response, *A Letter to Dr. Amos Hull, in Vindication of Capital Punishment*. Pastor of a Baptist congregation in Camillus, New York, Haynes apologized for addressing his comments to the aggrieved father: "Rest assured that nothing but a sense of duty to God and my country, could have induced me to interrupt your tranquility with the following epistle." However, Amos Hull's association with the 1821 anti-death penalty pamphlet accounted for Haynes' sense of urgency. "An address from *you*, on such a *subject*, at such a *time*, and thus *situated*, would naturally be overwhelming," observed Haynes, "and produce sensations and even sentiments in the publick mind, not easily to be erased." Haynes countered with a horrifying vision of an America without capital punishment. "Then savages of all descriptions might riot in scenes of blood and rapine with impunity," he predicted. Responding to specific arguments against capital punishment, Haynes contended that fickle public opinion had no legitimate place in matters of criminal justice. For example, Haynes commented on those who believed death too strong a penalty: "This may be the case with some weak minds, and tender hearts, who have no fixed principles of right and wrong . . . and with whom ever fluctuating caprice is the only standard by which to judge of things." Those who believed public executions turned criminals into heroes were surely "the more stupid and senseless part of the community, who are governed more by their passions than by sound judgment." All told, the public opinion should carry no more weight than the "sick-bed repentance" of the convicted murderer.[44]

The legitimacy of public opinion suffered in the wake of Morris Hull's execution. Critics not only lambasted the public as fickle, but also accused them of undermining the efficacy of punishments. Proposals to hide executions behind prison walls and to strip the governor of the pardoning power marked a significant denial of the public's role in criminal justice. Legal scholars have argued that the early republic witnessed efforts to place certain issues within the realm of political discussion and to rule others outside the bounds of appropriate discourse. For instance, jurists sanctified property rights in such a way as to remove them from the realm of debate.[45] The effort to situate criminal justice off-limits for public discussion marked strong resistance to the growing power of public opinion. The post-execution backlash on the part of prominent commentators suggested a disagreement as to who constituted "the public." The public surfacing during the Hull case was not a legitimate manifestation. Elite commentators had long dismissed the public as embodied in mob activity and other popular protests. Yet here was public participation in a sustained and informed debate. To Niles, Raymond, and others, it was still a public not to be trusted—a public that proved itself morally bankrupt in coming to Hull's defense. But such anti-democratic sentiments did not stop there. The solution—removing the pardon power from elected officials—promised an equally anti-democratic outcome. To that end, the Hull case highlights the ambivalence at the center of early republic political culture. The voices claiming to speak to and for society multiplied, but some of those voices sought to close down discussion rather than expand its scope and participants.[46]

Most telling, however, interested parties debated the legitimacy of public opinion before the public itself. Opponents of public participation in matters of criminal justice made their case in newspapers, pamphlets, and reports—all of which garnered a wide readership that included the elements of society whose voices were in question. Public opinion continued to shape penal practices in Maryland, where the governor maintained his pardoning power. Elsewhere, the public demanded alterations in the penitentiary system and continued to sway clemency decisions. In Baltimore itself, public opinion attested to the blurring of the elite and plebeian politics. The lower elements of society gained expression without using violence, while the elite realm of discourse found itself opened to an expansive community of readers and writers. To be sure, mob violence remained prevalent for much of the nineteenth century just as wealthy Baltimore residents were best situated to speak *to* the public and *as* the public. Public opinion's role in shaping political outcomes did not make Baltimore a democracy of equal voices. But it created a political culture recognizable to present-day observers—one with an emphasis on the creation and modification of public opinion. Democratic in theory more than in practice, our ambivalent legacy appears in instant polling, focus-group research, and test marketing.

¹ No one celebrates the beating of Frederick Douglass as a high point in the history of democracy in Baltimore. Nonetheless, for the apprentices committing this crime, the exclusion of African American workers was an issue of social justice. For plebeian violence in Baltimore, see Sherry Olson, *Baltimore: The Building of an American City*, revised edition (Baltimore: Johns Hopkins University Press, 1997), 98–101; Paul Gilje, "The Baltimore Riots of 1812 and the Breakdown of the Anglo-American Mob Tradition," *Journal of Social History*, 13 (1979): 547–64; David Grimsted, "Democratic Rioting: A Case Study of the Baltimore Bank Mob of 1835," in William L. O'Neill, ed., *Insights and Parallels: Problems and Issues of American Social History* (Minneapolis: Burgess Publishing Company, 1973), 125–91; Frederick Douglass, *Narrative of the Life of Frederick Douglass, An American Slave, Written by Himself* (1845; reprint, Boston: Bedford Books, 1993), 92.

² Stuart M. Blumin, *The Emergence of the Middle Class: Social Experience in the American City, 1760–1900* (New York: Cambridge University Press, 1989), 63. For Baltimore's "oligarchy," see Whitman H. Ridgway, *Community Leadership in Maryland, 1790–1840* (Chapel Hill: University of North Carolina Press, 1979), 71–95; Gary L. Browne, *Baltimore in the Nation, 1789–1861* (Chapel Hill: University of North Carolina Press, 1980), passim. On voluntary associations in Baltimore, see Joshua Civin, "Civic Experiments: Community-Building in Liverpool and Baltimore, 1785–1835" (Ph.D. diss., Oxford University, 2001); and Amy S. Greenberg, *Cause for Alarm: The Volunteer Fire Department in the Nineteenth-Century City* (Princeton: Princeton University Press, 1998). The notion of a bourgeois public sphere derives from Jurgen Habermas, *The Structural Transformation of the Public Sphere: An Inquiry into a Category of Bourgeois Society*, trans. Thomas Burger (Cambridge, Mass.: MIT Press, 1989).

³ Richard D. Brown, *The Strength of a People: The Idea of an Informed Citizenry in America, 1650–1870* (Chapel Hill: University of North Carolina Press, 1996), 90–91. See also Seth Cotlar, "In Paine's Absence: The Trans-Atlantic Dynamics of American Popular Political Thought, 1789–1804" (Ph.D. diss., Northwestern, 2000).

⁴ Joyce Appleby, *Inheriting the Revolution: The First Generation of Americans* (Cambridge: Belknap Press of Harvard University Press, 2000), 34–40 (quote on 40); Gordon S. Wood, *The Radicalism of the American Revolution* (New York: Alfred A. Knopf, 1992), 363–65.

⁵ Murders, trials, and executions have proven particularly fruitful in linking local events to broader social, cultural, and political developments. See, among others, Natalie Zemon Davis, *The Return of Martin Guerre* (Cambridge: Harvard University Press, 1983); Davis, *Fiction in the Archives: Pardon Tales and their Tellers in Sixteenth-Century France* (Stanford: Stanford University Press, 1987); Sarah Maza, *Private Lives and Public Affairs: The Cause Celebres of Prerevolutionary France* (Berkeley: University of California Press, 1993); Patricia C. Cohen, *The Murder of Helen Jewett: The Life and Death of a Prostitute in Nineteenth-Century New York* (New York: Alfred A. Knopf, 1998); Alan Taylor,

"'The Unhappy Stephen Arnold': An Episode of Murder and Penitence in the Early Republic," in *Through a Glass Darkly: Reflections on Personal Identity in Early America*, edited by Ronald Hoffman et al. (Chapel Hill: University of North Carolina Press, 1998), 96–121; Michael Grossberg, *A Judgment for Solomon: the d'Hauteville Case and Legal Experience in Antebellum America* (New York: Cambridge University Press, 1996); Irene Q. Brown and Richard D. Brown, *Deliver Us from Evil: Rape, Incest, and the Gallows in the Early Republic* (Cambridge: Harvard University Press, forthcoming).

[6] For the execution of Hare and Alexander, see *Niles' Weekly Register*, May 16, 1818; *The Life and Dying Confession of Joseph Hare, the Noted Robber who was executed at Baltimore in September last for Robbing the Mail* (Auburn, N.Y.: D. Rumsey, 1818). For Tyson's plea in court, see *Baltimore American*, April 18, 1820.

[7] Karen Halttunen, "Humanitarianism and the Pornography of Pain in Anglo-American Culture," *American Historical Review*, 100 (1995): 303–34. For examples in the Hull case, see *Baltimore American*, March 27, 1820; *Niles' Weekly Register*, April 1, 1820.

[8] *Baltimore American*, March 31, 1820. Although the outcome of Davis's trial is unknown, he reportedly pledged to divulge no additional information regarding the conspiracy without assurances of a presidential pardon.

[9] Ibid., April 1, 1820.

[10] Ibid.

[11] Ibid., March 27, 1820.

[12] Ibid., April 20, 1820.

[13] *Life and Confession of John Tuhi, (A Youth of 17 Years,) who was executed at Utica (N.Y.) on Friday, July 25, 1817, for the Murder of his Brother Joseph Tuhi* (n.p., 1817), 9–12.

[14] Ezekial Bacon to Hon. John Quincy Adams, April 20, 1820; N. Williams to Hon. Smith Thompson, April 20, 1820; Morris J. Miller to Hon. John C. Calhoun, April 20, 1820, in Governor and Council (Pardon Papers), S-1061-20, folders 57, 67, and 69, Maryland State Archives, Annapolis.

[15] It remains unclear if Amos Hull released the letter to the public, or whether Morris did so through his jailers. The letter was dated April 23 and made referred to the fact that Amos was supposedly on his way to Baltimore. If Amos set out from Utica on the April 20 (with his letters of introduction), it may have taken him more than a week to reach Baltimore, even if he took the water route down the Susquehanna. He may have received the letter on the road, or if his trip lasted longer, may have seen it first in the newspaper.

[16] *Baltimore American*, May. 3, 1820.

[17] *Baltimore Morning Chronicle*, April 27, 1820.

[18] Jim Rice, "'This Province, So Meanly and Thinly Inhabited': Punishing Maryland's Criminals," *Journal of the Early Republic*, 19 (1999): 39–41. The pardon papers have become a fruitful source for Maryland social historians. Two essays reliant upon pardon testimony appear in the recent anthology, Christine Daniels and Michael V. Kennedy, eds., *Over the Threshold: Intimate Violence in Early America* (New York: Routledge, 1999). See Jim Rice, "Laying Claim to Elizabeth Shoemaker: Family Violence on Baltimore's Waterfront," 185–201; T.

Stephen Whitman, "'I Have Got the Gun and Will Do as I Please with Her': African-Americans and Violence in Maryland, 1782–1830," 254–67. For the political aspects of the pardoning system in nineteenth-century America, see Scott P. Culclasure, "Edward Isham and Criminal Justice for the Poor White in Antebellum North Carolina," in Charles C. Bolton and Culclasure, eds., *The Confessions of Edward Isham: A Poor White Life of the Old South* (Athens: University of Georgia Press, 1998), 71–84.

[19] J. P. K. Henshaw to Governor Samuel Sprigg, May 5, 1820, and W. E. Wyatt to Governor Samuel Sprigg, May 5, 1820, in Pardon papers, S-1061-20, folder 57.

[20] Ibid. For Hutton's kidnapping charges in Richmond, see *The Life and Confessions of Peregrine Hutton, who, with his companion, Morris N. B. Hull, was executed in Baltimore, July 14, 1820* (Baltimore: Benjamin Edes, 1820). This document also reveals some of the accusations Hutton made against Hull from within the prison. For example, Hutton indicated that Hull had made his way to New York City in early 1820 from a Canadian counterfeiting ring.

[21] W. E. Wyatt to Sprigg, May 5, 1820; Edward Johnson et al. to Sprigg, no date; Thomas Stansbury to Sprigg, May 8, 1820, in Pardon papers, S-1061-20, folder 57.

[22] Jesse Talbot to Sprigg, May 5, 1820; Dr. David Reese to Sprigg, June 2, 1820 in ibid.

[23] Amos Hull to Sprigg, no date, in ibid.

[24] Stansbury to Sprigg, May 8, 1820, in ibid.; E. Anthony Rotundo, *American Manhood: Transformations in Masculinity from the Revolution to the Modern Era* (New York: Basic Books, 1993), 25–27. Amos Hull later described himself as "suffering under the greatest calamity that can befall a father." See *Remarks on Capital Punishments, to which are added, Letters of Morris N. B. Hull* (Utica: William Williams, 1821), 40.

[25] Reese to Sprigg, June 2, 1820; Governor Daniel Tompkins to Sprigg, June 1, 1820, in Pardon papers, S-1061-20, folder 57; Taylor, "The Unhappy Stephen Arnold," 116–17.

[26] Rice, "Punishing Maryland's Criminals," 15–42; Michael Meranze, *Laboratories of Virtue: Punishment, Revolution, and Authority in Philadelphia, 1760–1835* (Chapel Hill: University of North Carolina Press, 1996); Louis P. Masur, *Rites of Execution: Capital Punishment and the Transformation of American Culture, 1776–1865* (New York: Oxford University Press, 1989); Myra Glenn, *Campaigns Against Corporal Punishment: Prisoners, Sailors, Women, and Children in Antebellum America* (Albany: SUNY Press, 1984).

[27] *Baltimore American*, May 5, 1820; [William Williams], *"An Appeal to the Citizens of Baltimore, recapitulating, generally, the facts that go to extenuate the guilt of Morris N. B. Hull, one of the Mail Robbers, who is now under the sentence of death,"* [1820], Broadsides Collection, Maryland Historical Society.

[28] *Baltimore American*, April 14, 1820.

[29] Thanks to Joshua Civin for alerting me to this useful connection. David S. Bogen, "The Scandal of Smith and Buchanan: The Skeletons in the *McCulloch vs. Maryland* Closet," *Maryland Law Forum*, 9 (June 1985): 125–32. For court papers, see Maryland *v*. Buchanan, 5 H.&J. 317 (1821).

[30] *Baltimore American*, May 8, 1820.

[31] Beatriz Hardy raised these possibilities in her comments at the Baltimore History Conference, September 25, 1999.

[32] Pardon papers, S-1061-19, folder 8.

[33] S. Tyndale to Sprigg, June 10, 1820, and undated Philadelphia petitions, in Pardon papers, S-1061-20, folders 44, 57, and 64; *Baltimore Morning Chronicle*, June 8, 1820. On the Hull pseudo-memoir, see *Baltimore American*, July 12, 1820. On the larger circulation of murder narratives, see Karen Halttunen, *Murder Most Foul: The Killer and the American Gothic Imagination* (Cambridge: Harvard University Press, 1998); Ann Fabian, *The Unvarnished Truth: Personal Narratives in Nineteenth-Century America* (Berkeley: University of California Press, 2000), 49–78; Joseph P. Reidy, "The World of Nineteenth-Century Condemned Men," in Bolton and Culclasure, eds., *Confessions of Edward Isham*, 101–16.

[34] David Reese's letter quoted in [Williams], "Appeal to the Citizens of Baltimore"; *Baltimore Morning Chronicle*, June 8, 1820; *Baltimore American*, July 1, 1820. Incidentally, Mrs. Heaps received a five-year annual pension of $100 from the U.S. Congress. See the *American*, May 13, 1820.

[35] *Baltimore Morning Chronicle*, June 30, July 10, 1820; *Baltimore American*, July 11, 1820; *The Life and Confessions of Peregrine Hutton* (Baltimore: Benjamin Edes, 1820).

[36] *Baltimore Morning Chronicle*, July 10, July 13, 1820; *Baltimore American*, July 14, 15, 17, 1820. The *American* of the twentieth reprinted Hull's speech from the gallows. He played the role of the good penitent, advising "youths by my example to avoid bad company" and proclaiming faith that the blood of Christ would cleanse his soul. But Hull also testified to the ebb and flow of public support: "I am called this day to suffer for my crime. I have been condemned by the severity of the law for that only crime; and it is but a few days ago that I entertained as much hope of living as any person in good health. I had a father, an affectionate father, whose influence was used in my behalf. I had friends too who interested themselves for my youth—thanks for their kindness; but to-day what are my hopes?—the gallows and a coffin." Interestingly, Hull's final words appeared somewhat differently in an 1821 anti-capital punishment pamphlet. There, Hull praised his father and friends but did not invoke their specific efforts to generate a pardon. In this version, he asked "God to forgive the unkindness wherever it has existed that would represent my guilt greater than it was and my life more criminal than it has been." See *Remarks on Capital Punishments, to which are added, Letters of Morris N. B. Hull* (Utica: William Williams, 1821), 38–39.

[37] *Niles' Weekly Register*, July 22, 1820.

[38] On women's engagement in public affairs, see Elizabeth R. Varon, *We Mean to Be Counted: White Women and Politics in Antebellum America* (Chapel Hill: University of North Carolina Press, 1998); Nancy Isenberg, *Sex & Citizenship in Antebellum America* (Chapel Hill: University of North Carolina Press, 1998); Lori D. Ginzberg, *Woman and the Work of Benevolence: Morality, Politics, and Class in the 19th-Century United States* (New Haven: Yale University Press,

1990); Mary Ryan, *Women in Public: Between Banners and Ballots, 1825–1880* (Baltimore: Johns Hopkins University Press, 1990).

[39] *Baltimore Morning Chronicle*, July 18, 19, 1820.

[40] Michael Meranze uses the 1823 hanging of William Gross, the last man publicly executed in nineteenth-century Philadelphia, to explain this point. See *Laboratories of Virtue*, 24–26, 48–53.

[41] Masur, *Rites of Execution*, 94–113.

[42] *Baltimore Morning Chronicle*, July 19, 1820.

[43] Daniel Raymond, *The Elements of Political Economy, in Two Parts* (Baltimore: F. Lucas, 1823), volume II, appendix, 430–31.

[44] *Remarks on Capital Punishments, to which are added, Letters of Morris N. B. Hull* (Utica: William Williams, 1821); Sylvanus Haynes, *A Letter to Dr. Amos G. Hull, in Vindication of Capital Punishments; being a reply to a pamphlet which was written at his suggestion and published at his request; in which the doctrine of capital punishments is opposed in all cases; with an appendix on murder and manslaughter* (Auburn, N.Y.: Thomas M. Skinner, 1822). New York did not abolish the death penalty for another twenty years. See John L. O'Sullivan, *Report in Favor of the Abolition of the Punishment of Death . . .* (New York: J. & H. G. Langley, 1841).

[45] Jennifer Nedelsky, *Private Property and the Limits of American Constitutionalism: The Madisonian Framework and Its Legacy* (Chicago: University of Chicago Press, 1990); Christopher Tomlins, "Law, Police, and the Pursuit of Happiness in the New American Republic," *Studies in American Political Development*, 4 (1990): 3–34; Morton J. Horowitz, *The Transformation of American Law, 1780–1860* (Cambridge: Harvard University Press, 1977).

[46] This tension is at the center of a number of studies in the "newest political history" of the early republic. See David Waldstreicher, *In the Midst of Perpetual Fetes: The Making of American Nationalism, 1776–1820* (Chapel Hill: University of North Carolina Press, 1997); Peter Thompson, *Rum Punch and Revolution: Taverngoing and Public Life in Eighteenth-Century Philadelphia* (Philadelphia: University of Pennsylvania Press, 1999); Saul Cornell, *The Other Founders: Anti-Federalism and the Dissenting Tradition in America, 1788–1828* (Chapel Hill: University of North Carolina Press, 1999).

FRANK TOWERS

Secession in an Urban Context: Municipal Reform and the Coming of the Civil War in Baltimore

JOSEPH ARNOLD'S WARNING against viewing the course of Baltimore history as inevitable will find ready acceptance among those interested in the outbreak of the Civil War in Maryland. Baltimore provided some tantalizing expressions of support for secession that have fueled debate as to whether Maryland, with her largest city leading the way, might have joined the Confederacy had the coercive powers of the federal government not intervened. Hints of a secessionist majority in Baltimore appeared in the 49 percent plurality garnered by Southern and States' Rights Democrat John C. Breckinridge at the November 6, 1860, presidential election—a result above his statewide showing that helped him carry Maryland—and the April 19, 1861, clash between Union troops traveling to Washington and armed civilians that resulted in at least twenty-one deaths and more than one hundred injuries. While arguing that "Unionism . . . was always uppermost in Maryland," modern-day scholars emphasize the contingency of events that blew the city back and forth between sectional poles analogous to the course of a small ship in a stormy sea. Accordingly, Constitutional Unionist John Bell's association with the unpopular American Party helped Breckinridge, and support for Southern rights ebbed during the winter's secession-related business failures but surged again after Lincoln's post-Sumter mobilization of the

Frank Towers is an associate professor of history at Colorado State University. He is completing a book manuscript entitled *The Coming of the Civil War in the Urban South: The Politics of Free Labor and Mob Violence in Baltimore* for the University Press of Virginia.

army. The April riot produced a backlash, and by mid-summer "the high tide of southern sentiment had receded and left the state on Union ground."[1]

While nothing was inevitable about the outbreak of the Civil War, Baltimoreans had so many reasons to remain in the Union that a popular majority for secession had little chance of taking hold. Located on the sectional border, Baltimore was an industrializing port more like Philadelphia and New York than Charleston, South Carolina, or an Alabama plantation. In 1860, Baltimore had 212,000 people, one-fourth foreign-born, one-seventh free black, and less than 2 percent slaves or slaveowners. After a 700 percent increase in the value of its manufactures since 1840, the city boasted the largest industrial workforce in the South and the sixth largest in the nation. Integration into the industrializing economy of the North found political expression from 1854 to 1860 in the reigning American Party, also called Know Nothings because of their origins as a secret society. Party politics had been thrown into confusion by the collapse of the Whigs over cultural and sectional disputes. In the South, Know Nothings challenged increasingly proslavery Democrats by criticizing the alleged corruption of American culture and living standards by European immigrants and advancing traditional Whig support for the federal Union and state aid to industry. And while they were hardly abolitionists, most took Congressman Henry Winter Davis's advice that, "the way to settle the slavery question is to be silent on it." Social similarity to northeastern cities, economic ties to the free states, a tradition of political Unionism, and fear of becoming the war's front line predisposed most Baltimoreans to reject secession.[2]

Understanding these conditions helps dispel Confederate might-have-been scenarios, but the question remains as to why Baltimore had such significant manifestations of Southern sympathy. The ability of secession to strike a chord with a sizeable minority of a city whose social reality poorly fit Southern nationalist visions of a slave-holding agricultural republic indicates that secession had a Janus-faced appeal that went beyond defending slavery and state sovereignty. Analyzing the war's outbreak in Baltimore strictly in terms of sectional issues obscures how local social and political conflicts associated with the rise of the American Party had shaped the wartime allegiances of urban residents. Baltimore secessionists came from a coalition of conservative businessmen, partisan Democrats, and beleaguered immigrant workers that had spent six years battling Know Nothing rule. By 1861 slavery and states' rights had become interwoven with the local objectives of ending corruption in city government, restoring order to city streets, and stopping labor unrest. To achieve these goals, urban conservatives strengthened preexisting ties to southern Maryland slaveholders who wielded influence in the General Assembly, and with their help the Democrat-inspired City Reform Association defeated the Know Nothings in 1860 only to lose power after the April 1861 riot. The fight for municipal reform had prepared a larger than expected group of Baltimoreans to opt for disunion rather than live under a reinvigorated Know Nothing regime emboldened by new federal allies in the Lincoln administration.

Baltimore's path to the Civil War resonated with the experience of city dwellers nationwide. Since the rise of mass parties in the 1830s, politicians had talked about class, culture, and sectionalism while trying to prevent social divisions related to these issues from dividing the voting base and policy choices. In the 1850s, the increasing volatility of these issues helped destroy Jacksonian party competition simultaneous with the spread of cities of more than 100,000 people beyond the Mid-Atlantic coast. Unfettered by strong national parties and supported by a growing number of working-class votes, prototypes of Gilded Age political machines emerged to challenge the elite of businessmen and party veterans that had heretofore run cities, and who counterattacked by arguing that the "best element" should govern, and popular participation and the power of parties should be curbed.[3] The emerging battle over boss rule cut across regions, but municipal reformers in the late antebellum South faced political choices that could not be disentangled from the sectional conflict. Rural planters in state government rightly viewed the expanded wage-earning electorate of large industrializing cities as a base of slave-state Unionism—St. Louis voted for Lincoln, New Orleans and Baltimore had long-lasting Know Nothing regimes, and workers in all three cities rallied to the Union banner after federal occupation—and they offered to help reformers in the urban elite restrict the power of municipal government. By 1861, reformers accepted secession as a way to preempt aid to their machine opponents from the Lincoln administration. Their criticism of party spirit as the cause of urban ills found common ideological ground with Southern nationalists who railed against political parties as corrupt tools of anti-slavery demagogues. Urban reformers and Lower South disunionists had different priorities, but whatever popularity secession had outside the planter class stemmed in part from the adaptability of its republican themes to local circumstances.[4]

Baltimore's secessionist minority came together through involvement in the campaign against the American Party. After bloody election riots in 1856, Democrats demanded a complete overhaul of municipal party politics and asked that state militia police the polls, a request that began a drive to circumvent the local Know Nothing majority by appealing to state government. In the spring of 1857, Democratic Governor T. Watkins Ligon had used state troops to break a strike on the Baltimore and Ohio Railroad, and he agreed to deploy them at the fall election. He relented after Mayor Thomas Swann promised to call up extra police and Baltimore regiments in the state militia threatened to disregard his order. Swann's preparations notwithstanding, mobs again assaulted Democratic voters, infuriating Ligon, who said that the American Party, "is an essential tyranny. It sways a spurious sceptre, over a people despoiled of their rights, and its career must be in profligate antagonism with law, order, and good government."[5]

The conflict between state and local government sharpened in 1858 because of an ambitious Know Nothing scheme to amend the Maryland constitution. One proposal would have apportioned legislative seats solely on population and thereby increased Baltimore's share of the House of Delegates to one-third. Having replaced Ligon with American Thomas Hicks, Know Nothings also tried to reconvert elected judgeships to appointments by the governor. They also asked the legislature "to lend its co-operation in abolishing the law which now admits the foreign element to participation in the affairs of your government." The plan expanded representation for the American Party's urban electoral base, cut seats for rural slaveholding counties, and bolstered Know Nothing municipal dominance by disfranchising naturalized voters and removing popular control over some statewide elected offices likely to go to Democrats.[6]

Constitutional reform alarmed rural proslavery Democrats who increasingly regarded Baltimore Know Nothings as threats to slavery and the traditional dominance of rural counties in state government. Calling the apportionment idea "Red-Republican," Upper Marlboro Democrat Edward Belt asked his rural brethren, "if our representation be stricken down, where is our Slavery interest?" Belt conjured up the demon of Baltimore's municipal "corporation sitting on the throne of power, the emblems of Maryland lying at its feet

. . . holding in its right hand the scourge that is all powerful even under existing laws, and just grasping with its left the legislative power itself; so that in the future *its* will may be the Law!" In a May referendum, Maryland voters rejected the plan despite overwhelming approval in Baltimore. After meeting with Democrats in his birthplace of Frederick, Supreme Court Chief Justice Roger B. Taney was "very indignant at the state of things [in Baltimore] . . . and does not seem able to comprehend how it can exist." The implications of expanding the power of Baltimore Know Nothings in Maryland politics helped persuade rural Democrats to support state intervention in municipal affairs.[7]

By the fall of 1859 the simultaneous escalation of the municipal battle and the national slavery controversy had divided city residents into warring camps that increasingly viewed the two struggles as interconnected. On October 16, John Brown attacked a federal arsenal on Maryland's border in the hopes of sparking a slave revolution. Panicked slaveholders responded by trying to re-enslave or banish free blacks. The plan won little support in Baltimore, where free blacks played a vital role as unskilled wage labor, but, occurring in the wake of riots aimed at driving black ship caulkers from their jobs, Brown's raid added to the urban elite's concerns about the changing racial status quo. The prospect of an election on November 2 added to the tension produced by sectional conflict and labor strife. At a rally held a week before the vote, Henry Winter Davis spoke beneath a transparency depicting an assault on George William Brown, a leader of the officially nonpartisan City Reform Association that emerged in 1858 and worked closely with Democrats in Baltimore and Annapolis. Days later, the Blood Tubs knocked unconscious a Democratic congressional candidate and the Tiger gang broke up a south-side Reform rally and threatened those who tried to vote. Second-generation German merchant Frederick W. Brune, Brown's business partner and brother-in-law, commented that "the outrageous exhibition . . . has . . . disgusted many thinking persons. I hope and pray there will be a bloodless revolution achieved here on Wednesday next." Brune's belief that an election for ten state assembly seats and two congressmen would be a vehicle for revolution was as unfounded as his hope that the contest would be bloodless.[8]

Events in south Baltimore's Fifteenth Ward exemplified how social divisions had attached themselves to the party battle and how this fusion of

"Procession of Rowdies through the Streets of Baltimore." (Maryland Historical Society.)

electoral and social conflicts had in turn polarized city politics. On election-day morning, George and Adam Barkly Kyle Jr., two aspiring merchants in their late twenties, prepared to head to the polls. Their father, a prosperous, Irish Protestant slaveowner, had been a Whig but had switched to the Democrats because of grievances against the American Party that included indulgence of working-class gangs; allegations of collusion with northern Republicans—a charge reinforced by Davis's vote for a Republican Speaker of the House in 1859; and nativist attacks on Kyle's countrymen. The Kyle brothers planned to distribute Reform ballots and, expecting trouble, they carried guns and knives for themselves and other Reformers who had promised to monitor the polls. Their decision to arm themselves had a lot to do with the election-day plans of another prominent Fifteenth Warder, Joseph Edwards Jr. While Edwards and the Kyles shared the legal and cultural privileges that went along with being white and male in nineteenth-century America, their backgrounds differed sharply. Edwards intermittently ran a tavern and performed casual manual work. His father, a Maryland native, was a day laborer who had amassed only $300 in property by age sixty-four and who instead of living with servants took in five boarders to supplement his income. A neighbor's claim that, "every man, woman and even child, who could talk, residing in the fifteenth ward, knows Edwards," referred to his reputation as leader of the Tiger American club, one of the working-class gangs that the American Party relied on to promote their cause and intimidate opposing voters. As part of this coercive strategy, the city council located the Fifteenth Ward polls at Edwards's former tavern and placed the neighboring Seventeenth Ward voting booth just two squares away in what one observer believed "was generally looked upon as a hard neighborhood."[9]

Around 8:30 that morning Edwards encountered the Kyle brothers en route to voting, and, spying their ballots, he told them "don't worry, you'll get plenty of tickets later." The Kyles spent a tense two hours at the polls in which outnumbered Reformers suffered verbal insults and occasional rough treatment from the Tigers. At half past ten, Edwards called out "snatch the tickets from them sons of bitches" and another man yelled "kill the rascals." The mob then surrounded and beat the Kyle brothers. George escaped with severe injuries, but Adam, who ran into the first dwelling with an unlocked door, was trapped. Ignoring the protests of the family inside, the Tigers broke in, dragged Kyle from the second floor, and killed him as he lay on the stairs. No arrests were made, and the American Party won 75 percent of the city's vote. In wards fifteen and seventeen they limited Reformers to only 136 of the 1,840 ballots cast.[10]

Two days later, leaders of the Reform Association and many of Baltimore's wealthiest businessmen turned out for Kyle's funeral. Their procession, which "number[ed] an unusual quantity of private carriages followed by hundreds of gentlemen arm in arm, four by four," attracted the city's attention, and the speeches at the ceremony condemned not only Know Nothingism but a system of party politics that they believed ruthlessly pursued partisan victory at the expense of responsible government and civic order. "How dreadful that such should be the result of excitement growing out of what some might say good to the government," lamented the wife of a southern Maryland congressman, "politics is an evil instead of a blessing, and I should be truly happy to see less interest taken in it." Reverend John C. Backus praised

Kyle as a man "forgetful of personal risk or the demands of business, and impelled by a principle independent of self. . . . He went forth to defend those rights, which in a civil relation were most dear to every citizen, and to rescue the city from the reproach which it bore. . . . He was not a politician, he had not given himself up to the men who aspire to control political parties, but he stood up as all citizens should do to discharge their duties." Backus portrayed Kyle as a martyr to the ideal of the virtuous republican citizen who had an innate dislike for professional politics but was ready to risk all for the public good.[11]

While the Reform discussion of Kyle's murder concentrated on the broad theme of restoring good government without regard to class or sectionalism, the contrast between Kyle, a rich man connected to the mercantile elite and proslavery Democrats, and Edwards, a poor man who used the resources of working-class culture to gain power within the American Party, dramatized the close correspondence between social divisions and party differences. Not only was compromise unthinkable, but every issue that involved the parties had become another point of conflict between wealthy Southern sympathizers and Unionist workers.

For example, reformers thwarted Mayor Swann's seemingly innocuous plan for a commuter railway by mixing allegations of Know Nothing abolitionism into charges that a city government beholden to wage earners had harmed business and encouraged public disorder. A group led by a Know Nothing state legislator won the city contract to build the railway, beating out a Democratic businessman, and then sold its interest to a Philadelphia consortium headed by Republican Jonathan Brock, who not only offered bribes and subcontracts to firms run by American Party city councilmen but was also friends with Republican Senator Simon Cameron, who, according to one of the contractors, had made "some reference to the possession of a road that had considerable patronage, and might be useful for political purposes." Proslavery voters and businessmen fighting to prevent New York and Philadelphia from sapping Baltimore's commercial opportunities turned out at anti-Brock rallies and declared that "we are in this, as in every other public matter especially jealous of our rights as southerners, when they are invaded by sinister and dishonorable means by northern men, who are more than suspected of hostility towards our institutions." Labor militancy also worried Brock's foes. Police refused requests to disperse the pickets, forcing the builders to forfeit their contract to a company willing to raise pay. In March 1859, a Know Nothing official paid the Tigers and other political clubs to break up one of these rallies, and in June two hundred workers demonstrated against the low wages paid for track construction jobs. Laborers celebrated with a banner that read "Victory Gained," while critics protested that, "those who had charge of [the railway's] management subjected it in a great measure to the influence of men notorious as the most lawless in this community." In the winter of 1859–60, Brock's opponents inundated the legislature with petitions and filed an injunction challenging the city's authority to charter a railroad. The intense General Assembly debate sparked a knife fight in the state house rotunda and ended with the suspension of Brock's charter. Although Brock eventually completed the railway, in the spring of 1860 Reformers had convinced the state to strike back at their municipal enemies by associating a prosaic public works project with sectionalism, class, and partisan advantage.[12]

Reformers saw the refusal of police to break up the railway pickets as symptomatic of city government's support for labor militancy. During an 1857 strike on the B&O, police had refused to clear a blockade of the tracks, and in the caulker riots of 1858 and 1859 the Tiger gang had not only driven blacks from shipyard jobs but also assaulted prominent Democratic shipbuilders while police stood idle. Even though Swann was a former railroad president and most major Know Nothing leaders were well-off businessmen, their party's indulgence of working-class supporters nurtured the growing preference of wealthy men for the Reform cause. Roughly four fifths of the Reform leaders were merchants and professionals and a large contingent served on the Board of Trade. Concern for public morals, initially an issue claimed by the Know Nothings, went along with class-based preferences for the Reform movement. Most Reformers were Democrats, but out of 208 Reform Association officers, forty-eight had been Whigs or Americans, and one-third held a post in a moral reform organization or church bureaucracy. George P. Kane, one of the Whig converts, told a Democratic senator that "the good gentlemen of the late Whig party have redeemed the slate . . . [while] your rank and file upon whom you have so much relied are now the bravest soldiers of the K N clubs." The national failure of political nativism, the Panic of 1857, and the crisis over slavery's expansion pushed Know Nothings to highlight class and sectionalism over religion and culture, a shift that along with corruption and violence drove some upper-class moral reformers out of the party.[13]

After the 1859 elections, the Reform Association asked the General Assembly's new Democratic majority to clean up what one delegate called a "God-forsaken and God-accursed city." Reformers successfully lobbied for passage of the Baltimore Bills, laws that gave the state control over the city's police, militia volunteers, and juries, and reduced polling place crowds by subdividing each ward into four election precincts. The legislature unseated the Baltimore delegation on the grounds that fraud and intimidation invalidated their election, and it removed a city criminal court judge who habitually acquitted Know Nothing defendants. Finally, if local officials failed to keep the peace, the state militia now had unambiguous authority to suppress civil disorder. Reformers argued that, "as long as lawlessness was supreme here, it was idle to hope for better times, for neither capital nor enterprise can develop themselves unless protection is assured them." They lobbied for these measures as cures for labor violence and economic depression, while rural Democrats tacked on their own concerns about runaway municipal power by amending the police bill to bar "Black Republicans" from the force. That stipulation and the straight partisan vote on the Baltimore Bills showed how the class and corruption issues of urban Reformers had become alloyed to the party and sectional concerns of rural legislators.[14]

The Democratic legislature staffed the police department's new governing board with men sympathetic to their views on slavery and the Know Nothings. Chairman Charles Howard, a speaker at Kyle's funeral and an 1859 Reform candidate, belonged to a leading Democratic family and had close ties to proslavery politicians through his presidency of the Maryland Colonization Society. John W. Davis had been a Democratic state legislator and Customs appointee and William Gatchell, a slaveholder, ran a business with a co-owner of the *Exchange*, the organ of the Reform campaign. Flour merchant Charles Hinks, brother of a former Know Nothing mayor now in the Reform Association, had called for better enforcement of the Fugitive Slave Law. George P. Kane, the Police Marshal, was a second-generation Irishman and a slaveowner who offered to resign after Lincoln's election. He thought Know Nothing "bullies" had defrauded him of a city council seat in 1856 and he combated their nativism through his leadership of the Hibernian Society.[15] Invested with power in February, the new board purged the force of Know Nothings—only four of fifty-nine officers identified in correspondence were Swann holdovers—made efforts to root out corruption, and began arresting violent gang members. Among the notable cases, in August 1860 Joseph Edwards and several other Tigers went on trial for the murder of Adam Kyle. "What a great change since November last," remarked Frederick Brune in the fall of 1860, "the rowdies are nowhere, except in jail."[16]

Reformers saw the 1860 city elections as a battle for honest, nonpartisan government against the forces of violence and corruption. Set against the backdrop of Know Nothing outrages and claims that "the blood of the Kyles cries from the ground," Reformers pledged "the retrenchment of expenditures to the lowest point" and vowed to "zealously cooperate with, and cordially aid, the Police Board . . . in its efforts to preserve and conserve the peace of the city, and redeem it from the disgrace of past lawlessness." Hitting their broadest theme, Reform editors stated that, "while, therefore, we earnestly desire to see the present administration of the city wholly gotten rid of . . . that desire is altogether secondary to the paramount anxiety which we feel for the suppression of partisan municipal government altogether." George William Brown, the Reform mayoral nominee, like most of his colleagues was a veteran politician, but he nevertheless presented himself as an anti-party administrator who reluctantly came forward in order to save the people from corrupt politicians. Prophesying victory, Brown gloated that "the politicians are not as well satisfied as the people," but "if I should be defeated . . . I should grieve that the cause should be lost, but not for myself." Rather than purify government with new men, Old Line Whigs and Democrats suspended party differences to reinstate in office Baltimore's traditional core of political professionals and drive out Know Nothings who had disrupted established government routines and agitated divisive social questions.[17]

This appeal and the help of friendly police brought Reformers a decisive victory in 1860, but it would be a distortion to assume that if their opponents criticized party spirit then Know Nothings defended it. Decrying self-interested partisanship, Daniel H. McPhail, the state lottery commissioner and a gang favorite, turned down the 1858 mayoral nomination because "the seeking of office with me . . . is considered in direct contravention of the tenets of the American party." Baltimore Know Nothings derided the Vigilance Committee that tried to oust the New Orleans American Party regime as a crass ploy designed to put government into "the arms of the old Democratic wire workers," and McPhail warned that "already have desperate politicians . . . begun to talk of a Vigilance committee in the 'Monumental city.'" Criticizing the use of state militia in municipal elections, Governor Hicks said that, "the reverence for law and order, and for the ascertained popular will . . . seems to be in danger of utter extinguishment by that violent spirit of party, which can invoke such means to overawe the free right of suffrage, and which may finally attempt to secure to itself the possession or continuance of power at the expense of civil war." By the late 1850s anti-partyism had become a popular theme of political culture and Hicks showed that despite its use by opponents, it could also connect municipal and sectional conflicts in ways favorable to the American Party.[18]

Dual local and national crises threatened to disrupt civic order and finally did so in April 1861. Until that time, the Reform administration kept its municipal opponents in check, and few Baltimoreans advocated either outright secession or unconditional Unionism. Within an overall consensus that valued peace and preservation of the Union with slavery, political participants divided between firm Unionism on one hand and sympathy with the South and a more conditional Unionism on the other. An activist core from the Reform coalition of businessmen, immigrants, and career politicians turned out for Breckinridge in November, rallied for the South and fought the union troops that winter. As staunch allies of the new city government, Southern Rights Reformers kept alive the partisan hatreds that Brown's campaign had officially sought to resolve.

The outlines of Southern Rights support appear in the contrast between the October 10 municipal election and the balloting for president in November. Brown's overwhelming majority in October—he won every ward—included votes from Know Nothings. William Schley, a Unionist and American, admitted that his party's municipal slate had been defeated "by our own votes." Brown did particularly well in the wealthiest wards and fared poorly in ones with concentrations of native-born workers, further indication that businessmen had abandoned the Know Nothings. In the presidential contest, those voters joined more ardent Know Nothings in backing Constitutional Unionist John Bell, who not only did well in the American Party's westside stronghold but also won three of the five wards with high concentrations of white-collar workers. The association of Know Nothings with Unionism made Brown, a pro-Bell Reformer, "dislike the company in which it places me," and convinced some of his supporters to vote for Breckinridge who polled better than Brown among blue-collar voters and whose pattern of support correlated strongly with that of Democrats before the rise of the American Party in 1854. In short, Breckinridge rode on Reform coattails, but he lost the support of Brown voters outside of the old Jacksonian Democratic base.[19]

For pro-Breckinridge Reformers, restoring the traditional elite to office and quashing the disruptive politics of the late 1850s could only be secured when Know Nothings lost the chance to regain power via federal intervention. The *Exchange* tried to fuse local and sectional arguments by telling readers that, "the Bell and Everett party is . . . only the discarded and defeated Know Nothing faction," and the "plainest duty of the people of Maryland" was to "defend the principles for which the South now contends." The discrepancy between the Brown and Breckinridge votes bears out the argument that city Unionists drew strength from the business community, but it also foreshadowed disagreement among Reformers that would hamper Brown's efforts to navigate the sectional conflict as he tried to eradicate Know Nothing corruption.[20]

The pattern also characterized support for the winter's public meetings held by Unionists and Southern sympathizers. A majority of rally officers had been active in party politics and among Unionists Know Nothings and Whigs predominated but enough Democrats joined them to lend credence to Schley's January boast that "the Union meeting here was a crusher, composed as it was of all parties." Their opposition drew more exclusively on Democrats who were over half of the ninety-three officers of Southern Rights meetings as compared to only six Whigs and Americans.[21]

Although distracted by the sectional crisis, the Brown administration largely succeeded in cleansing city government of Know Nothing partisans and dismantling Swann's patronage machine. Brown followed through on his campaign promise to sack all municipal employees "concerned in the many outrages that have been perpetrated on the citizens of Baltimore for the last five or six years."[22] To rein in public works spending, Reformers eliminated or consolidated several departments, held up construction of the city pas-

senger railroad, cut money to deepen the harbor, and forced private sub-
scribers to fund the purchase of Druid Hill Park. Secession-related hard times,
spending on militia, and inherited debt prevented Reformers from balancing
the books in their short reign, but they slowed the growth rate of municipal
borrowing by a fourth and nearly halved the floating debt used to pay off
existing claims.[23]

Spending cuts pleased businessmen unhappy about debt's impact on
commerce and taxes, but they angered working-class voters who welcomed
Know Nothing public works relief after the Panic of 1857 and who had lost
jobs in the secession-related economic slowdown. As early as November
1860 a merchant noted "an utter want of confidence" among his colleagues.
Two banks failed and port arrivals and rail traffic fell below their 1856 levels.
Canneries and foundries reported layoffs, and a builder claimed that, "there
is much less doing at this moment than ever before in my knowledge." In
the first half of March 1861 over five thousand people sought aid from the
Poor Association, more than in the entire month a year earlier, and according
to one estimate fifteen thousand laborers were out of work. The crisis continued into late April when a Baltimorean observed that, "all kinds of business that I know anything about is protracted. I really do not know where
very many get bread."[24]

Calls for relief mounted in the spring. One group asked for public works
jobs on the grounds that "a large number of Mechanics and laboring men
have been thrown out of employment and . . . many are suffering for the
necessaries of life." East-side "citizens and tax payers" urged the city council
to build roads to ease the burden on private charities. "Many there are in our
midst that are entirely destitute of food to support their needful wants,
although the more fortunate have given liberally yet it does not appear
reasonably that this class can give that relief that would be desirable." Petitioned steadily since February, on March 27 the council appropriated $20,000
for park building.[25]

Negotiations for public works touched on old wounds related to the
labor activism of the 1850s. On April 5, a new unemployed association led
by Thomas Saville, an ex-Know Nothing policeman and future Union volunteer, proposed a march with banners reading "Work or Bread!" and claimed
that, "the merchants and bosses desired to crush the poor working man."
Arguing that the relief daily wage of seventy-five cents could not support

families, he warned that, "it is necessary that something should be done in relieving the necessities of the unemployed, otherwise, as necessity knows no law, and self-preservation is the first law of nature, they will be forced to seek for sustenance for themselves and families in any manner that presents itself." Although some Democratic leaders had endorsed the earlier relief campaign, only one of the April 5 officers had been a politician while eight were veterans of the Know Nothing police or gangs.[26]

Angry Reformers viewed this and other labor unrest as a question of law and order. The city council refused to consider the April petition, and the *Exchange* wrote that, "when the threat is openly made, that if [the city council] do not give bread . . . bread will be taken by force in spite of them, they will owe it to themselves and the people they represent, to make the most determined stand, at the threshold, against any and every such inadmissible and criminal resolution." The next week, Reformers applied this doctrine to a strike at the iron foundry of Adam Denmead, a Whig and early Know Nothing who bolted to run for state office as a Reformer in 1859. When some employees turned out to protest wage cuts Denmead quickly convinced a judge to issue warrants for strike leaders, one of whom went to jail for conspiracy.[27]

Remarkably, both sides backed away from a showdown. Saville's group toned down its rhetoric, telling the council on April 11 that it felt "grateful to your honorable body for the appropriation of $20,000 you have already made, and feel assured that it is only necessary to make known to your honorable body the sufferings now in our midst to procure your sympathy and aid." Accepting this overture, the city spent an additional $22,918 to dredge the harbor and Jones' Falls. Despite their rhetoric, Reformers created more than one thousand relief jobs in hopes of containing labor conflict that had helped bring them to power but that now, in combination with national events, threatened their destruction.[28]

Treading on the heels of the past decade's public disorder, the secession crisis invited rioting. On February 23, between 10,000 and 15,000 people who had gathered to meet Lincoln en route to his inauguration demonstrated in anger upon learning that he had passed through Baltimore secretly the night before, an act perceived as Lincoln's "imputation on their character." By April, each morning witnessed scrapes between Unionists and Southern sympathizers who were among the crowds reading breaking stories posted outside newspaper offices. The firing on Fort Sumter on April 12 and Lincoln's call three days later for 75,000 volunteers to defend federal property in the seceding states enflamed these smoldering sectional feelings. "Never before," a reporter observed, "have the citizens . . . been laboring under such a perfect *furore* of excitement." On the fifteenth, two thousand Unionists and Southern sympathizers clashed downtown and smaller battles broke out at flag raisings and rallies. Northern troops began arriving in Baltimore en route to defending Washington, D.C., an act Southern sympathizers viewed as provocation, yet although crowds menaced, the first federal soldiers passed without bloodshed.[29]

The explosion occurred on April 19, when 1,700 Union troops arrived at President Street Station, just east of today's Inner Harbor, and tried to make their way by foot and horse-drawn streetcar to the Washington-bound train at Camden Station on the southwest side. For four hours a crowd of thousands jeered, set up barricades, and physically assaulted Massachusetts and Pennsylvania volunteers as they tried to move along Pratt Street. Friends of the Union battled on the side of the troops, and some fighting occurred away from the rail stations. Southern sympathizers destroyed the presses of the German language anti-slavery newspapers. On the south side's Federal Hill, between one hundred and five hundred workingmen, including some ex-Tigers, routed a smaller party trying to fire a salute to the Confederacy. The political elite fell out at city hall, where a Democratic judge threatened to cut off the nose and ears of his Unionist colleague, Hugh Lennox Bond. The violence ended when the 6th Massachusetts Regiment departed for Washington and the hapless Pennsylvania volunteers either fled on foot or returned north on the train that brought them. Nine soldiers and twelve civilians died in the riot. Scores more were injured.[30]

During the war Baltimore women on both sides of the sectional conflict took on public roles for their cause, but they were less visible during the riot. One exception was Ann Manley, a brothel keeper married to a Know Nothing gang member and constable, who provided refuge for the fleeing Pennsylvanians. At the other end of polite society, Adeline Tyler, a New Englander working at an Episcopal Church hospital, defied Southern opinion by nursing four wounded soldiers held at the central police station.[31]

A three-week period of "armed neutrality" followed in which Southern sympathizing Reformers pushed city government towards secession. Municipal officials enrolled approximately fifteen thousand men into militia units to defend Baltimore from invasion. Although he denied the riot's secessionist impulse, Brown admitted that militia volunteers "hoped for war," and many later fought for the Confederacy. Militiamen raided armories and gun shops. Aided by Kane and Brown, militia commander Isaac Ridgway Trimble, later a Confederate general, bought munitions from Virginia. North and South Carolina also sent arms, and secessionists at Harpers Ferry debated marching to Baltimore. Governor Hicks had enough doubts about the militia's loyalty to confiscate their weapons in late May.[32]

In late April, city government garrisoned itself against federal attack. Police and militia destroyed rail and harbor connections to the North, cut the telegraph to Washington, and patrolled the outskirts of the city with an eye on Union encampments at Cockeysville and Fort McHenry. Brown embargoed commerce and asked local financiers for $500,000. Bowing to intense pressure, Hicks convened a special legislative session. On April 24 Baltimore elected an uncontested Southern and States' Rights ticket that led a failed fight for secession. Prominent Unionists like Henry Winter Davis and abolitionist rabbi David Einhorn fled north, while police and militia arrested and disarmed those who stayed behind. When Henry Hoffman, Lincoln's choice to head Baltimore's Customs House, tried to enter the city on April 22, train passengers cried that a "Black Republican traitor . . . was aboard & ought at once be taken from the cars." Hoffman reached Baltimore, but after seeing "the excited state of feeling" he returned to his native Cumberland. That weekend mobs raided the armory of the German Turner militia and stoned the home of another Lincoln appointee, prompting Brown to order that national flags be lowered to discourage attacks on Unionist homes. Although they would later deny it, Lincoln believed that Brown and other city officials had shown their "unmistakable complicity with those in armed rebellion against the Government of the United States."[33]

Despite this outpouring of Southern sympathy, a week after the riot a few Unionists demonstrated in public. By early May they had regrouped and were agitating to end the embargo and disperse pro-Southern militia. Meanwhile federal troops had occupied Annapolis and secured the rail connections around Baltimore. On May 13 General Benjamin Butler peacefully entered the city, and within a week the Union army had established military control that would last until 1865. By the end of the summer Reform leaders

The riot of April 19, 1861, on Pratt Street in Baltimore. (Maryland Historical Society.)

including Brown and the Southern Rights delegates had been jailed for treason while many of those who escaped arrest had joined the Confederate
military.[34]

The April 19 rioters and the supporters of armed neutrality are prime
subjects for analyzing the constituency of secession in slave-state cities like
Baltimore. Most important in this group were "gentlemen of property and
standing" who had close ties to water-born commerce and the Democratic
party. They were joined by a smaller number of immigrant workers, many
of them Irish. These groups forged a patron-client alliance resembling that
of black caulkers and white shipbuilders or New York's draft resisting Irish
dockers and Democratic merchants trading with the South. Critical assistance
came from Baltimore government and the federally controlled Customs service, an island of Democratic power during the late 1850s and a resource for
partisan violence. This Southern sympathizing minority traced its lineage
back to the six-year struggle against the Know Nothings.[35]

Social data can be found for 159 men identified as either attacking the troops on April 19 or demonstrating for the South—something like hurrahing for Jefferson Davis or marching with a South Carolina flag.[36] It is plausible to assume they led the attack on Northern volunteers because police quickly released most rioters leaving no record and most of these named offenders were tried weeks and months later by a new Unionist administration seeking to make examples of notorious cases. Although more local businessmen devoted their energies to preserving the Union, the most common occupations for rioters were merchant, clerk, or another commercial pursuit, followed by a smaller number of immigrant workers. More than half of the identifiable rioters practiced non-manual trades, over half were employed in commerce or transportation, and less than one-eighth worked in industry. The mob averaged $9,879 in personal wealth as compared to $779 for the entire Baltimore working-age population, and more rioters owned upwards of $1,000 than had no property in a city where the median holding was zero. As one trader wrote, "the merchants and all the best citizens (not the rowdies) armed themselves to prevent more troops from passing through the city."[37]

Most of the rioters hailed from Maryland or another slave state (68 percent), but while very few had Northern roots, one-fourth came from a foreign country. Irish workers seem to have sympathized with the South to a greater degree than Germans, the other significant non-Anglo immigrant bloc. The Irish made up the largest group of foreigners rioting on April 19. Irish surnames stand out in the April 24 poll book, and a smaller share of Maryland's Irish fought for the Union than did Germans. Nine of the seventeen Irish rioters identified in census records practiced unskilled and semi-skilled trades, and they were all but two of the rioters holding such occupations for whom nativity could be determined. In addition to Irish laborers, other subsets of the working class took part in the riot. George Konig, a second-generation German tavern keeper and Democratic brawler, carried the Palmetto flag that the mob forced Massachusetts volunteers to walk behind. Corsican barber Cypriano Ferrandini allegedly plotted Lincoln's assassination in February, and he helped threaten Bond during the riot. African American sailors helped merchants construct barricades on Pratt Street and cheered Jefferson Davis. These rioters represented the various elements of low-skilled minority labor that nativist gangs had targeted in election brawls and hate strikes during the 1850s.[38]

The demographic backgrounds of the rioters resembled those of the 9,578 men who voted on April 24. In terms of class and ethnicity, wealthy Maryland natives and poor immigrants comprised the bulk of the voters while the middle class of skilled artisans shunned the polls. Voters held a median of $500 in property and their per capita wealth was ten times that of all white Baltimoreans. Two-fifths of the voters worked in commerce as compared to one-eighth of the city. Skilled artisans were under-represented in comparison to their proportions in the general population and electorate, whereas unskilled and semi-skilled workers, who normally voted at half the rate of their eligibility, matched their share of the electorate. The Irish, 8 percent of Baltimore whites, made up 14 percent of the voters, and Germans turned out at a rate just ahead of their 17 percent share of the white population. Three-fourths of low-skilled voters were born abroad, half in Ireland. Conversely, American natives, two-thirds of them Marylanders, made up 91 percent of high white-collar Southern Rights voters. Combining occupation and nativity, wealthy Maryland-born merchants were the most numerous followed by penniless Irish laborers. Immigrant common laborers had innumerable informal contacts with Baltimore-bred merchants and clerks who hired them on a need basis to move their commodities from wharf to market to rail depot. Their common battle against the Know Nothings reinforced that bond, and their alliance continued to hold in the crisis atmosphere that followed the riot.[39]

In line with the dynamics of municipal reform, on April 24 propertyless immigrants voted for wealthy men rather than their fellow workers. Reform publicist and attorney Severn Teackle Wallis led the Southern Rights delegation. Other candidates included Frederick Brune's brother, John, a merchant who presided over the Poor Association and the Board of Trade; T. Parkin Scott, a Catholic attorney and outspoken foe of nativism; and iron-maker Ross Winans, whose opposition to strikes in 1853 and 1857 led him to the Reform cause and whose high profile among secessionists—he manufactured weapons for the South and told an April 18 rally to "repel, if need be, any invader who may come to establish a military despotism over us"—made him the first Baltimorean arrested for treason against the federal government. The non-elected leadership "was composed chiefly of old democrats" according to an insider and included Adam Kyle Sr., who wanted to run to avenge "the assassination of his gallant son, by the roughs at the polls."[40]

Military support for Southern rights came from "law and order" militia companies organized in the wake of Kyle's murder and John Brown's raid with the help of a $70,000 General Assembly appropriation. The Maryland Guard, co-founded by George Kyle, was the most important of these companies. One volunteer stated that on April 19 "we were on the side of the mob and we were sorely exercised in our mind as to how far our duty required us to go in the matter." Afterwards, the unit helped police burn the railroad bridges and arrest and disarm Unionists. Unlike working-class gangs and fire companies, young Democrats from merchant families predominated in the militia units. Sixty-nine percent of the Maryland Guard's 303 members were clerks, merchants, or customs officials, and almost all (95 percent) held white-collar jobs. Confirming a federal officer's October assertion that, "the Maryland Guard is in Virginia fighting for secession," forty-nine out of 111 Guardsmen sampled, including Kyle, fought for the Confederacy, a rate five times higher than that for white men statewide. Maryland Guardsmen belonged to prominent families like the Gilmors and the Howards, and they helped channel the energy of Reformers in the mercantile elite into the campaign against federal coercion.[41]

"Should this continue," wrote a Baltimore clerk a week after Lincoln's election, "I think all the merchants have to go overboard which are heavy engaged with the Southern States." The majority of businessmen, including heads of large firms like Alexander Brown and Sons and eventually John W. Garrett at the B&O, backed the Union and did so in part because of extensive trade with the free states. The minority of commercial men involved in secession-related activities did business in the South and wanted to curtail growing indebtedness to Northern creditors. In the 1850s, they had expanded markets in the South and Latin America, with some successes in dry goods, textiles, and fertilizers. Rioters working in commission houses involved in these efforts could find an economic logic in secession, especially when business interests dovetailed with family and politics. After the riot, Samuel Wethered, a textile maker with Southern investments, urged his brother-in-law Daniel Barringer, a leading North Carolina politician, to send "arms and men" to stop the approaching "hordes from the North."[42]

Like Wethered, other rich secessionists probably gave less priority to the long-term economics of their actions than they did to their political ties to Reformers and Democrats who played key roles in the riot and armed neutrality defense. Shouting "keep back, men, or I shoot," Marshal Kane enabled the Massachusetts volunteers to escape by placing himself and fifty officers between them and the mob. Police wanted to avoid the consequences attending federal casualties, and the mob cooperated because it considered police to be allies in their larger cause—for example, Kane, according to an eyewitness, dispersed a crowd threatening the B&O's offices "amid deafening cheers [and] . . . the assurance of those present that they would do whatever he directed"—however police efforts to avoid bloodshed should not be taken as support for the Union. Kane later served as a Confederate colonel. During the riot he walked with a rioter carrying a South Carolina flag and telegraphed Frederick secessionist Bradley T. Johnston to "send expresses over the mountains and valleys of Maryland for the riflemen to come without delay. Fresh hordes will be down on us tomorrow. We will fight them and whip them or die." Police quickly released the few rioters they chose to apprehend. One officer told rioters he would make no arrests and urged them to loot arms stored at city hall; another claimed that Officer Dull was disliked "as he was a Union man." A Maryland Guardsman recalled that after the riot city government directed his unit to "assist the police to scatter the body of armed men who called themselves 'Union' men. . . . Word was passed around among the men to give them no quarter if we got a chance to attack them." These actions along with federal arms seizures and cutting transport and communications persuaded U.S. authorities to arrest Kane and the Police Board for treason.[43]

Along with police, state troops that defended the city in late April had earlier fought Know Nothings and workers. In 1857, the First Light Division put down the B&O strike and stood ready to guard Baltimore polls that fall, and after John Brown's raid it patrolled the vicinity of Harpers Ferry. In 1860 a volunteer wrote that "notwithstanding all the combined efforts of political traducers and enemies, who joined in the *denunciation of the military* because of its honest readiness to oppose rowdyism and support the civil authority . . . [the Division was] now ready to act and do their duty under the better auspices of our happy reformation." Their chief, George Hume Steuart, a slaveowner who would command the Confederacy's Maryland Line, believed the secessionist fable that black votes in the free states had given Lincoln the presidency and protested as "a violation of my rights . . . the deliberate and intentional extension of the elective franchise to a single negro." Like other urban secessionists, militia volunteers blended local partisan grudges with racial and proslavery arguments publicized farther south.[44]

The experience Reformers and militia volunteers had in combating strikers and gangs predisposed them to view all local Unionists as Know Nothing rowdies. A secessionist paper identified Unionists who rioted on April 19 as "ex-members of Mayor Swann's police and Joe Edwards' crew of Tigers Eubolts &c.!" A merchant agreed that "all the disorder we have now is from the old clubs of 'Tigers, Roughs, and Plugs,' who are to a man 'Black Republicans,' and the only ones that we have in Baltimore." A militia volunteer claimed that city Unionists "were the same lot of Roughs whose killing of Adam Kyle was the reason for the formation of the Maryland Guard." McHenry Howard, Charles Howard's son, linked the battle against gangs to the defense of Southern rights. "The outbreak of April 19th was not a return of mob law as Northern papers say. The roughs are Unionists. It resulted from the irrepressible indignation of the people at seeing armed men pass over our soil to subjugate our brethren of the South." The "roughs" had connections to the American Party of the 1850s, just as Howard, a Maryland Guardsman and future Confederate officer, did to the Democrats. While Baltimore secessionists shared the concern of most Confederates for states' rights, their explanations of the riot exhibited a visceral partisan dislike for their local enemies that many conflated with opposition to federal coercion.[45]

This connection of sectionalism and party politics got a boost from Southern sympathizers in the Customs service appointed by Democratic presidents. At least eleven Customs employees rioted on April 19. They paraded with captured Massachusetts rifles and proclaimed "this will tell the time of day." Collector of the Port John Thompson Mason used his office as the headquarters for Southern Rights organizing, joined the April riot, and later took a commission in the Confederate navy. In early May, thirty-seven Customs officials followed Mason's earlier decision to resign in protest of Lincoln's policies.[46]

During the height of Know Nothing election violence, Democrats used the Customs House as a paramilitary base not unlike the function of taverns for nativist gangs. John Lutz and Samuel McElwee, Customs workers involved in the attack on Union troops, had brawled for Democrats at the Eighth Ward polls, and Democratic gang members sometimes received bail money from Customs officials. Augustus Pennington, a Fifteenth Ward Reform candidate in 1859, had been threatened on election eve and was attending to the wounded Kyle brothers the next day when friends urged him to find cover. "I proceeded down to the United States Customs House," Pennington said, "which I considered the only safe place in the city except the eighth ward." What organization the 1861 riot had came from armed Customs workers like Lutz, captain of the Customs police, who was observed "leading a crowd and saying he knew where to get guns." The ascendancy of Southern sympathizers in late April owed more to their control of the means of violence—as manifested in the actions of police, militia volunteers, and federal employees—than it did to a non-existent majority sentiment for secession.[47]

Some of the most lucrative federal patronage was in the Customs service—Mason earned $6,000 a year and controlled a hundred appointments, many of which paid $1,000 annually—and Baltimore, America's fourth most profitable port, had one of the larger Customs payrolls. In the 1850s, Democrats cut off from municipal patronage rewarded local partisans with federal jobs from the Pierce and Buchanan administrations. Top Customs jobs went to merchants affiliated with the Democratic Party—for example, Charles Howard passed his $1,500 clerkship on to his son William in 1858—while lower paying positions were awarded to working-class partisans like Franklin "Patty" Naff, lead brawler for the New Market Fire Company, who was hired as a watchman in 1857. Lincoln's victory ended Democratic control of the Customs House and closed off an important counterweight to Know Nothing control of city government. Early in 1861, a Democratic patronage official lamented that "it is all a scramble now for the spoils, and the American party are making desperate efforts to get control of the Balto Post Office and Custom House." Customs officials had close ties to Democratic merchants trading on the seas, and in 1861 these groups stood together in defiance of the new Republican federal administration that threatened the commerce of the slave states and the political fortunes of Democrats.[48]

The minority of immigrants backing secession further demonstrated its flexible appeal. Some were wealthy merchants like the Brunes, Kyles, and Robert W. Davis, an Irishman shot by Massachusetts troops whose funeral, like Kyle's, became a political platform. The Friedenwalds, a family of German Jewish dry goods merchants that traded extensively in the Upper South, advanced familiar ideas about abolitionist fanaticism and financial ruin, but they also connected states' rights arguments to German liberal fears of government tyranny. After Lincoln's election, Moses Friedenwald wrote that, "if there is yet a bosom in the Old World wherein there is a spark for the freedom of man let it be smothered. Man must be oppressed, the Iron heel of tyranny must be felt, self government, I say, is a failure." A year later, Jonas Friedenwald, then a captain in a Virginia regiment, claimed that Union victory would "palsy the fervent emigrant from attempting to embark to a land of dissension, the asylum of the oppressed of all nations will be a land without law and Liberty." All sides claimed to defend freedom, but for immigrants involved in Southern commerce and suspicious of Know Nothing Unionists, the Confederacy looked like the better defender of civil liberty and economic opportunity.[49]

As the demographic data show, upper-class leaders of the secession movement had some success in attracting immigrant workers near the bottom of the economy. Catholic slaveowners in southern Maryland, Catholic politicians T. Parkin Scott and Roger B. Taney, and the Church newspaper, the *Catholic Mirror*, lobbied the South's cause with Baltimore's Irish. Secessionist editor Thomas Hall, one of Davis's pallbearers, played on the cultural insecurity produced during the Know Nothing era: "The idea of Irishmen coming on here to fight the battles of a party that a very few years ago deprived them of the right to carry arms belonging to the state in Massachusetts, while the negro enjoyed the privilege of forming military companies—thus making the negro not equal but superior to the adopted citizen!" Long the targets of nativist politicians, some Irish workers allied with these wealthy Southern sympathizers rather than cast their lot with former enemies that now dominated the Union movement.[50]

Secession's wealthy leaders were drawing workers to them via patron-client relationships that Democrats had earlier used to appeal to minority workers persecuted by the American Party. Unlike New York's Civil War draft protesters, Baltimore's anti-Union rioters left African Americans alone, and although Reform police monitored free black assemblies, a late April conference of the African Methodist Episcopal Church offered a "vote of thanks" to city officials for their protection, and some black sailors joined the April riot. Addressing the unemployed, Hall promised that "there will be work enough for all, to the remotest generation, in supplying the demands of Southern Commerce." A Reform public works recipient claimed that on April 20 a factory owner "asked me if I was out of work. [He] asked me to join the Southern Army," and a machinist accused of making Confederate arms explained that "he was a Union man, but had to work for a living." Notwithstanding the April strike, Reformer Adam Denmead built weapons for the militia, and his employees were among the few industrial workers demonstrating for secession. Cypriano Ferrandini cut the hair of the mercantile elite at Barnum's Hotel, a rallying point for the April riot, and he used those connections to finance a militia unit that he commanded during the 1857 B&O strike. On April 22 a friend urged Mayor Brown to buy arms, expel federal troops from Maryland, and fund soup kitchens like one started by Ross Winans' son and the widow of secessionist merchant George S. Brown. "It is important not only in view of the calls of humanity," read the advice, "but for other reasons which your known intelligence must perceive." By linking Southern rights to unemployment relief, the writer reminded Brown of the local and national dimensions of the crisis and urged that patron-client relationships be used to broaden secession's appeal beyond a clique of wealthy merchants.[51]

Social and economic considerations that had become entangled with partisan antipathy for Know Nothings and Unionists say a great deal about the motivation of Baltimore's Southern sympathizers that cannot be gleaned from their public statements alone. In the sectional debate all sides made the popular and uncontroversial case that the single-minded pursuit of party victory and the rewards of office had contributed to crisis of the Union. Hours after the riot, Wallis told a crowd to "stand together hereafter under the old flag of Maryland, forgetting all parties and distinctions, and may the blood which has been spilt, this day among us, be the seal of the covenant of our reunion in the holy cause of the South." The *South* accused Unionists of seeking "to breed dissensions and beget a spirit of party among the people." Defending Brown's administration, the *Sun* warned that "there is an implacable spirit of party, to which the peace of this city is always exposed, and which no truth, no experience, no sense of propriety can allay or appease." For their part, city Unionists urged "our fellow citizens" to act "without respect to party political relations or opinions for the sake of our common country." Congressman J. Morrison Harris criticized "the lust of the Democratic party, that induced it to stir up the agitation of this slavery question . . . ," and Unionist Brantz Mayer believed that "men, not actuated by true patriotism, but by false issues which are to subserve selfish or sectional interests, have introduced perilous discussions in the legislative halls." Republicanism did not so much determine sectional allegiance as it shaped understanding of the stakes involved in the conflict. Baltimoreans who looked to political leaders for guidance learned that parties owned some of the blame for the crisis, that one side or the other conspired against the Republic's principles, and that the threat was dangerous enough to warrant a resort to arms.[52]

Historians' ship-at-sea metaphor for Baltimore's entry in the Civil War overstates the vacillation of opinion, but it provides insight into the way that partisan differences intensified during the secession crisis. Just after Lincoln's election, Frederick Brune claimed that "we ought not to aim to get out of the union, but to maintain our Honor and safety in the Union." Seven months later, he had moved closer to secession, saying that he wanted to "show . . . the Northern people that while there is one man left in our state they will never yield."[53] By that time, the Reform administration and its friends were in a corner. Union on the South's terms was no longer viable and the harder choice of secession or a nation led by the Republicans presented itself. Many chose the latter, but in late April 1861 those who had earlier disavowed outright secession took it up as a lesser evil to living under a federal administration they thoroughly disliked and one that might soon return their local enemies to power.

The core group that moved from Reform to Breckinridge to decrying federal coercion and ultimately to secession failed miserably in bringing the rest of the city along to their final destination. Furthermore, while they had success against the Know Nothings, their revolution against political parties did not work out exactly as planned. Unlike the Lower South's revival of one-party, or "no party," government in the late 1850s—something Confederate nationalists praised as a return to the virtues of the early republic—big cities like Baltimore had socially diverse electorates that had been polarized in local struggles and could not be easily reunified, especially by leaders strongly identified with recent conflicts. If the elimination of party competition made the lower South look northward for the ever-present threat to republican liberty, then anti-party rhetoric in cities like Baltimore encouraged a search for local as well as external agents of tyranny. Instead of

Federal troops searching Baltimore police headquarters for concealed arms. (*Frank Leslie's Illustrated Newspaper,* July 13, 1861.)

resolving local partisan differences, secession raised the stakes in an already bitter struggle.[54]

The hardening of these divisions to the point of war had national and local dimensions. Slavery's status in the federal government and nativism shook apart the controlled competition of Jacksonian parties nationally, but the disruption of democracy at the local level followed a somewhat different path. In Baltimore, the politicization of ethnic and class conflict by the Know Nothings initially invigorated a system of party competition in danger of collapsing due to voter indifference. However many soon perceived the anti-toxin of popular mobilization to be worse than the disease of elite consensus. The tactics of machine politics, particularly coercion, persuaded Reformers to adopt their own drastic measures, such as inviting the state legislature to redraw the lines of municipal power and bombarding voters with the message that strong party organizations like the Know Nothings brought economic ruin, government corruption, and civil disorder. Local polarization coincided with the national escalation of sectional conflict and prepared the ground for civil war within the city and nation.

Instead of restoring republican consensus, the breakdown of normal party politics generated lasting hatreds. While sitting in a federal prison in 1863 former militia commander Isaac Ridgway Trimble promised Unionists that, "your women shall dream of bloody massacres and pale faces hung with locks stiffened by gory blood. . . . The whole land shall be to you a curse and the favour of a just God shall rest upon it; *never.*" Trimble no longer looked at politics as a gentleman's game where shared social status and mutual interests outweighed policy differences between parties. Neither did the Baltimorean who told Governor Hicks in late April 1861 that "your destiny is fixed. It is resolved that if it takes twenty years [you will] . . . be shot privately for being a damn black republican." That summer Unionist Anna Ella Carroll adopted the equally hard view that, "there can be no equivocal position. . . . He who is not with the Government is against it." Baltimore, like the rest of the country, had gone to war.[55]

Notes

[1] Jean H. Baker, *The Politics of Continuity: Maryland Political Parties from 1858 to 1870* (Baltimore: The Johns Hopkins University Press, 1973), 44 (quotation), 54. Also see William J. Evitts, *A Matter of Allegiances: Maryland from 1850 to 1861* (Baltimore: Johns Hopkins University Press, 1974), 152, 190; Kevin Conley Ruffner, *Maryland's Blue and Gray: A Border States' Union and Confederate Junior Officer Corps* (Baton Rouge: Louisiana State University Press, 1997), 30; Robert J. Brugger, *Maryland: A Middle Temperament, 1634–1980* (Baltimore: Johns Hopkins University Press, 1988), 272; William B. Catton, "The Baltimore Business Community and the Secession Crisis, 1860–61" (M.A. thesis, University of Maryland, 1952), 53. Northerners Abraham Lincoln and Stephen Douglas had little support in what was after all a southern city.

[2] Jane C. Bernstein, "From Anonymity to Unity: The Baltimore Iron Workers' Strike of 1853," (M.A. thesis, University of Maryland, College Park, 1989), 7; U.S. Department of Commerce, Bureau of the Census, *Manufactures of the United States in 1860: Compiled from the Original Returns of the Eighth Census* (Washington, 1865), 222–23; Gary L. Browne, *Baltimore in the Nation, 1789–1861* (Chapel Hill: University of North Carolina Press, 1980), 168–169, 172–75; Brugger, *Maryland*, 262 (Davis quoted).

[3] Philip J. Ethington, *The Public City: The Political Construction of Urban Life in San Francisco, 1850–1900* (New York: Cambridge University Press, 1994), 129; Mary P. Ryan, *Civic Wars: Democracy and Public Life in the American City*

During the Nineteenth Century (Berkeley: University of California Press, 1997), 150; Jon C. Teaford, *The Unheralded Triumph: City Government in America, 1870–1900* (Baltimore: Johns Hopkins University Press, 1984), 9.

[4] Michael P. Johnson, *Toward a Patriarchal Republic: The Secession of Georgia* (Baton Rouge: Louisiana State University Press, 1977), 80–81; William L. Barney, *The Secessionist Impulse: Alabama and Mississippi in 1860* (Princeton: Princeton University Press, 1974), 37; William W. Freehling, *The Road to Disunion: Volume I: Secessionists at Bay* (New York: Oxford University Press, 1990), 49–50; Ted Tunnell, *Crucible of Reconstruction: War, Radicalism and Race in Louisiana, 1862–1877* (Baton Rouge: Louisiana State University Press, 1984), 20; George C. Rable, *The Confederate Republic: A Revolution Against Politics* (Chapel Hill: University of North Carolina Press, 1994).

[5] *Baltimore Republican*, October 5, 1857; Evitts, *A Matter of Allegiances*, 116–17; correspondence between T. Watkins Ligon and Thomas Swann, October 28, 1857, and Reverdy Johnson, et al. to Ligon, n.d. [October 1857], Governor's Letterbook, 1854–64, Maryland State Archives, Annapolis (hereafter MSA); Lawrence F. Schmeckebier, *History of the Know Nothing Party in Maryland* (Baltimore: Johns Hopkins University Press, 1899), 77; T. Watkins Ligon, *Message of the Executive of Maryland, to the General Assembly of Maryland* (Annapolis, 1858), 21, 25, 26 (quotation).

[6] *Baltimore Clipper*, May 20, 1858; Richard R. Duncan, "The Era of the Civil War," in Richard Walsh and William Lloyd Fox eds., *Maryland: A History* (Baltimore: Maryland Historical Society, 1983), 309–39, 326–27; Thomas Swann, *Mayor's Message and Annual Reports of the City's Departments to the Mayor and City Council of Baltimore, 1858* (Baltimore, 1858), 26 (quotation), 19, 24–25.

[7] Edward W. Belt, *The Reform Conspiracy* (Baltimore, 1858), 35, 39, 40; Frederick Brune to Emily Brune, November 8, 1859, box 14, Brune-Randall Papers, Special Collections, Maryland Historical Society, Baltimore (hereafter MdHSSC).

[8] Gerald S. Henig, *Henry Winter Davis: Antebellum and Civil War Congressman from Maryland* (New York: Twayne Publishers, 1973), 116; Evitts, *A Matter of Allegiances*, 128; *Baltimore American*, November 3–15, 1859; William P. Preston Papers, Historical Manuscripts and Archives Department, McKeldin Library, University of Maryland. Frank Towers, "Job Busting at Baltimore Shipyards: Racial Violence in the Civil War–Era South," *Journal of Southern History*, 66 (May 2000): 221–56. Frederick W. Brune to Emily Brune, October 29, 1859, box 14, Brune-Randall Family Papers, MdHSSC.

[9] Manuscript Census Returns, Eighth Census of the United States, 1860, Baltimore City, Schedule I, Population (hereinafter cited as 1860 U.S. Census, Baltimore City, Pop.), National Archives Microfilm Series M-653, rolls T-464, 15th Ward, p. 408, 511; James E. P. Boulden, *The Presbyterians of Baltimore: Their Churches and Historic Grave-Yards* (Baltimore, 1875), 79; *Baltimore American*, May 12, 1851; J. Thomas Scharf, *History of Maryland from the Earliest Period to the Present Day* (1879; Reprt. Hatboro, Pa.: Tradition Press, 1967), 3:267; *Baltimore Sun*, January 26 (first quotation) and 31, 1861; Maryland General Assembly, House of Delegates, *Baltimore City Contested Election—Papers in the Contested*

Election from Baltimore City, 1859: Adam Denmead, E. Wyatt Blanchard, Francis B. Loney et al. vs. Charles L. Kraft, Thomas Booze, Robert L. Seth et al. (Annapolis, 1860), 78–79, 277 (second quotation) (hereinafter, Maryland, *Baltimore Contested Election, 1859*).

[10] *Baltimore American,* November 4, 1859; *Baltimore Sun,* January 26, 1861 (Edwards quoted); *Baltimore Exchange,* August 31, 1860; Coroner's inquest, n.d. [1859] Health Department Records, ser. 1, box 26, RG 19, Baltimore City Archives, hereafter BCA; *Baltimore Clipper* October 4, 1860; Maryland, *Baltimore Contested Election, 1859,* 236–51.

[11] Mrs. Benjamin G. Harris Diaries, November 4, 1859, MdHSSC; *Baltimore American,* November 5, 1859.

[12] Maryland, House of Delegates, "Evidence Taken before the Committee on Corporations Relative to the Baltimore City Passenger Railroad," Document 2 in Maryland, General Assembly, *Documents, 1859* (Annapolis, 1860), 8, 15 (contractor quoted), 30, 54, 88–91, 107–8, 161; Maryland, House of Delegates, *Majority Report of the Committee on Corporations . . . Relative to the Baltimore City Passenger Railroad* (Annapolis, 1860); J. Thomas Scharf, *History of Baltimore City and County from the Earliest Period to the Present Day: Including Biographical Sketches of Their Representative Men* (Philadelphia, 1881), 363–64; *Sun* June 3, 4, 7, and 8 (marchers quoted), 1859; *Baltimore Clipper,* June 3, 1859. *Baltimore Exchange,* February 3, 7 (first rally quotation), 10 and 13, 1860; John B. Seidenstricker, *Proceedings of a Town Meeting of Citizens of Baltimore Relative to the City Passenger Railway Company* (Annapolis, 1860), 4 (second quotation).

[13] *[Baltimore] The South,* April 30, 1861 (quotation). Baker, *The Politics of Continuity,* 43; Evitts, *A Matter of Allegiances,* 149. *Baltimore American,* November 1, 1859. George P. Kane to James A. Pearce, November 19, 1859, James Alfred Pearce Papers, MdHSSC.

The backgrounds of politicians in this study come from political reporting in local newspapers for the years 1840–66, including the *[Baltimore] American Democrat, Baltimore American, Clipper, Republican, Exchange, Patriot,* and *Sun.* Housed at the BCA are City of Baltimore, *Members of the City Council, Their Clerks, and the Officers of the Corporation,* 1840–1866, Mayor's Papers, RG 9, ser. 2, City Council Papers, RG 16, ser. 1. Useful personal papers at the MdHSSC are the Howard family, William P. Preston, Thomas Swann, James Alfred Pearce, J. Morrison Harris, Henry Winter Davis, the Mayer family, the Glenn family, and the Brune-Randall Papers. Over 1,500 politicians are in the database.

[14] *Baltimore Exchange,* February 2, 3, March 1, 16 (quotation), 1860; *The Laws of Maryland,* 1860, ch. 7; Baker, *The Politics of Continuity,* 27, 31; Henig, *Henry Winter Davis,* 138; Evitts, *A Matter of Allegiances,* 132.

[15] John Everett et al. to Franklin Pearce, March, 20, 1853, vertical file, MdHSSC; *Baltimore American,* January 9, 1857, November 3 and 4, 1859; William W. Glenn to William H. Gatchell, August 11, 1859, William W. Glenn Papers, MdHSSC; Ralph Clayton, *Black Baltimore, 1820–1870* (Bowie, Md.: Heritage Books, 1987), 64–65; Clinton McCabe, *History of the Baltimore Police Department, 1774–1907* (Baltimore: Fleet-McGinley Co., Printers, 1907), 31; *Baltimore Republican,* January 3, 1856, September 25, November 2, December 10, 1857.

[16] Letters Sent by the Baltimore Board of Police, 1861, Military Records, Middle Department, RG 393, part 4, National Archives and Records Administration, Washington, D.C. (hereafter NARA); Charles Howard, et al., to Benjamin Herring, n.d. [February 1861], box 117, Baltimore City Council Papers; *Baltimore Clipper*, August 31, October 3, 1860; *Baltimore Sun*, November 1, 1860; *Baltimore Exchange*, February 11, August 15, 17, 31, September 8, 1860; R. S. Teal to George P. Kane, April 13, 1861, Provost Marshal, letters received, part 1, box 1, Military Records, Middle Department, NARA; Frederick W. Brune to Emily Brune, October 10, 1860, box 14, Brune-Randall Papers.

[17] George W. Brown to Frederick W. Brune, August 7, 30, September 6, 1860, box 6, Brune-Randall Papers; *Baltimore American*, October 13, 1859; *Baltimore Exchange*, September 7, 25, 1860, October 6, 10 (campaign quotations), 1860.

[18] McPhail quoted in *Baltimore Clipper*, June 5, 9, 1858; Thomas H. Hicks, *The Inaugural Address of Thomas H. Hicks, Governor of Maryland, January 13, 1858* (Annapolis, 1858), 10–11.

[19] George Brown to Frederick Brune, July 13, 1860, box 6, Brune-Randall Papers; William Louis Schley to Thomas Hicks, January 16, 1861, Thomas Hicks Papers, MdHSSC; *Baltimore Exchange*, October 23, 1860; Baker, *The Politics of Continuity*, 39, 42; Evitts, *A Matter of Allegiances*, 143–44; Peyton McCrary, Clark Miller, and Dale Baum, "Class and Party in the Secession Crisis: Voting Behavior in the Deep South, 1856–1861," *Journal of Interdisciplinary History*, 8 (1978): 429–57, 454; *[Baltimore] Daily Exchange*, October 11, 1860; *Baltimore Sun* November 7, 1860.

Data on ward makeup come from the 1860 federal census of population presented in Joseph Garonzik, "Urbanization and the Black Population of Baltimore, 1850–1870," (Ph.D. diss., State University of New York at Stony Brook, 1974), 57, and my own sample of 4,000 names from the 1850 manuscript census. The Democratic vote pattern comes from election returns printed in newspapers from 1845 to 1860. Correlation coefficients: White-collar workers, Brown 0.09, Breckinridge -0.37; manual workers, Brown -0.23, Breckinridge 0.25; Democratic vote 1845–1852, Brown 0.23, Breckinridge 0.56. Both correlated above 0.66 for foreign-born voters and below -.66 for native-born.

[20] *Baltimore Exchange*, November 6, 1860. In addition to Baker, Evitts, and Catton see Carl M. Frasure, "Union Sentiment in Maryland," *Maryland Historical Magazine*, 24 (1929): 210–24.

[21] *Sun* January 7 and February 1, 1861; Matthew Page Andrews, "History of Baltimore: From 1850 to the Close of the Civil War," in Clayton Coleman Hall, ed., *Baltimore: Its History and Its People, Vol. I—History* (New York, 1912), 151–237, 166–67; David Perine Scrapbook, Perine Papers, MdHSSC.

[22] *Baltimore Sun*, January 9, 11, 22 and 26, 1861. For resignations see "Law and Order" to George W. Brown, n.d. [1861] (quotation), William Thompson to George William Brown, November 12, 1860, Jehu B. Askew to Brown, November 21, 1860 and other letters in box 30, Mayor's Papers, RG 9, ser.2, BCA.

[23] Resolutions to economize on expenditures, November 22, 1860, box 119, Baltimore City Council Papers; Simon J. Martenet to George W. Brown, February 15, 1861, box 30, Mayor's Correspondence; *Baltimore American*, February 22,

1861; J. H. Hollander, *The Financial History of Baltimore* (Baltimore, 1899), 209, 218, 233–35, 270, 278, 310, 326, 384–85.

[24] F. W. Brune to Emily Brune, November 29, 1860, box 14, Brune-Randall Papers; Catton, "The Baltimore Business Community," 53; *Baltimore Exchange,* March 14, 26, 30, April 1, 1861; Catherine N. Smith to Nelly, May 10, 1861, Civil War File, MdHSSC.

[25] Mechanics and Workingmen's petition to the Mayor and City Council, March 4, 1861, box 30, Mayor's Papers, BCA; Peter Mowel et al. to the Mayor and City Council of Baltimore, March 4, 1861 (second quotation), Joint Standing Committee on Ways and Means, Baltimore City Council, March 27, 1861, and other petitions of the Mechanics and Workingmen's Association, City Council Papers, box 120, are in box 120. *Baltimore Exchange,* April 4, 5, 1861.

[26] *Baltimore Exchange,* April 6, 9, 1861.

[27] Ibid., April 9, 12, 1861.

[28] Petition of William L. Garrittee and Others . . . , April 10, 1861, box 120, Baltimore City Council Papers; *Baltimore Exchange,* April 11, 1861. Saville refused to endorse the petition. List of employees on Druid Hill Park improvements, April 21–27, 1861, Vouchers, 1861, ser. 3, box 184, RG 41, BCA; *Second Annual Report of the Park Commission of the City of Baltimore, 1861* (Baltimore, 1862), Published Reports, RG 68, ser. 22, BCA.

[29] Evitts, *A Matter of Allegiances,* 174; *Baltimore American,* February 25, 1861; Daniel M. Barringer to Elizabeth Wethered Barringer, February 24, 1861, Daniel M. Barringer Papers, box 3, Southern Historical Collection, Wilson Library, University of North Carolina–Chapel Hill; *Baltimore Exchange,* April 15 (quotation), 16–19, 1861; Harold R. Manakee, *Maryland in the Civil War* (Baltimore: Maryland Historical Society, 1961), 31; Matthew Page Andrews, "Passage of the Sixth Massachusetts Regiment Through Baltimore, April 19, 1861," *Maryland Historical Magazine,* 14 (1919): 60–73, 63–64.

[30] Matthew Ellenberger, "Whigs in the Streets? Baltimore Republicanism in the Spring of 1861," *Maryland Historical Magazine,* 86 (1991): 23–38; Charles B. Clark, "Baltimore and the Attack on the 6th Massachusetts Regiment, April 19, 1861," *Maryland Historical Magazine,* 56 (1961): 39–71; Andrews, "Passage of the Sixth Massachusetts." For casualties and crowd numbers see Frank Towers, "'A Vociferous Army of Howling Wolves': Baltimore's Civil War Riot of April 19, 1861," *The Maryland Historian,* 23 (1992): 1–28. Hugh Bond's reminiscences are in James M. Harris Papers, box 5, MdHSSC; *Baltimore Clipper,* April 20, 1861.

[31] Frank Moore, *The Civil War in Song and Story* (1882, Rpt.. New York, 1889), 36; Adeline Tyler, Dielman File, MdHS.

[32] Arms deals are documented in the Isaac Ridgway Trimble Papers, MdHSSC. Leonard Passano to George P. Kane, April 22, 1861; Joseph Boury to George William Brown April 22, 1861; John Friese to Kane, April 22, 1861; Magruder, Taylor and Roberts to G. W. Brown, April 22, 1861, Provost Marshal, letters received. City Hall Guards Autograph List, 1861, Civil War File, MdHSSC; *The South,* April 22, 1861; George William Brown, *Baltimore and the Nineteenth of April, 1861: A Study of the War* (1887; repr. Baltimore: Johns Hopkins University Press, 2001), 63; George L. P. Radcliffe, *Governor Thomas Hicks of Maryland and*

the Civil War in Baltimore (Baltimore: The Johns Hopkins University Press, 1901), 97.

³³ *The South*, April 23, 1861; *Baltimore Sun*, April 30, 1861; *Baltimore American*, April 22, 1861; Radcliffe, *Governor Thomas H. Hicks*, 65–67; Henry W. Hoffman to Samuel P. Chase, April 23, 1861, in John Niven, et al., eds., *The Salmon P. Chase Papers: vol. 3. Correspondence, 1858–March 1863* (Kent, Ohio: Kent State University Press, 1995), 59. Lincoln quoted in Frank K. Howard to the *Maryland Times*, September 22, 1861, Abraham Lincoln Papers, Manuscripts Division, Library of Congress, Washington, D.C. (hereafter LC).

³⁴ *Baltimore American*, April 30, May 2, 6, 8 and 13, 1861; *Baltimore Sun*, May 3, 1861; Horace Abbott and Sons, et al., to the Mayor and City Council, May 4, 1861, box 119, City Council Papers.

³⁵ Iver Bernstein, *The New York City Draft Riots: Their Significance for American Society and Politics in the Age of the Civil War* (New York: Oxford University Press, 1990), 117–123.

³⁶ David Creamer, Notes and Memorandum Taken in 1861, in Reference to the Riots in Baltimore &c. Before the U.S. Grand Jury, June Term, 1861, copy at MdHSSC; *Baltimore Sun* April 20, May 6, September 6, 18, November 7, 1861; *Baltimore Exchange*, June 27, 1861; *Baltimore American*, April 20, May 10, 1861; *The South*, April 22, May 4, 1861; *Baltimore Republican*, April 20, 1861; *Baltimore Clipper*, May 10, 1861; Magistrate's Reports for the quarter ending July 1, 1861, Reports and Returns, RG 41, ser. 1, boxes 81 and 82, BCA; Maryland, House of Delegates, *Evidence of the Contested Election in the Case of Ridgely vs. Grason, to the General Assembly* (Annapolis: Richard P. Baily, 1865), 24, 39, 44, 76. Demographic sources: 1860 U.S. Census, Baltimore City, Pop.; John W. Woods, *Woods' Baltimore Directory for 1858–'59* (Baltimore, 1859); John W. Woods, *Woods' Baltimore City Directory . . . Ending Year 1860* (Baltimore, 1861); Baltimore City General Property Tax Records. Assessor's Tax Books, 1856–1861; Ruffner, *Maryland's Blue and Gray*.

³⁷ Jabez David Pratt to John C. Pratt, April 27, 1861 (quotation), Civil War File, MdHSSC; Brown, *Baltimore and the Nineteenth of April*, 50, 45; Francis X. Ward to Richard D. Fisher, November 8, 1909, Reminiscences of April 19, 1861, Civil War File, MdHSSC; Creamer, Notes and Memorandum, 1. Occupation = 118 identifiable cases; 14 merchants; 15 clerks. Place of birth=80 cases; 18 Irish, 50 Maryland-born, 6 Northerners. Wealth = 82 cases.

³⁸ Creamer, Notes and Memorandum, 6, 23, 26, 27, 30; *Baltimore Sun*, September 12, 1861; Various contributors, *Baltimore: Its History and Its People, Vol. 3, Biography* (New York, 1912), 594–97. Black sailors are in the *Baltimore Exchange*, April 20, 1861; Andrews, "The Passage of the Sixth Massachusetts," 67; Scharf, *History of Baltimore City and County*, 789.

³⁹ n.a., *Poll Book, 24 April 1861* (Baltimore, n.d. [1861]), at the MdHS Library; 1860 U.S. Census, Baltimore City, Pop. Ten percent of the names from each voting precinct were matched with the 1860 census. The average voter owned $8,109. Place of birth: Maryland 52%, North 8%, South 6%, Ireland 14%, Germany 18%, other foreign-born, 2%; N=985. Like other voters, the vast majority of these men were married and headed households.

[40] Ellenberger, "Whigs in the Streets?" 36; Ross Winans and Co., Day Book, May 4, 1861, Ross Winans Papers, MdHSSC; *Baltimore Sun*, April 23 and May 9, 1861; *The South*, April 25, 1861; Evitts, *A Matter of Allegiances*, 190; *Baltimore American*, April 23, 1861; *Republican*, April 22, 30, 1861; William W. Glenn, *Between North and South: A Maryland Journalist Views the Civil War: The Narrative of William Wilkins Glenn, 1861–1869*, Bayly Ellen Marks and Mark Norton Schatz, eds. (Rutherford, N.J.: Fairleigh-Dickinson University Press, 1976) 31–32.

[41] Radcliffe, *Governor Thomas H. Hicks*, 15; Isaac F. Nicholson, "The Maryland Guard Battalion, 1860–61," *Maryland Historical Magazine*, 6 (1911): 117–31. Daniel M. Thomas to "My Dear Sister," April 21, 1861 (quotation), Daniel M. Thomas Papers, MdHSSC; Creamer, Notes and Memorandum, 28; Tunstall Smith, ed., *Richard Snowden Andrews: A Memoir* (Baltimore: The Sun, 1910), 33. *The War of Rebellion: A Compilation of the Official Records of the Union and Confederate Armies* (Washington, 1880), ser. 1, vol. II, 10, 20. Clerk to the General Auditor, October 2, 1861 (quotation), Register of Letters Received and Endorsements Sent, July 1861–June 1862, Military Records, Middle Department, part 1; Maryland Guard Register, Adjutant General's Papers, MSA; 53rd Regiment, Maryland Volunteers, Descriptive Book, MdHSSC; Daniel D. Hartzler, *Marylanders in the Confederacy* (Westminster, Md.: Family Line Publications, 1986).

[42] Jonas Friedenwald to Aaron Friedenwald, November 11, 1860, Friedenwald Papers, Jewish Historical Society, Baltimore. Alexander Brown and Sons to Edinburgh, April 18, 1861, Letters, 1859–1861, Alexander Brown and Sons Papers, LC; Catton, "The Baltimore Business Community," 18, 22–23, 29–30, 112; Brown, *Baltimore in the Nation*, 171; Baltimore Board of Trade, Minute Book, May 3, 1852 and May 12, 1853, Baltimore Board of Trade Records, MdHSSC; Samuel Wethered to Daniel M. Barringer, April 19, 1861, box 3, Barringer Papers.

[43] Brown, *Baltimore and the Nineteenth of April, 1861*, 51 (first quotation); Andrews, "Passage of the Sixth Massachusetts," 70–71; Scharf, *History of Baltimore City and County*, 791; *Baltimore Exchange*, April 20, 1861 (B&O quotation). Washington Hands, Civil War Notebook, microfilm at the MdHS Library; *Baltimore American*, April 20, 1861; Creamer, Notes and Memorandum, 3–5, 7, 17–18, 22 (Dull quotation), 23–24, 27, 33–34, 36; Clark, "Baltimore and the Attack on the Sixth Massachusetts Regiment," 50–51 (Kane's telegram), 65; Isaac Ridgway Trimble to Lt. Col. Morris A. Moore, April 30, 1861, Trimble Papers; Charles Howard to General Mason, April 30, 1861, and Howard to Col. Benjamin F. Huger, May 3, 1861, Letters Sent by the Baltimore Board of Police. William Bowly Wilson, Reminiscences of the Nineteenth of April 1861, Civil War File, MdHSSC (final quotation).

[44] *Baltimore Sun*, May 1–8, 1857; *Republican*, October 29, 1857; Duncan, "The Era of the Civil War," 322–25; *Baltimore Exchange*, February 14, 17, 18, 20 (quotation), 1861; George H. Steuart to the *National Intelligencer*, November 19, 1860, box 3, James Steuart Papers, MdHSSC; Hartzler, *Marylanders in the Confederacy*, 10.

[45] *The South*, April 28, 1861; Jabez David Pratt to John C. Pratt, April 27, 1861; Wilson, Reminiscences of the Nineteenth of April 1861; McHenry Howard to Francis G. Wood, May 17, 1861, McHenry Howard Papers, MdHSSC;

[46] Creamer, Notes and Memorandum, 12 (quotation), 17; Hartzler, *Mary-*

landers in the Confederacy, 220; Glenn, Between North and South, 21; Baltimore Sun, May 6, 1861.

[47] American Democrat, October 30, 1855; Return of Basil Root Justice of the Peace, December 1855–October 31, 1856, Reports and Returns; Baltimore American, October 16, 1857, April 20, 1861; Republican, September 11, October 6, 1856 November 5, 1857, January 7, 1858; Baltimore Sun, October 14, 1858; Baltimore Clipper, April 21, 1857; Secretary of State, Register of Officers, and Agents, Civil, Military, and Naval in the Service of the United States, 1859 (Washington, 1859), 64. Maryland, Baltimore City Contested Election, 1859, 305 (first quotation); Creamer, Notes and Memorandum, 12 (second quotation).

[48] John Thompson Mason to Howell Cobb, Secretary of the Treasury, September 14, 1857, Customs House Nominations for Delaware, Maryland, Georgetown, District of Columbia, and Virginia, 1857–1861, and John L. Proud to Edward Bates, U.S. Attorney General, March 20, 1861, Applications for Appointment as Customs Service Officers, both in Treasury Department, Civil Records, RG 56, NARA; Secretary of State, Register of Officers . . . 1859; Edward Spencer to Braddie Spencer, n.d. [1861] (quotation), in the possession of George M. Anderson, S.J., Rockville, Maryland.

[49] Andrews, "The Passage of the Sixth Massachusetts," 71; Dieter Cunz, The Maryland Germans: A History (Princeton: Princeton University Press, 1948), 284–316; Moses Friedenwald to Aaron Friedenwald, November 12, 1860 and Jonas Friedenwald to Aaron Friedenwald, November 22, 1861, Friedenwald Papers; Philip Kahn Jr., The Four Seasons of Baltimore's Needle Trades (Baltimore, 1989), 26–27.

[50] Thomas Spalding, The Premier See: A History of the Archdiocese of Baltimore, 1789–1989 (Baltimore: Johns Hopkins University Press, 1989), 175–76; The South, April 30, 1861.

[51] Charles Howard to George P. Kane, March 14, 1861, Letters Sent by the Baltimore Board of Police; Baltimore Sun, May 8, 1861; Louis Clifton to George P. Kane, April 18, 1861, box 1, Provost Marshal, Letters Received; Creamer, Notes and Memorandum, 1–2, 21; Ferrandini and Lincoln Plot of February 1861, Vertical File, Maryland Room, Enoch Pratt Free Library, Baltimore; Baltimore Clipper, May 4, 1857; Bond Reminiscences. For Denmead's employees see 53rd Regiment, Descriptive Book; Maryland Guard Register, 1861; Washington Hands, Civil War Notebook; C. E. Brooke to George William Brown, August 28, 1861, box 30, Mayor's Correspondence. Thomas Winans, Soup House Account Book, June 1861 to May 1862, Winans Papers, MdHSSC; David Keene to George William Brown, April 22, 1861, Civil War Papers, RG 56, ser 1., box 1, BCA.

[52] Republican, April 20, 1861 (Wallis quoted); The South, April 28, 1861; Baltimore Sun, May 2; Baltimore American, May 6, 1861; James Morrison Harris, State of the Union (n.p., n.d. [1861]), Rare Book Room, Wilson Library, University of North Carolina, Chapel Hill; Brantz Mayer, "True Americanism, Considered in the Lives of Calhoun, Webster, and Clay," February 21, 1860, in box 2, Mayer-Roszel Papers, MdHSSC.

[53] F. W. Brune to Emily Brune, November 27, 1860, May 27, 1861, box 14, Brune-Randall Papers, MdHSSC.

[54] Michael F. Holt, *The Political Crisis of the 1850s* (New York: John Wiley, 1978), 211, 238, 244; Paul D. Escott, *After Secession: Jefferson Davis and the Failure of Confederate Nationalism* (Baton Rouge: Louisiana State University Press, 1978), 40; Lacy K. Ford Jr., *The Origins of Southern Radicalism* (New York: Oxford University Press, 1988), 338–40; Anthony Gene Carey, *Parties, Slavery, and the Union in Antebellum Georgia* (Athens: University of Georgia Press, 1997) 166, 240.

[55] William Starr Myers, ed. "The Civil War Diary of General Isaac Ridgway Trimble," *Maryland Historical Magazine*, 17 (1922): 1–19, 16; Southern Rights to Thomas Hicks, April 23, 1861, Hicks Papers, MdHSSC; Anna Ella Carroll, *Reply to the Speech of the Hon. J. C. Breckinridge* (Washington, 1861), 4.

RICHARD PAUL FUKE

Race and Public Policy in Post-Emancipation Baltimore

AFTER EMANCIPATION on November 1, 1864, black and white Baltimoreans faced each other across a racial divide no longer defined by slavery. On several occasions this confrontation riveted the attention of the entire city and threw its citizens into a heated discussion of urban race relations. In 1865, white shipyard workers struck against black caulkers. In 1866, a race riot disrupted a Methodist camp meeting. In 1867, a white police officer shot and killed a black woman, and parading black militiamen fatally shot a white bystander. Significant in their own right, these events served as flash points in an ongoing debate over the place of African Americans in Baltimore's post-emancipation society.

The September 1865 shipyard strike pitted several hundred black caulkers against the combined forces of the city's white labor associations. Determined to push black labor out of the East Baltimore shipyards, white caulkers, carpenters, joiners, and painters walked off the job on September 26, threatening not to return until black caulkers were fired. John J. Abrahams and Son, the principal shipyard affected, after being initially sympathetic toward its black workers, eventually succumbed to sustained white pressure. On October 25, a month after the strike began, Abrahams and other East Baltimore shipyards agreed to expel all of their black caulkers by the spring of 1866. Henceforth they were to be hired only if there were no whites available. Throughout the month-long confrontation, the feelings of

Richard Paul Fuke is Associate Professor of History at Wilfrid Laurier University in Waterloo, Ontario, Canada. He is the author of *Imperfect Equality: African Americans and the Confines of White Racial Attitudes in Post-Emancipation Maryland* (New York: Fordham University Press, 1999).

both blacks and whites remained highly charged, the former insisting on their right to work for whomever chose to hire them, and the latter remaining determined to establish the supremacy of white labor over black.[1]

The August 1866 Methodist camp meeting south of Baltimore at Hanover Switch in Anne Arundel County disintegrated into a pitched midnight battle between local whites and black worshippers. Although the latter were generally confined to an area separate from whites and in charge of many of their own services, the occurrence of any joint worship aroused the ire of neighboring whites to the point that some felt compelled to invade the campsite. A several-hour melee ensued during which both blacks and whites fired pistols at each other, incurring injuries in the process. As with the caulkers' strike a year earlier, the Hanover Switch riot attracted city-wide attention and drove a wedge between the black and white communities. Clearly black Methodists sought to enlarge their freedom to associate with whites. Equally clearly, other whites tried to stop them from doing so.[2]

In September 1867, during a neighborhood scuffle, Gottleib Frey, a city police officer, shot and killed Eliza Murray, a black resident living in South Baltimore. Evidence conflicted and opinions divided sharply. The police and white witnesses accepted Frey's claim that his pistol discharged accidentally. Black witnesses insisted that Frey had shot his victim deliberately. In the end, the Baltimore Criminal Court grand jury sided with Frey. In response, in a mass meeting at the Douglass Institute, Baltimore's black leaders condemned the "murder" of Eliza Murray, and asked "whether the colored people can have . . . protection." The whole affair, they said, was "a specimen of the justice meted out to colored people in this city."[3]

Barely a month later, the killing of a white man, Charles Ellermeyer, by a member or members of a black "militia" unit, raised a heated public debate over the question of whether or not black veterans and their postwar military regiments ought to parade on city streets with loaded muskets. Uniforms and guns represented highly visible symbols of racial equality, the possession of which placed the black man on the same footing as the white. Of the various regimental activities, none were more popular than full dress parades through the central core of the city. Nothing, however, could be better calculated to anger whites. In 1866, black regiments clashed in open fist fights with white spectators on three occasions, during one of which shots were fired from both sides. In 1867, regiments encountered thrown

Maryland camp meeting. (Maryland Historical Society.)

bricks and pistol shots on several occasions. In October 1867, the escalation of such violence reached its peak when the rear guard of a regiment known as the Butler Guards wheeled and fired into the crowd killing a bystander. Ensuing public pressure secured a ban on all such black militia parades, and city police confiscated as many regimental firearms as they could find.[4]

The lasting impact of these events, however, lay deeper than circumstantial detail. Alone, and in combination with the others, they helped determine the post-emancipation attitudes of white Baltimoreans toward black people in their midst and the public policies designed to express them. Between 1864 and 1867, the city experienced tremendous change. Emancipation in 1864, the shift from a war-time to peace-time economy, and the sudden migration of several thousand rural freed people into their city forced white Baltimoreans to confront the presence of African Americans in new and different ways. Out of this process emerged patterns of thought and action that would shape the city's race relations for years to come.

Between 1860 and 1870 the United States Census reported a 42 percent growth in the city's black population, from 27,898 to 39,558.[5] Of Baltimore's 54,936 new arrivals during the decade, 11,660 or 21 percent were black. During the same period, the census reported a decline in the

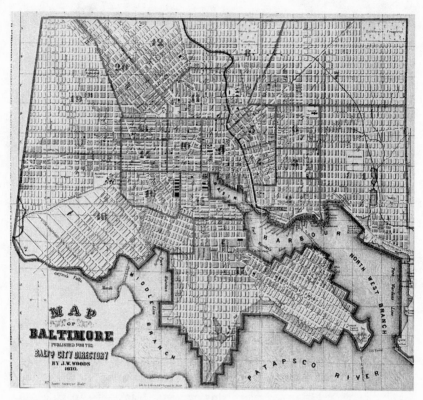

Map of Baltimore showing the election districts in 1870. (Maryland Historical Society.)

black population of all but one of the six rural counties in southern Maryland and in four of eight on the Eastern Shore.[6] A week after Governor Bradford's emancipation proclamation, the Quaker Friends Association in Aid of Freedmen observed that "the faces of the newly-freed population are naturally turned toward the City of Baltimore."[7] In January 1866 the city Trustees of the Poor reported that "a large mass of colored persons . . . have been thrown from the several counties of the State upon the City of Baltimore."[8] Five months later, the *Baltimore Gazette* referred to "the great influx of negroes in the city since the emancipation."[9]

The arrival of so many rural black people in such a short period of time severely challenged and almost overwhelmed Baltimore's capacity to absorb them. Within a month of emancipation, the Friends' Association reported "many calls from women with children . . . who have neither food nor shelter."[10] "We find more suffering than we are able to alleviate," it added in January 1865. "They [are in] want of the most necessary food and clothing, and have crowded into alleys and cellars."[11] These conditions attracted the attention of many others but not always with the Friends' sympathy. "The great influx of negroes in the city since the emancipation has become a nuisance," complained the *Baltimore Gazette* in June 1866. "So great has become the evil that the Marshal of Police has been constrained to cry out against it. . . . They come to the city without the means of support and . . . depend on what they can pick up to satisfy the demands of hunger, and seek shelter at night in the police stations."[12] The *Baltimore Sun* was equally alarmed. "Many freedmen . . . are now loafing about the wharfs acquiring vicious habits, or obtaining the means of a precarious existence only by the few jobs they procure."[13]

Under the circumstances, Baltimore proved ill-equipped to handle so many people. Without enough immediately available jobs or homes to offer black migrants, and in the absence of municipal services designed to find them, city officials, particularly the Trustees of the Poor, were hard-pressed to respond. In the face of limited municipal resources, and the absence of any help from the state, blacks turned to the United States government. Immediately after emancipation, General Lew Wallace, commander of the Eighth Army Corps, set up a "Freedman's Bureau," to help destitute blacks, but despite his plans to commandeer a Baltimore building known as the "Maryland Club" and to assess contributions from known "rebel sympathizers," little came of it. The army's successor, the Freedmen's Bureau, did not do much better. In 1866, the Bureau established a district headquarters in Baltimore, but relief for indigent migrants was not high among its priorities.[14] Even black migrants' most outspoken supporters had their doubts about too much philanthropy. "We say to our colored people in all kindliness as well as in earnestness," admonished the *Baltimore American*, "[that] they should depend mainly upon their own exertions, and not upon extraneous aid."[15]

In the end, blacks' needs either went unmet, as migrants spent their nights on the street or in police station houses, or they were provided for by the black community itself. Ultimately, the latter had to assume primary responsibility for its indigent population. To the extent that Baltimore eventually absorbed so many black migrants without even greater disruption or dislocation, it depended on the generosity—especially for relief and hous-ing—of its twenty-five thousand free black residents. Ultimately, the vast majority of migrants to Baltimore eventually found their way into its black economy and community. The steady climb in the city's total population, its growing number of black residents, and the increased number of black house-holders in the city directories between 1864 and 1871 testified to the long-run success of most in finding homes and work. By 1868, the *Woods' City Directory* counted eight thousand employed black heads of households, a 100 percent increase from four years earlier.[16] More specifically, the number of day laborers grew from 883 in 1864 to 2,644 in 1870, laundresses from 616 to 2,206, waiters from 350 to 798, porters from 294 to 474, draymen from 288 to 423, and cooks from 176 to 565.[17]

Clearly, like most of the twenty-five thousand free blacks before them, rural migrants found jobs in Baltimore by swelling the ranks of the city's unskilled labor force. That they managed to do so may have reflected in part a healthy postwar economy, but the nature of their inclusion also indicated change and cost to the black community which absorbed them. Specifically, migration contributed to substantially increased numbers of women working as domestic servants and laundresses and men as day laborers, while at the same time, the percentage of semi-skilled, skilled, and professional blacks declined.[18] With respect to housing, a similar situation prevailed. A large number of female servants found homes with whites, but others had to find theirs within or alongside already existing black neighborhoods next to or mixed together with white. Increasingly, blacks crowded into cellars and alley-way apartments of already occupied buildings, and although the num-ber of actual black dwellings listed by the United States Census increased between 1860 and 1870, the availability of new housing clearly did not keep pace. From time to time the substandard condition of much of that housing attracted the attention of city authorities.[19] During the cholera out-break of October 1866, for example, city health officials reported that sev-eral dwellings on Elbow Lane were "in a state of indescribable filth, there being as many as eighty persons in one and no adequate means of ventila-tion or cleanliness."[20]

Black Baltimoreans' efforts to cope with such circumstances attracted widespread attention from white observers who heralded blacks' success in addressing black homelessness and joblessness. "There are over thirty thou-

Photograph of Baltimore Harbor taken from Federal Hill in 1872. (Maryland Historical Society.)

sand colored people in Baltimore," explained the *Baltimore American*,

> We doubt whether, among the same number of our citizens simi-
> larly situated . . . and dependent upon employment as common
> laborers for subsistence, there will be found more activity and suc-
> cessful industry and less absolute pauperism, mendacity and want.
> . . . We do not believe that the statistics show a material over propor-
> tion of crime or disease, and death among them. Certainly their
> efforts to improve themselves . . . deserves the highest commenda-
> tion, and must surprise everyone acquainted with the facts.[21]

In fact, the *American* exaggerated the capacity of the black community
to solve the problems caused by the influx of rural migrants into the city.
Throughout the several-year period following emancipation, unemployment—or at best underemployment—remained chronic for many blacks,
housing was still inadequate, crowded, and hard to find, the police station

houses full of temporary lodgers, and the almshouse too frequently a destination of last resort.[22] Clearly, black Baltimoreans did the best they could under difficult circumstances. Equally clearly, they did so without a lot of help from the white community. In the absence of greater support from the city, state, or federal governments, the long-term absorption of so many people imposed additional social costs not only on the black community but on the entire city.

These were reflected especially in patterns of crime and arrests and in the reaction to both, especially by city newspapers and the Baltimore police force. Beginning immediately after emancipation, black Baltimoreans fell afoul of the law in unprecedented numbers, a fact that exacerbated tensions both within the black community and between it and neighboring whites. Between 1864 and 1870, a growing number of blacks were charged with petty theft, assault, and disorderly conduct.[23] The picture that emerged from the records of justice of the peace, the Baltimore Criminal Court and the city jail was clearly that of a class of people chronically at odds with the police and the justice system. Such was particularly the case with female servants charged by their employers with theft, intoxicated men and women accused of disorderly conduct or assault, and juveniles, particularly boys— whose presence on the city's streets expanded dramatically during these years—arrested for a litany of petty offences.[24]

The Democratic and conservative *Baltimore Gazette* was quick to attribute the relationship between crime and the black migrant to the latter's inherent shortcomings. "His habits are generally shiftless and desultory," the *Gazette* explained in November 1865, and nothing short of subjecting him to a certain measure of control, through the influence of just laws . . . can prevent him from becoming a burthen and an annoyance to the community in which he resides in consequence of his idle ways and of those habits of petty larceny to which so many of the race seem naturally addicted."[25] The radical *Baltimore American* shared the *Gazette's* and *Sun's* concern about black people's characteristics but believed they were habits imposed by slavery. "Complaints of theft and worthlessness are frequently urged against our free colored population," it argued in November 1864. "This is the inevitable consequence of social degradation and this degradation in an offspring or reflex of Slavery."[26]

Indeed, most radicals shared conservative fears of black behavioral ten-

"The Arrival of Freedmen and Their Families at Baltimore, Maryland—An Everyday Scene." (From *Frank Leslie's Illustrated Newspaper*, September 30, 1865.)

dencies but argued that education, opportunity, and just treatment under the law would reform recently freed slaves into productive citizens. "If . . . the colored people are left in hopeless ignorance and without education," argued Hugh Lennox Bond, radical judge of the Baltimore Criminal Court, "[they will] grow more vicious till their presence is intolerable and requires ten times the pecuniary expense in police regulations that their education would require."[27] It was, explained John Ware of the Baltimore Association for the Moral and Educational Improvement of the Colored People:

> incumbent upon us to educate them beyond the temptations of vagabondism, vice, and criminality to which they are liable, and by which they are beset so long, as they are in a condition of mental inferiority and moral darkness. . . . The slave a dangerous element as a slave before is a more dangerous element as a free man now. . . . He is without the wonted restraint. He is ignorant, he may become vagabond, and then vicious, and then—why, danger—new

laws, new jails, new police, the cumbersome, costly, superficial, tardy, uncertain cure. . . . Neglect this *now*, this golden opportunity, . . . and the curse will come. The horde of ignorant, unrestrained men, women, and children will be upon you.—Your city will be the charnel house of vagabondism and vice and crime. . . . Already they come. . . . They must be met by prisons and punishments, or by *education*.[28]

The degree and intensity of public attention to migration, poverty, and crime and whites' explanation of the relationship of each to the other made it difficult for blacks to defend themselves. Nor was it made any easier when the city's main law enforcement agency—the police—operated on the basis of such assumptions. From the start, the police were quick to call attention to the presence of rural migrants, to seek their removal to the counties from whence they came, and—when that failed—to keep a close eye on their behavior.[29] Such vigilance led to constant police scrutiny of the black community and the instant deployment of armed squads whenever blacks participated in public occasions either on their own or with whites. In short, the actions of the police served as a constant reminder of white Baltimoreans' perception of not only blacks' place in the community, but also of the connection between them and civil disorder. "The negro population of Baltimore have lately become . . . 'irrepressible,'" complained the *Baltimore Gazette* in November 1865, "and collisions between them and the whites are quite frequent,"[30] Two months earlier, the *Gazette* had gone so far as to celebrate the police roundup of "twenty-seven darkies, who were standing on the pavement in front of the Orchard St. African Church, and . . . [who] were lodged in the Station house. Justice Dryden imposed a fine of one dollar and costs upon each of them for obstructing the footway." Blocking the streets outside their churches was, the *Gazette* explained, "a habit indulged in by negroes," something which "the police intend to abate."[31]

The conservative *Gazette* was quick to notice such things and provided a virtual running commentary on blacks and their run-ins with the police.[32] Although its tabloid approach to black-police relations, and its approval of prompt police action articulated only a portion of the white community's response, its obvious concern resonated with many, including those with quite opposite opinions. Blacks and white radicals were equally disturbed at the occurrence of such confrontations but blamed the police for much of the tension behind them. In the aftermath of the fatal police shooting of Eliza Taylor in September 1867, the *Baltimore American* responded critically. "A colored woman was killed," it said, "under circumstances which show the spirit of hate and oppression cherished toward that portion of the population by many of the police."[33] Upon the acquittal of the police officer on charges of murder, a meeting of black leaders in Baltimore said much the same thing. As reported by the *American:*

> The President [George A. Hackett] stated the object of the meeting, quoting the Declaration of Independence in proof of the fact that "all men were created free and equal." He referred to the fact that the colored people have no friends in Baltimore in the Governor or the police, and cited the action of the Grand Jury in discharging the Policeman Frey, charged with the murder of the colored woman, Eliza Taylor.[34]

Such tensions provided the essential backdrop for interracial violence. Competition for jobs often led directly to physical confrontation, but more importantly, the broad demographic and economic changes which shaped post-emancipation Baltimore, and the attitudes they engendered among whites, created a gulf of misunderstanding and hence tension between blacks and whites. Insofar as most of the latter attributed blacks' economic plight to inherent racial characteristics, it was perhaps inevitable that white Baltimoreans should respond awkwardly and inappropriately to such tension. Too often they saw it in terms of blacks' "demoralized" state and attributed poverty and crime to the character flaws of an idle and degenerated people. As such, the actions of urban blacks threatened the peace and good order of the community and called for appropriate legislation and vigilant police protection.

Not surprisingly, conservative Democrats who had opposed emancipation in the first place resisted change of any sort, blamed blacks themselves for most racial conflict, and saw the latter as the consequence of misguided efforts to force the issue of civil rights. But reactionaries did not monopolize the debate. A vocal radical or Republican minority fought to enlarge the political, social and economic opportunities offered blacks in their city and did so with an outspoken energy that belied their numbers. For all that Democrats came to dominate the political scene, the discussion of post-emancipation race relations was challenged by their Republican opponents. They constituted a dynamic element of the debate and as such helped shape the contours of white racial attitudes and policy. But radicals also suffered their limitations. While supporting black Baltimoreans' aspirations for full civil and political rights and equal economic opportunities, they failed to supply the mechanisms required to guarantee them. Such failure, in the end, proved crucial. Republican attitudes helped fashion a liberal mind-set that contributed to vigorous debate but which ultimately failed to surmount barriers of its own making.

That Democrats might refuse to respond to the challenges offered by African Americans in post-emancipation Baltimore was hardly surprising. Conservatives maintained that blacks were inherently incapable of function-ing on the same social or economic plane as whites. As a consequence they believed the denial of equal rights of any sort to blacks justified and viewed the effort to force the "intermingling" or "amalgamation" of such unequals with extreme distaste. Theirs was a white man's society; one which must be protected from all debilitating influences if its strength and integrity were to prevail. "The negro and the white man belong to two distinct races," ex-plained the *Baltimore Gazette*. "Providence, for some wise purpose has so determined it."[35] "History furnishes . . . no record of a successful intermin-gling," added the *Baltimore Sun*, "between the great divisions of mankind."[36] In a letter to the radical *Baltimore American* in September 1865, a conser-vative correspondent argued, "There is a natural antipathy between the white man and the black which neither time nor association can remove."[37] And as the *Gazette* reiterated:

> Between the blacks and the whites in this country the differences— moral, mental, and physical—are far more strongly marked than between those of any two . . . nations. . . . They are of such a character as to forever preclude such a blending of the Caucasian and the negro on this Continent. . . . Nature has her laws and man must bond to their inexorable dictates.[38]

Republican attitudes were more complicated and thus more difficult to assess. On the one hand, radicals professed open support to the prospect of equal rights for blacks in Baltimore. In response to the white shipyard workers' strike in 1865, the *Baltimore American* asserted, "It is monstrous to assume that because these men are black they are not to be permitted to earn a living. . . . They have a right under the law, and a moral right to do their best at any honest calling they can put their hands to, and no man or set of men can gainsay it."[39] In defense of black Methodists at the Hanover Switch riot in 1866, the Reverend James Lanahan, the meeting's white presiding elder, pointed to "those memorable words in the Declaration of Independence, which declared that . . . [everyone was] 'entitled to life, liberty and the pursuit of happiness.'"[40] In defending the right of black militias to parade with muskets in 1867, the *Baltimore American* proclaimed "these men are citizens of the United States. As men they are entitled to bear arms. They are entitled to the protection of the police when they do it, and are not to be called 'damned niggers' and kicked and cuffed along the street and beaten with espantoons on the slightest provocation."[41]

Furthermore, radicals responded angrily to the treatment black Baltimoreans received on a daily basis. "It is our misfortune to live in a community full of the traditions and customs of slavery, which regard the negro as something less than a man," editorialized the *American*. "The majority of our citizens are full of these prejudices, and are not willing to do justice to the blacks."[42] Hugh Lennox Bond warned of the effect of such opinion. "Without the cultivation of a healthy moral sentiment," he argued, "the feeling of caste will not only prevail, but be widespread. There will ultimately become dominant the . . . idea that the negro is not a man."[43] Radicals decried the treatment of blacks on Baltimore's streets and in its places of employment and spoke out frequently against it.

Finally, radicals believed totally in the efficacy of a liberal mid-nineteenth century reform agenda. Access to education, civil rights, the ballot, and freedom from economic restraint, were guarantees, they believed, of black Baltimoreans' eventual success. As Bond explained, "We are determined this class of people shall have the opportunity to get out of the slough. . . . [I]f we would now make them free and equal citizens, we will find it still more necessary to give them facilities for acquiring knowledge."[44] Similarly, radicals believed, the right to vote would ensure the acquisition of civil and political rights, and free access to employment would guarantee economic opportunity based solely on merit. As one Radical observer said in response to the shipyard strike, "Every man has a right to work where he can and for whom he can with the full protection of the laws."[45]

Once all of this was said, such assurance barely concealed fatal shortcomings within Republican racial attitudes. To start with, the latter were based on a surprisingly negative view of the very people they were intended to help. Indeed radicals seemed at times to direct their reform agenda more at the need to civilize a savage race than to open the door to equality for its own sake. In defending blacks' right to worship freely at the 1866 Hanover Switch camp meeting, the *Baltimore American* warned of the consequences of doing otherwise. "We all know what the negroes are at present time—they are ignorant, idle, and vicious. . . . [I]t behooves every man to labor with all his might to elevate and ameliorate the condition of this race. . . . As they are now, they are little better than so many savages."[46] Radical educator John Fathergill Waterhouse Ware struck the same tone in support of black education. "It is incumbent upon us," he said, "to educate them beyond the temptations of vagabondism, vice, and criminality to which they are liable."[47]

Second, despite their commitment to helping blacks, radicals refused to push such support beyond a philosophical minimum. "We do not encourage any benevolence toward them," explained Bond, "which does not tend to make the colored man feel his duty and capacity to support himself. Whatever can educate his mind and equip his body for self-care is in the right direction. Everything else tends to lager houses, idleness, vice."[48] On another occasion Bond added, "If he can get a living, let him get it; if he cannot, let him go without, only throw no obstacles in his way."[49] To Bond and his fellow Radicals, it was a case of "root hog, or die," a somewhat less optimistic version of twentieth-century "rugged individualism." Either way, it stopped well short of what some prominent radicals—Charles Sumner of Massachusetts and Thaddeus Stevens of Pennsylvania, to name two—were beginning to advocate on the subjects of universal suffrage and federal land distribution.

Clearly radical opinion shared many of the well-established limitations of mid-nineteenth-century liberal thought. There were points beyond which such men as Hugh Lennox Bond would not go in their honest efforts to assist blacks, and there were economic principles whose sacrosanct nature transcended all other considerations. All this being said, it is remarkable that white radicals could stick to such a narrow agenda in the face of everything going on around them. The rapidity of post-emancipation change in Baltimore was stunning. Within months of emancipation, several thousand rural blacks flooded the city. Their presence and needs were objects of constant newspaper attention. Eventually, the city's economy would absorb these people and more, but in the early going, levels of unemployment and poverty were high. Crime statistics escalated, especially among women and children, a disproportionate number of whom were black. As much as Bond, Ware, the Baltimore Association, and others might continue to talk about the efficacy of education, the ballot, and contracts freely entered into, it was clear for anyone who cared to see that such nostrums no longer worked.

Interestingly, however, outside the confines of ideological debate there were some who were beginning to see. In 1867, in a poignant reflection on the problems faced by many blacks in Baltimore, the Grand Jury of the Criminal Court commented on the occupants of the city jail. "We have found confined," it said:

> quite a number of young negroes of both sexes between the ages of ten and fifteen years. Most of them are committed by magistrates upon trivial charges, and after an imprisonment of ten to thirty days are discharged. . . . [O]f this class many are discharged, not from the want of legal evidence of guilt, but from a belief in the minds of the jurors that from their youth and ignorance of right from wrong, they are not morally accountable to the law for their actions. But imprisonment in idleness, and contact with older prisoners hardens them in guilt and gives new lessons in the school for crime.[50]

It was a compelling observation, one echoed and enlarged by the official visitors to the Maryland State Penitentiary. "Here, then, lies the precise cause of the present difficulty," they offered, "the vast number of idle, unemployed blacks who have been thrown upon the public by the events of the past two or three years." In the light of such circumstances, the visitors called attention to the absence of appropriate municipal facilities. And although, typically, they laid the blame for such absence beyond Baltimore's borders, their assessment managed at least partially to surmount the barriers of ideological debate:

> We have been compelled time after time to forego presenting especially juvenile colored thieves for punishment because neither state authority nor private beneficence has yet provided any house of correction for this class. . . . they are multiplying rapidly and becoming criminals of a larger growth. We have to look helplessly on while the negro boys attain their growth in vice and stature finally to be sent to the state Penitentiary to herd there with hundreds in a single room unemployed and with every opportunity to become worse and merely because no adequate provision has been made to punish or correct them at an earlier age.[51]

Restricted by their traditional focus, the best Baltimore's white conservatives could offer was a behavioral analysis of such crime based on blacks' alleged inferiority. Radicals held out hope but still relied essentially on an oft-repeated recitation of the preventive efficacy of schools, ballots, and contracts. And when conservatives blamed crime upon black people's natural indolence and savagery, radicals proved ill-prepared to respond. Their own agenda for greater black access to civil, political, and educational rights was predicated on a similar assessment of black people and their characteristics. Indeed, radicals' inability to respond to the specifics of urban crime with anything other than ideological orthodoxy, seemed to characterize their response to a number of alarming problems staring them directly in the face.

That people's action is historically shaped by the nature of their attitudinal boundaries goes almost without saying. In a very real sense white conservatives and radicals failed to confront urban problems squarely because the solutions were beyond their ken. In the report of the visitors to the city jail, it is possible however, to identify the beginnings of a more sophisticated or "modern" critique of racial confrontation that transcended the limitations of a familiar mid-nineteenth century ideological debate. As Baltimore confronted the presence of powerful post-emancipation forces affecting its society and economy, some began to recognize that its institutions and those of the state and federal government operating in its midst would eventually be forced to play a much more vigorous role in meeting the needs of the

House of Reformation and Instruction for Colored Children, 1870. (Maryland Historical Society.)

community. As much as conservatives and radicals might still argue over the definition of such needs and the extent to which anyone should respond to them, the necessity for some sort of action grew out of the very mechanics of urban government. The *nature* of this response relied less on attitudes and more on the simple need for action.

Indeed, the forces of change were already at work. While the debate over the city's social responsibility remained locked in traditional arguments between 1864 and 1870, isolated events conspired to encourage a more pragmatic—indeed bureaucratic—approach to urban problems, one shaped by practical necessities which surmounted the ideological restrictions of the Civil War generation. The cholera epidemic of 1866 forced Baltimore to respond with a public health program directed at all citizens, regardless of their race. The obvious success of the Quaker-inspired Baltimore Association for the Moral and Educational Improvement of the Colored People in establishing schools for black children encouraged some public financial support from the start and finally, in 1870, the takeover of these schools by the city board of education. That same year, the state of Maryland built its first reformatory for black youth in the city.[52]

Be that as it may, the city's response had clearly been tentative, timid, and slow. By 1870, much had happened to force Baltimore's African American population into new and rigid social and economic compartments. Whether it was in the area of occupations, housing, relief, education, or relations with the police or media, whites reacted initially with fear and alarm to the sudden presence of freed men, women, and children in their midst. In the process they responded defensively and relied heavily on established attitudes which no longer reflected the needs of the community. In other words, they failed to meet the challenge presented by this substantial addition to the city's population and work force amidst what was by all contemporary accounts a period of economic growth. Furthermore, in a pattern already well-established and destined to be repeated, white Baltimoreans left black Baltimoreans alone, essentially to fend for themselves.

Notes

[1] *Baltimore Gazette,* September 27, 28, 1865; *Baltimore Sun,* September 27, October 2, 25, 1865; *Baltimore American,* September 27, 28, October 27, 28, November 6, 8, 1865; *New York Tribune,* September 1, 1870. See also Richard Paul Fuke, *Imperfect Equality: African Americans and the Confines of White Racial Attitudes in Post-Emancipation Maryland* (New York: Fordham University Press, 1999), 131–35; Bettye C. Thomas, "A Nineteenth Century Black Operated Shipyard, 1866–1884: Reflections upon Its Inception and Ownership," *Journal of Negro History,* 59 (January 1974): 1–12.

[2] *Baltimore Sun,* September 1, 3, 5, 8, 15, 18, 23, 25, October 20, 1866; *Baltimore American,* September 1, 3, 5, 6, 8, 11, 12, 17, 18, 19, 21, 24, October 19, 20, December 24, 1866; *Baltimore Gazette,* September 3, 14, 18, 26, 1866; *Annapolis Gazette,* September 6, 20, October 25, 1866; Fuke, *Imperfect Equality,* 206.

[3] *Baltimore American,* September 23, October 8, 1867; Fuke, *Imperfect Equality,* 131.

[4] *Baltimore Gazette,* May 10, August 18, 1866, July 3, October 18, 19, 21, 22, 26, November 8, 1867; *Baltimore Sun,* May 10, 1866, July 3, October 18, 19, 21, 22, 26, 29, November 15, 1867; *Baltimore American,* August 18, 1866, July 3, 4, August 5, September 5, October 18, 19, 21, 22, 23, 29, 1867; Fuke, *Imperfect Equality,* 204.

[5] U.S. Bureau of the Census, *Population of the United States in 1870* (Washington, 1872), 163.

[6] U.S. Bureau of the Census, *A Compendium of the Ninth Census, June 1,*

1870 (Washington, 1872), 10–11; U.S. Bureau of the Census, *Population of the United States in 1870*, 163–65.

[7] *Baltimore American*, November 10, 1864.

[8] Report of the Trustees of the Poor, January 1866. Contained in *Ordinances of the Mayor and City Council of Baltimore, Passed at the Session of 1866, To Which is Annexed the Mayor's Communication, Reports of City Officers, and a List of the Members of the City Council, and Officers of the Corporation* (Baltimore, 1866), 329.

[9] *Baltimore Gazette*, June 2, 1866; *Baltimore American*, July 31, 1867.

[10] *Communication from Major Genl. Lew Wallace, In Relation to the Freedman's Bureau, to the General Assembly of Maryland* (Annapolis, 1865) 66, which appears as Document J in Maryland, General Assembly, House of Delegates, *Journal of Proceedings, January Session, 1865* (Annapolis, 1865).

[11] *Ibid.*, 80; *Baltimore American*, February 7, 1865.

[12] *Baltimore Gazette*, June 2, 1866.

[13] *Baltimore Sun*, August 9, 1865.

[14] *The Statutes at Large of the United States of America*, Vol. XIV: December 1865 to March 1867 (Boston, 1868), 174; E. M. Gregory to O. O. Howard, November 3, 1866, Volume 3 (Register of Letters Sent, Assistant Commissioner, April 1, 1866 to August 17, 1868), Records of the Bureau of Refugees, Freedmen, and Abandoned Lands, District of Maryland, Record Group 105, National Archives, Washington, D.C.

[15] *Baltimore American*, November 11, 1864.

[16] *Woods' Baltimore City Directory, Ending Year 1864* (Baltimore, 1865), 443–84; *Woods' Baltimore City Directory, 1867–1868* (Baltimore, 1868), 564–626.

[17] Ibid., 443–84; *Woods' Baltimore City Directory, 1867–1868* 564–626; *Woods's Baltimore City Directory, 1871* (Baltimore, 1871), 667–757.

[18] Ibid.

[19] Ibid.

[20] *Baltimore Sun*, October 15, 1866.

[21] Ibid., November 19, 1866.

[22] Reports of the Trustees of the Poor, January 1, 1865-1872, and Reports of the Police Commissioner, January 1, 1865–1872, as found in *The Ordinances of the City Council of Baltimore* (Baltimore, 1865–1872).

[23] Reports of the Visitors to the Baltimore City Jail, January 1, 1865–1871, as found in *The Ordinances of the Mayor and City Council of Baltimore [1865–1871]* (Baltimore, 1865–72).

[24] Ibid.

[25] *Baltimore Gazette*, November 3, 1865.

[26] *Baltimore American*, November 14, 1864.

[27] *Easton Gazette*, January 7, 1865.

[28] *Baltimore American*, March 15, 1865.

[29] *Journal of Proceedings of the First Branch City Council of Baltimore At the Session of 1866* (Baltimore, 1866), 646; *Baltimore Gazette*, June 2, 1866.

[30] *Baltimore Gazette*, November 2, 1865.

[31] Ibid., September 22, 1865.

[32] See for example, ibid., December 29, 1864, May 15, 27, June 13, July 20, August 5, November 1, 2, 3, 27, 1865.

[33] *Baltimore American*, September 23, 1867.

[34] Ibid., October 8, 1867.

[35] *Baltimore Gazette*, July 39, 1865.

[36] *Baltimore Sun*, July 27, 1865.

[37] *Baltimore American*, September 5, 1865.

[38] *Baltimore Gazette*, April 18, 1866 .

[39] *Baltimore American*, October 3, 1865.

[40] Ibid., September 18, 1866.

[41] Ibid., October 19, 1867.

[42] Ibid., November 18, 1867.

[43] Ibid., March 31, 1866.

[44] Hugh Lennox Bond to Kate Bond, January 1, 1865, Bond-McCulloch Family Papers, MS 1159, Maryland Historical Society, Baltimore, Md.; *Baltimore Gazette*, May 11, 1865.

[45] *Baltimore American*. October 3, 1865.

[46] Ibid., September 17, 1866.

[47] Ibid., March 15, 1865.

[48] *American Missionary*, 2nd Ser., 9 (April 1, 1865), 80.

[49] *Baltimore American*, November 24, 1866.

[50] *Memorial of the Grand Jury of Baltimore City Praying that a Place of Punishment May be Provided for Minor Colored Children* (Annapolis, 1867), which appears as Document X in *Journal of Proceedings of the House of Delegates, January Session, 1867* (Annapolis, 1867); *Baltimore Sun*, February 18, 1867; *Baltimore American*; February 16, 1867.

[51] Ibid.

[52] Richard Paul Fuke, "The Baltimore Association for the Moral and Educational Improvement of the Colored People," *Maryland Historical Magazine*, 66 (Winter 1971): 369–404; Fuke, *Imperfect Equality*, 127–29, 197.

JESSICA I. ELFENBEIN

"A Place of Resort and Help for Their Young Men": Baltimore's Black YMCA, 1885–1925

THE YOUNG MEN'S CHRISTIAN ASSOCIATION (YMCA) has long been a mainstay in West Baltimore, the city's oldest and perhaps most significant African American neighborhood. Known simply as the "Colored YMCA" in its pre-1900, pre–Druid Hill Avenue days, the story of the Druid Hill Avenue YMCA's establishment and growth (when it has been told at all), has, ironically, been white-washed.[1] It has been told in the tradition of celebratory history: *viz.* A group of upstanding black men came together to do good in and for their community. Despite great odds and limited resources, they succeeded. Their legacy continues today.[2] Although this version of the Druid Hill Avenue YMCA's history is not untrue, it raises questions far more provocative than those it answers. Why, for example, would men persevere in their efforts to be accepted by a club that didn't want them? Where did the white YMCA stand on matters of race? How close was the white YMCA's rhetoric to reality? Once created, what was the relationship between the black YMCA and the community? What role did the black press play in this institution's expansion? How important were issues of class?

To better understand this story, it is helpful to review briefly both the history of the Baltimore YMCA and the national YMCA's handling of the race issue. In November 1852, the white Maryland Baptist Union issued the call

Jessica I. Elfenbein is Associate Professor of History and Director of the Center for Regional and Baltimore Studies at the University of Baltimore. She is the author of *Civics, Commerce and Community: The History of the Washington, D.C. Board of Trade, 1889–1989* and *The Making of a Modern City: Philanthropy, Civic Culture and the Baltimore YMCA*.

that led to the establishment of a YMCA in Baltimore, among the first in the United States. From the beginning the white YMCA used pantheistic and catholic rhetoric to describe its simple goal of leading men to Jesus by offering an attractive alternative to the myriad temptations industrial cities posed to young men "adrift."[3] From its inception, Baltimore's YMCA was exclusively white. Yet, by the mid-nineteenth century, the city's African American community was sizable, long established, and predominantly free.[4]

The exclusion of African Americans from the YMCA was not unique to Baltimore. Before the Civil War most YMCAs simply evaded the issue of race. In Baltimore, as in most associations nationally, partisan political talk was forbidden. During Reconstruction, the YMCA nationally began to encourage a jim crow policy by allowing African Americans to organize their own branches and "join the Christian brotherhood on 'separate-but-equal' terms." The black elite welcomed the YMCA's tripartite mission to develop the body, mind, and spirit, and embraced the association's character building programs, viewing them as a means for racial advancement.[5]

In 1876, the International YMCA (the national policy group to which local YMCAs belonged) appointed its first secretary to promote association work among African Americans in the South. From 1876 to 1891, two white men served successively as the YMCA's International Secretary for "colored work."[6] In 1890, William A. Hunton, a Canadian, was appointed to the position, becoming the highest-ranking black YMCA official in the United States. Hunton assisted African Americans as they established YMCAs in cities. Under his leadership Baltimore's Colored YMCA became a reality. The branch prospered under Jesse E. Moorland, who in 1898 was hired as Hunton's assistant. Hunton then turned his attention to college work, and Moorland took charge of helping urban YMCAs with fundraising and membership drives. Upon Hunton's death in 1916, Moorland became the senior African American International Secretary.[7]

The roots and antecedents of Baltimore's black YMCA go back to 1869 when Bishop Alexander Wayman of the Bethel A.M.E. Church invited fellow clergy to join him in the formation of a Pastors' Union to "discuss all problems affecting Negroes, including drunkenness and idleness and the possibility of establishing a Colored YMCA," an idea which did not then materialize.[8] In 1885 a precursor to Baltimore's colored YMCA began at the Old Union Baptist church, located at Guilford Avenue near Lexington Street. The

Bishop Alexander Wayman of the Bethel A.M.E. Church, in 1869. (Courtesy, University of Baltimore Educational Foundation.)

group's work was limited to discussions of religious issues. Members held meetings at their homes. In 1888 this group began calling itself "the Colored YMCA."[9] Those active in the early work of the Colored YMCA included: W. T. Greenwood (the first president); F. C. Lewis; Milton N. White; M. B. Mayfield; J. H. Murphy Sr.; R. Mattell; M. Williams; T. H. Smith; R. Hall; and T. Alexander Date.

The next year, the white Central YMCA (whose records mentioned race for the first time in 1883 when its leaders denied rental of their hall to "colored people") appointed a committee which, after considering "the question of a Branch of our association for Colored Men," recommended an indefinite postponement.[10] More fruitful efforts began in March 1891, when representatives of two black groups visited Secretary William Morriss, the Baltimore YMCA's General Secretary from 1882 to 1923, hoping to enlist his support for the creation of a black YMCA branch. The time was ripe. Not only was Hunton newly appointed as Secretary for Colored Work, but the deterioration of race relations and the tightening of the color line nationally affected the YMCA, which, at its national convention in 1891, "officially acknowledged the long-established de facto segregation of African Americans." That year, too, delegates to the national convention recognized "Colored Associations" as legitimate facets of the national YMCA work.[11] Both local African American groups and the YMCA's International Committee lobbied the Baltimore association. Acceding to their requests, as well as to those of his own executive committee, Morriss attended a convention of "Colored Associations" at Richmond, Virginia.[12] His attendance notwithstanding, no immediate action resulted.

Despite the lack of substantial support from the local white YMCA leaders, some young men persevered in their efforts to create a black association in Baltimore. In 1892 an interdenominational group of church-going young black men who desired to be "under the direction . . . of the YMCA of Maryland" worked with an advisory committee of seven black clergy to lobby for the YMCA's blessing. They also sought a meeting place "centrally located in the city where young men who are victims of evil association may be gathered and led into Christian society." It was, the clergy reported, difficult to "save our young men from the many agents of vice which are actively at work in this city." Although the churches and Sunday schools were "doing good work," additional help was needed. The black clergy's rhetoric mirrored language white clergy used in the 1850s and again in the 1870s and 1880s to convince their congregants and other concerned citizens of the need for a YMCA for white young men. The language is eerily familiar.[13]

The dearth of organizations serving young black people in Baltimore in the late nineteenth century bears out the clergy's concerns. In 1892 researchers for Baltimore's Charity Organization Society (COS) identified only the House of Reformation and the Industrial Home for Colored Girls as providing services to "colored minors."[14] These organizations were inappropriate for the constituency defined by the young men hoping to organize a YMCA. Hunton, the International Secretary of Colored Work, came to Baltimore in the summer of 1892, remarkably at Central YMCA's invitation, to "look over the field," confer and advise. Hunton asked YMCA president Joshua Levering for support, estimating that it would cost about $1,400 to operate the Colored YMCA for the first year. Of this he thought that $500 could be raised "from the colored people, from all sources, membership fees, baths, entertainment, etc." Hunton wished for "means for physical cleanliness . . . reading room, library and night school, and the other uplifting influences of a 'Christian home away from home.'"[15]

The white YMCA's response was tepid at best. The YMCA board resolved: "We cannot see our way clear . . . to appropriate from our already overtaxed treasury the sum that seems to be necessary to put this Association in good working order." Based on consultations with friends "who are especially interested in the work among colored young men," a special fund was proposed, but here too the Central YMCA hedged, reporting "of this we cannot be at all sure."[16]

Despite the Central YMCA's reticence and their leaders' conclusion that "it was thought best by them and by us not to organize as a branch but as an independent Association, under their own direct management," the black community organized a YMCA in 1892. They rented a twelve-room house at 416 W. Biddle Street, where, Central believed, "they will be able to supply a much needed place of resort and help for their young men."[17] Their work was commended by Hunton under whose supervision the branch placed itself.

The 1890s were a decade of good intentions but limited action for Baltimore's Colored YMCA.[18] By 1896 the house on Biddle Street was sold and the branch was homeless. Central's response was long on high-minded lip service but short on meaningful financial support: "What a splendid thing it would be . . . if at this crisis, a building could be bought and equipped in first class style for the Association," the board minutes observed.[19] Central's leaders limited their financial support to forgiving a $12 debt owed by the Colored Branch, a gesture encouraged by Morriss who believed the black group's financial security to be so tenuous that without loan forgiveness the branch "may disband and a few of its official members assume its present obligations."[20]

The Colored YMCA instead maintained "steady work on a modest scale" at a smaller structure at 436 West Biddle Street.[21] But those efforts were not enough to address the needs of the black community as perceived both by black clergy, who were "anxious for the establishment of a well equipped" Colored YMCA, and by Central's white leaders, who reported that Baltimore's black population of about eighty-five thousand included fifteen thousand young men whose need for a YMCA was "very evident to any thoughtful citizen.[22]

In the quarter-century preceding World War I, young men from rural areas and graduates of historically black colleges made their way in great numbers to urban areas, attracted by the lure of jobs and better housing in the growing cities, and, oftentimes, also propelled by a desire to escape the racism and discrimination of their birthplaces. While the experience of the migrants who moved north between 1890 and 1915 has been largely eclipsed by the attention focused on the Great Migration, the harsh realities of their situation and the need to protect them from the city's evils was a primary goal not only of YMCA supporters in Baltimore but in other major cities, too. For example, in 1899, Reverend Dr. Charles T. Walker, the nationally known pastor of New York City's Mount Olivet Baptist Church, led the creation of a black YMCA to serve as a home of southern migrants in Manhattan. Walker raised money from his own congregants and the black community at large for a year's lease on a building on West 53rd Street, "the Main Street for respectable folk of Negro Tenderloin." Walker then successfully appealed to the white New York YMCA for membership for the branch. When the black population began to move to Harlem early in the twentieth century, a branch was created there. In 1919 the 53rd Street Branch relocated to Harlem where in the 1920s it became "the biggest Y in America."[23]

In Baltimore, despite the apparent, serious limitations of the local work, many applauded the contributions made by African American YMCAs nationally. A Dr. Talmage, whose weekly sermon appeared in the *Afro-American* newspaper, reported in 1898 that the country's YMCAs were doing "a glorious work. They have fine reading rooms, and all the influences are of the best kind, and are now adding gymnasiums and bowling alleys, where, without evil surroundings, our young men may get physical as well as spiritual improvement." This was important because, in Talmage's estimation, the community was "dwindling away to a narrow-chested, weak-armed, feeble-voiced race. When God calls us to work he wants physical as well as spiritual athletes."[24]

Many observers, both black and white, understood the efforts of the

YMCA as an important antidote to larger destructive societal trends. "Everything that the forces of evil can do to ruin these young men is being done, and the recent outbreaks of lawlessness and rowdyism is sufficient evidence of the power of the influences thus exerted," reported the Central YMCA's white leadership in 1899. Central's leaders proclaimed that what was needed to "place the [colored] branch on a firm basis" was "help from the white people."[25] That recognition notwithstanding, little tangible assistance followed.

In a June 1898 editorial, Baltimore's *Afro* criticized the racial policies of the local YMCA as representative of the racism racking institutions nationwide. "Our present Christian civilization and the institutions of the country are pervaded with an 'invisible' word, which is . . . productive of such results as are humiliating as well as exasperating to a large percentage of the people who make up this republic." At that time many predominantly black institutions and organizations were labeled "colored" while those white groups actively supporting jim crow policies did not identify their racial limitations by beginning their name with "white."

> Over the portals of the great majority of Christian churches are words although invisible, [which say] "for white people only." Ostensibly our white fellow citizens have not the courage to resurrect and re-establish the ante-bellum sign, "No Negroes and no dogs allowed in here," but in a striking hypocrisy indicative of supreme cowardice they are content to wound and outrage the feelings of their colored brethren by sailing under false colors. There ought to be some law, and it should be rigidly enforced, whereby every so-called public establishment, whether ecclesiastical or otherwise, whose business is conducted for white people alone, should state plainly this declaration in its charter and be placed in its forefront. To openly declare that an institution is for the public, and then deny a portion of that public its privilege on account of color is not only systematic lying but an outrage.

To prove that African Americans, "the most catholic minded of the people who make up the American public," were also "guilty of innocent, but systematic lying," the writer used the case of Baltimore's YMCA. The Central association, "although it would appear, on its face, as if it were for 'men' regardless of color," was restricted to whites only. The building on Biddle Street, the editorialist continued, "publicly and unwisely proclaims an untruth when it prefixes to its title 'colored'" when in fact it would "take men of all races." Therefore, only the Biddle Street branch could "justly, honestly, and honorably bear the title 'Y.M.C.A.'"[26]

Despite both the rhetoric and philosophy of inclusion, it appears that the Druid Hill YMCA's constituency was nearly all black. Given the exclusionary policies of so many other organizations and the growing need of the African American community in Baltimore, the black community embraced the association's efforts to provide services. On the eve of the twentieth century, the Colored YMCA's programs were expanded and professionalized. By February 1899, W. Edward Williams, a college graduate and the Colored YMCA's first paid secretary, whose hiring was "made possible by the generosity of the Central Association" which attempted (but failed) to raise $600 to cover his annual salary, was "in the field . . . actively engaged in pushing on the work." At the same time, W. H. Murray, a Baltimore public school vice principal, was elected president.[27] Williams and Murray were concerned about the thousands of black young men in Baltimore who were "looking, perhaps unconsciously for . . . help" from the risks the city posed: "the saloon, the club, and other places of evil," which opened attractive doors to them." With the exception of the church, Williams believed there was "no place of moral resort, of physical and mental and spiritual helpfulness to our young men" in the city. The result was they went astray and became "in large number rowdies."[28]

With that reality in mind, Williams helped craft the Colored Branch's mission:

> To band together young men whose lives and action will tell against rowdyism, impurity and vice in any form, and who will endeavor to bring other young men in touch with the YMCA. To make men workers, by securing work for them. To help them to be and keep pure, by giving them pure examples and bring them in touch with pure men. To help them towards intelligence, by supplying them means to profitably spend and improve their spare hours. To lead them to God; by living Godly lives ourselves and thus preach to them of the power and love of God.[29]

Williams succeeded in attracting members and funds. During his first year as secretary, paid membership increased from thirteen to 166 and contributions from the black community reached $500. Many of the new members worked for hotels or private families. They used the facilities most heavily from September through May. During the summer many members were "away in the country and at the seashore with the families of their employers and at the hotels."[30] Under Williams' leadership the branch purchased a building at the southeast corner of Hoffman Street and Druid Hill Avenue for $2,000, giving the branch its lasting moniker—the Druid Hill Avenue YMCA.[31]

Despite his successes, Williams left after two years "to accept the charge of a church in the city," Grace Presbyterian. Unlike William Morriss, he didn't believe the YMCA offered him the opportunity to do "the spiritual work" for which he was "better fitted." He leaned "too much toward the ministry or at least the Evangelistic work to be satisfied with the details of a local Secretary's work."[32] P. A. Goines, an experienced association worker and secretary in the YMCA's Army Department, replaced Williams.[33]

Chronic money problems plagued the black YMCA, whose leaders repeatedly urged all "white and colored friends" to give to save "from careless and sinful lives the thousands of young colored men of Baltimore." In reality self-help from within the black community accomplished much of what was achieved before 1915. In the first years, the largesse of Central included no cash, but "some of our old papers and magazines." In 1894 Central denied a request for financial aid, saying "it was impossible to assist." The following year, a request from Hunton generated $50 for the black association. The annual appropriation from Central to the Colored YMCA was the smallest made to any branch in Baltimore, averaging $100 or less. In 1900 the Druid Hill YMCA published a report highlighting the branch's financial, spiritual, intellectual, and physical accomplishments entitled, "What the Colored [YMCA] Has Done for Itself . . . Without Aid from the White People."[34]

Financial shortcomings were manifest in the building at Druid Hill Avenue and Hoffman Street, which had a small gym, reading room, and office.[35] Chronic underfunding caused chronic physical plant and equipment deficiencies. It took five years to raise funds sufficient to install baths, which was especially damning given the shortage of both indoor plumbing and public baths in Baltimore.[36]

The flawed facilities remained an issue even as the branch moved to another building five blocks north at 1619 Druid Hill Avenue in 1908 or 1909. Located in the Fourteenth Ward, where the black population would increase 67 percent between 1910 and 1920, the new building was just north of the Seventeenth Ward which, with a black population of 16,736 in 1920, would become the "center of the colored population."[37] Both the Fourteenth Ward and the southern part of the Seventeenth had increasingly serious housing and social problems. The small houses on alley streets were becoming overcrowded, with many housing two or three families, adversely affecting the health, social, and civic life beyond just the immediate area. Tuberculosis and venereal disease were especially serious threats, as was the shortage of safe recreational options.[38]

Like the earlier facilities, this one too, quickly proved wanting. Central reported that "In spite of limitations of an inadequate building . . . a fine work has been done for colored young men and boys. It speaks volumes for what might be done if facilities were provided in any way commensurate with those for white young men and boys."[39] Despite its shortcomings, the branch featured many of the same services offered by Central and other white branches, such as education, employment, and boarding house referrals.[40] Just as Central ministered to young men of or aspiring to the middle class, the Druid Hill branch was sometimes criticized for catering to the "'kid glove" class rather than helping those who really need help."[41] To ambitious young men, the branch offered Bible class, a literary society and an Employment Bureau to "secure work for members and other worthy men out of employment." Finding "Christian young men of good character" for positions like "porters, waiters, coachmen, footmen, [and] bell-boys" was the bureau's goal. A Junior Department was also created. Classes in English, first-aid, and physiology began in 1899. Arithmetic, short-hand, and political science were soon added.[42]

Educational offerings advanced careers. For example, George H. Arthur and W. H. Beckett studied religion as well as secular topics at the Druid Hill YMCA. They then earned highly coveted International certificates for their Bible Study examinations in 1903. Arthur, a five-year Druid Hill employee who worked first as janitor and later as typewriter and stenographer, left the YMCA to work for Chicago's police department, "all of his training for the position" having been gotten at the Druid Hill YMCA. Beckett left Baltimore for the YMCA Training School at Springfield, Massachusetts, which Secretary

Morriss had helped found, to study to become a secretary in the International YMCA's Colored Department.[43]

Some of Druid Hill's programs featured personal enrichment and culture. In 1899, Mary Richmond, General Secretary of the Baltimore Charity Organization Society, spoke on the "True Method of Giving Charity." Her speech was described as "the great event of the month." A lecture, "How to Lessen the Criminal Among Our People," attracted more than three hundred attendees in 1905.[44] In 1903 and 1904, Coleridge-Taylor's "Hiawatha" with a fifty-two-piece orchestra was presented. The branch's leaders were "convinced that the uplifting influences upon our own people of such music . . . is well worth the task of its management, especially when 'rag-time' music has even found its way in many of the Sunday Schools, to say nothing of the homes of the people." White members of Central's board of directors bought tickets, and a party of five whites occupied a box at the concert which was held at a black theatre.[45]

The colored work in Baltimore was very tightly linked to other black YMCA initiatives around the country. In December 1899, for example, Baltimore hosted the 11th Annual Conference of Colored YMCAs from Virginia, West Virginia, Maryland and Washington, D.C. Nearly six hundred men attended.[46] Like other black YMCAs nationally, Baltimore was profoundly affected when in December 1910, Julius Rosenwald, the president of Sears Roebuck, offered $25,000 to every community in the country that raised $75,000 toward the erection of a black YMCA over five years. He would give $25,000 after $50,000 raised locally was expended for land and building. In Baltimore, the white community raised $50,000, and the black community agreed to raise $25,000. After $15,000 of the $25,000 was paid, work on the new building would begin.[47]

Jesse E. Mooreland directed the November 1912 campaign to raise the $25,000 contribution from the black community. The new building was planned for a sixty by one hundred-foot lot on Druid Hill Avenue on the same block where the branch was already operating. Moorland was then a fifteen-year YMCA worker whom the *Afro* described as an "earnest Christian intensely interested in the uplift of young men, and full of optimism." He had already led similar fundraising drives in Chicago, Philadelphia, Atlanta, and Washington, D.C., among other cities.[48] In Baltimore, one hundred men volunteered in ten districts to solicit YMCA subscriptions from six thousand prospects over the ten days of the campaign. Their motto was "What others have done, we can do." Each volunteer got "a certificate empowering him with the authority to solicit funds." Anyone soliciting without a valid certificate was to be "handled according to law."[49]

The size and scope of the 1912 fundraising effort was unprecedented. Although the black community had given at "rallies for church purposes," never before, according to the *Afro*, had "large sums, such as fifty, one hundred and two hundred" dollars, been asked. But halfway through the campaign, less than a third of the $25,000 had been pledged. The "ridiculously small" contributions made by several "well to do men" surprised and dismayed the campaign's organizers and the editors of Baltimore's *Afro-American*, who believed that "many of our citizens do not realize what it really means to enter into a campaign of this kind."[50] Moorland urged every man "to give in keeping with his means." Those who earned their livelihood from the patronage of the black community were key. "The race made his success possible and he should be willing to give generously. . . . Those who owe their success to the race owe the race a duty and should discharge the same by being morally and financially in all movements that tend toward race betterment."[51]

The *Afro*'s editorial staff encouraged the community to participate fully while it chided black leaders to give generously. "These men owe it to themselves as well as to the people they serve to return something to those who have made it possible for them to be where they are." Those who were "giving five dollars where they ought to give fifty, and giving ten where they ought to give one hundred" were declared "a disgrace to the race." Some of the donations were "ridiculously small so much so that the individuals giving them ought to be heartily ashamed of themselves for even offering them." In contrast, those earning "a pittance" gave "more than the men who are making thousands." In response, the *Afro*'s writer proposed publishing a list of donors and amounts pledged "so that the people of the city will know in the future just upon whom they can depend."[52]

So big was the campaign that "all of the newspapers, especially the race papers" covered it. At its deadline, the campaign appeared to have succeeded, and the *Afro* reported that even the *Baltimore Sun* praised the black community for securing more than $31,000 in pledges. The *Afro* commented: "The colored people of Baltimore are to be congratulated for the splendid effort they made in raising $31,000 for a new building for the Y[MCA]. . . . $25,000 was the amount called for, but as Bishop Wayman used to say 'Colored folks in Baltimore always overdo the thing.' It was a glorious victory . . . both for the association and for Baltimore." The largest single donor was James W. Hughes, who subscribed $300 and was president of the association in July 1918, when the first public tours were given. Hughes proclaimed, "I am glad I gave my money. This building is needed and will be a God send to our People."[53]

The 1912 kudos proved premature. By 1915 only a third of the $31,000 pledged was in hand.[54] The balance proved elusive, causing both the building's delay and the need for additional fundraising. The *Afro-American* was again heavily involved, urging readers to "Make your Xmas and New Year's gift to the YMCA an investment that you will never regret. . . . Your gift . . . will help some boy and bless some man."[55] In December 1917, when the building's ground-breaking was held, nearly $9,000 was still needed to reach the $25,000 goal.[56] Nine months later, the Druid Hill YMCA held an "Over-the Top" campaign designed to collect $8,000 from the 1,375 people whose 1912 pledges remained unpaid. The YMCA's plan to publish "in the public press, a full and complete list of all the names of individuals who have paid no portion of the amount pledged by them" was softened when Druid Hill's leaders declared that "if each one . . . pays one dollar on their pledge, . . . we will have no need to publish any names."[57]

World War I complicated fundraising efforts because the black community was inundated with funding requests. Concurrent with appeals for the new building came requests to support black troops through military YMCAs.[58] As the new building was under construction the Druid Hill branch itself supported war work by providing social and recreational activities for black soldiers and sailors "who may have a few hours in Baltimore." The association's temporary recreation center at 1533 Druid Hill Avenue was used as "a real home" for soldiers on furlough in Baltimore. According to the *Afro*, "the Sammies know the value of the YMCA."[59]

Even as the Druid Hill YMCA served military men in town, events were held to generate interest and support for the new building. In February 1918 the *Afro* supported a membership campaign with a goal of a thousand new members. "A city with probably the largest colored population of any city in the Union, with the many men and boys who need just what the Association will be shortly so well equipped to furnish, ought to take first rank at least in matter of membership."[60] The day before the campaign's scheduled end, 242 more members were needed.[61] Secretary S. S. Booker made a final appeal to the congregation at Ames M.E. Church where the men then fanned out in different directions "each one determined to go the limit in order to win. The interest was at fever heat and everybody was talking about the campaign, No conversation was complete without the question — 'Are you a member of the "Y"?'" The men were successful. In the final day 328 new members were secured, bringing the total to 1,108.[62]

Despite the success of the membership campaign, when Druid Hill's cornerstone was laid in April 1918, six months after the second fundraiser began, more than $8,000 in pledges still remained unpaid. New sources were tapped. Black clergy passed the collection plate and sold souvenir bricks for a dollar. On YMCA Day, "every minister" in the black community was asked to speak of the YMCA's work and make an offering to the building fund. Pharmacists allowed their drugstores to be used as a distribution system for free tickets for a "monster patriotic mass meeting" at Ford's Theater on the YMCA's behalf.[63]

The *Afro* was unwaveringly committed to the YMCA. As pledges went unmet, the newspaper reported that the completion of the new building depended on black citizens paying their pledges. Failure was not an option. "The need for such a plant is too urgent, the time for it is most opportune and the generous gifts of our good white friends mean too much." Said Booker, "This is a 100 per cent proposition and I am confident that the citizens of Baltimore will put it thru with flying colors. Five other cities are doing the same thing this year and WE MUST DO IT, that's all."[64]

By the summer of 1918 the financial situation was critical, and the building was being erected on a "pay as you go loan" and "when the money gives out the work will stop." The campaign's 240 volunteers canvassed "home and church, minister and layman, shop and industrial plant" in order to attract notice from those whose pledges remained unpaid and from groups like "churches, social service clubs, business and professional clubs, to chauffeurs, waiters, janitors, porters, butlers, bellmen and workingmen of Baltimore for a united pull in the common cause." Unlike the 1912 campaign there was "no amount too small."[65]

The 1918 campaign started well. After ten days more than $2,500 in cash had been received, and the volunteers were "full of ginger and confident of getting $8,000 . . . and thus sav[ing] the honor and integrity of the colored citizens of Baltimore." Teams were organized at Sparrows Point and "at all the big firms of the city where a large number of colored men work." By October 1918 the campaign lagged. Only $3,000 of the required $8,000 had been raised, and there was cash enough for only two weeks of construction.[66]

To alleviate the cash shortage, short-term savings were realized by leaving the swimming pool unfinished, thus seriously compromising the YMCA's service to a recreation-hungry community. Despite that, the building's opening was celebrated. In his dedicatory address, Moorland sketched the history of the colored work in Baltimore, told of the new building campaign in 1912, and lauded Booker for his "indefatigable work in collecting the necessary pledges among the colored people." Booker in turn described his struggle to collect $25,000 in pledges made by the black community over his four-year tenure in Baltimore. He ended with an appeal to raise the $1,300 necessary to complete the fundraising![67] The *Afro* itself "had the honor and the privilege of giving the last hundred dollars," which allowed the association to "go over the top and emerge with every brick in the . . . structure paid for."[68] The building's opening festivities lasted for more than a week and featured events like Chauffeurs Night, Church Night, Organization Night, Boys Night, and a Patriotic Mass Meeting. Throughout the week the building was "thronged with visitors."[69]

Furnished, the building cost approximately $110,000, of which $25,000 came from the African American community, $50,000 from "White friends," and $25,000 from Rosenwald. At the opening, the Druid Hill YMCA had a mortgage of $12,000 but was current with all bills. Of all the black YMCA buildings then erected (including Washington, D.C., Philadelphia, Chicago, Indianapolis, Kansas City, and Cincinnati), Baltimore's was reportedly the only one in which the black community's quota had been fully paid at the time of the building's dedication.[70] The vagaries of fundraising and other budgetary problems helped the Druid Hill board decide that they would "be gratified to come under the control of the Baltimore Association," thereby becoming a formal branch of the Baltimore YMCA.[71]

The Central YMCA reported that the "thoroughly modern structure" designed and built by George R. Morris was "not only architecturally beautiful [and] semi-fireproof," it was also "thoroughly substantial and adapted to modern Association work." In addition to "commodious reception rooms" and "a fine gymnasium with running track," the building featured the unfinished swimming pool, separate Boys' and Men's departments, an auditorium and classrooms on the second floor, and fifty-two "simply but substantially furnished" dormitory rooms with a capacity of seventy-one boarders on the third and fourth floors.[72]

The building served both local residents and newcomers to the city. The dormitory provided an important base for newly arrived men. The 1920 federal census offers a snapshot of the Druid Hill YMCA's dormitory residents. All forty-two residents were literate and spoke English. Most were young (more than half between seventeen and twenty-six years of age), single, born in the region (nearly 75 percent were born in Maryland and Virginia), and employed. Many of the lodgers held service jobs with hotels or private families. The census-taker identified one-third of the residents as black and two-thirds as mulatto.[73]

Soon after the building's opening, the Central YMCA's leaders proclaimed that their investment at Druid Hill was "one of the best the Association . . . ever made." The building was "the central influence in the life of the colored population in this section of the city." Blacks and whites both saw the branch as an important center for the black community, "the center of the interdenominational religious life of the colored community" and "the center of the social and religious work among colored people."[74]

The new building was immediately popular. Its opening coincided with a population explosion in Baltimore. Between 1920 and 1924, the city's total population increased by more than fifty thousand to 785,242, of which there were 36,452 black boys and men between ten and forty-nine years of age.[75] In 1920, the Druid Hill YMCA's membership was 950. There were 101 students enrolled in educational classes and 312 in Bible studies. The dormitories were occupied by 1,875 different men. The branch matched forty-five men with churches and provided opportunities for 210 others to serve on a plethora of association committees.[76]

The YMCA's work, according to the *Afro*, was supported by "the leading colored people of the city" who would "increase their support when needed." The membership of the Druid Hill branch was then comprised of "ministers, teachers, lawyers, doctors, dentists, pharmacists, chauffeurs, con-

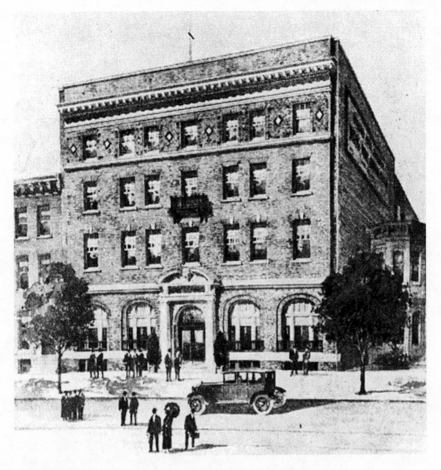

The Druid Hill Avenue YMCA, located at 1619 Druid Hill Avenue.

tractors, painters, waiters, porters, insurance men and laborers." The branch served as a community center by providing rooms for groups like the Medical Association, Teachers' Association, Male Ushers' Club and benevolent organizations.[77]

As the building's beauty and utility was celebrated, what was not apparent was that besides the unfinished swimming pool, other corners had been cut in the construction and finishing.[78] By 1924, the YMCA's own surveyors were struck by the poor conditions, observing "either the amount of the fund to be spent was fixed without regard to the standards of Association service or else it was assumed that the standards of equipment could be disregarded in a building for colored men and boys." The building was "exceedingly disappointing" and could not compare "for a moment" with the Central building, ten years its senior. The gym was too short for standard games. The combination of both intensive use (a thousand people used the building daily) and the poor quality of materials caused the locker rooms and showers to be in deplorable condition. The dormitories were the only part of the physical operation that met standards, but they were criticized for providing mostly double rooms. The lot itself was too small, and the building only half the size necessary to meet demand.[79]

Although there were clearly commonalities in the program of the Druid Hill YMCA and the association's white operations, there was also clear separation. Leaders of the white Central YMCA attempted to negotiate a modernity that was characterized by a profoundly racist society in which the Jim Crow edict of separate but equal long stood unchallenged by them and their peers. Where the white YMCA proved to be a pathbreaking organization in areas like adult and continuing education, vocational training, and even housing, in the area of race relations, Baltimore YMCA leaders both black and white long tolerated the status quo of racial segregation.

Notes

[1] Before 1890 there was no predominately African American residential area in Baltimore. Rather blacks lived throughout the city. In 1880 blacks constituted more than 10 percent of the city's population in fifteen of its twenty wards, yet no single ward was more than one-third black. Karen Olson, "Old West Baltimore: Segregation, African-American Culture, and the Struggle for Equality," in Elizabeth Fee, Linda Shopes, and Linda Zeidman, *The Baltimore Book: New Views of Local History* (Philadelphia: Temple University Press, 1991), 57–78.

[2] Dreck Spurlock Wilson, "Druid Hill Branch, Young Men's Christian Association: The First Hundred Years," *Maryland Historical Magazine,* 84 (1989): 135–46; and "The Druid Hill Branch YMCA: The First One Hundred Years, 1885–1985" (brochure), YMCA Vertical Files, Maryland Room, Enoch Pratt Free Library, Baltimore, Md.

[3] The standard history of the YMCA is C. Howard Hopkins, *History of the YMCA in North America* (New York: Association Press, 1951).

[4] For information on Baltimore's black community in the antebellum period, see Christopher Phillips, *Freedom's Port: The African American Community of Baltimore, 1790–1860* (Urbana: University of Illinois Press, 1997); William George Paul, "The Shadow of Equality: The Negro in Baltimore, 1864–1911" (Ph.D. diss., University of Wisconsin, 1972), see 14–30; and Ralph Clayton, *Black Baltimore,*

1820–1870 (Bowie, Md.: Heritage Books, 1987). Olson, "Old West Baltimore," has information on the making of community on the west side in the postbellum period.

⁵ Nina Mjagkij, *Light in the Darkness: African Americans and the YMCA, 1852–1946* (Lexington: University Press of Kentucky, 1994), 1.

⁶ The two were George D. Johnston and Henry Edwards Brown. Ibid., 3.

⁷ Ibid., 37–38, 50–51, 109.

⁸ Leroy Graham, *Baltimore: Nineteenth-Century Black Capital* (Washington, D.C.: University Press of America, 1982), 201.

⁹ Wilson, "Druid Hill Branch," 135–46; and Baltimore YMCA, *Druid Hill Avenue Branch: The YMCA and Negro Youth,* February 26, 1944, YMCA Papers, YMCA of Central Maryland Collection, University of Baltimore Archives (UBA).

¹⁰ Attempting to ensure that no such request would again arise, in 1883 the Central YMCA's board of directors set room rental fees at an astronomical minimum of $15 per night. In 1895 when Booker T. Washington, president of Tuskegee Institute, applied to rent the Central YMCA's hall for a lecture, the room rental issue was revisited. James Carey Thomas and Daniel Coit Gilman endorsed Washington's application. The board of directors, hoping that Washington would use rooms elsewhere, which in fact he ultimately did, gave Secretary Morriss "discretionary power" to respond to Washington's application. Baltimore YMCA, Minutes, Executive Committee, November 27, 1883, and Minutes, Board of Directors, October 30, 1895, and October 1, 1899, UBA.

¹¹ Mjagkij, *Light in the Darkness,* 49.

¹² The 1891 Convention followed one held in Nashville in 1890. Mjagkij, *Light in the Darkness,* 137. Baltimore YMCA, Minutes, Board of Directors, April 7, 1891, UBA.

¹³ The seven clergymen were: W. M. Alexander, Patterson Avenue Baptist; Harvey Johnson, Union Baptist; W. Brown, Knox Presbyterian; E. F. Eggleton, Grace Presbyterian; J. W. Norris; Trinity A.M.E.; and I. I. Thomas, Centennial A.M.E. Baltimore YMCA, Minutes, Board of Directors, April 5, 1892, UBA.

¹⁴ Charity Organization Society, *Directory of the Charitable and Beneficent Organizations of Baltimore and Maryland* (Baltimore: 1892), 103–5.

¹⁵ Baltimore YMCA, Minutes, Board of Directors, April 5, 1892, and October 4, 1892. UBA; William A. Hunton, "The Association Among Colored Men," *Men,* December 18, 1897, 249 as cited in Mjagkij, *Light in the Darkness,* 41.

¹⁶ Baltimore YMCA, Minutes, Board of Directors, September 6, 1892, UBA.

¹⁷ *Baltimore Afro-American,* November 16, 1912; and Baltimore YMCA, *1893 Annual Report,* 10.

¹⁸ Many in the black community considered only initiatives from the mid-1890s on as part of the history of the Druid Hill Branch. At the dedication of the new building "older men who helped to start the work more than 20 years ago" told the "real history of the association." *Baltimore Afro-American,* December 20, 1918.

¹⁹ Baltimore YMCA, *Association Bulletin,* January 1896, UBA.

²⁰ Baltimore YMCA, Minutes, Board of Directors, February 1898.

²¹ *Baltimore Afro-American,* November 16, 1912.

[22] Baltimore YMCA, *Association Bulletin,* January 1899, UBA.

[23] Gilbert Osofsky, *Harlem: The Making of a Ghetto, Negro New York, 1890–1930* (New York: Harper-Collins Publisher, 1963), 15, 80, 151 & 219 fn. 70.

[24] *Baltimore Afro American,* July 2, 1898. The literature on "muscular Christianity" is important to this discussion.

[25] Baltimore YMCA, *Association Bulletin,* January 1899, UBA.

[26] *Baltimore Afro-American,* June 25, 1898.

[27] *Association Bulletin,* February 1899, UBA.

[28] Baltimore YMCA, *Association Bulletin,* September 1899, 5; Minutes, Board of Directors, June 6, 1899, UBA.

[29] Baltimore YMCA, *Association Bulletin,* September 1899, 5, UBA.

[30] Baltimore YMCA, *1900 Annual Report,* 36; Minutes, Board of Directors, June 6, 1899; and August 1900, UBA.

[31] *Baltimore Afro-American,* November 16, 1912; Wilson, "Druid Hill Branch," 139.

[32] W. Edward Williams to J. E. Moorland, November 3, 1900, as cited in Mjagkij, *Light in the Darkness,* 56.

[33] Baltimore YMCA, Minutes, Board of Directors, December 1900; and January 3, 1901, UBA. Goines came to Baltimore from Atlantic City at Mooreland's recommendation. He left the Druid Hill YMCA about 1908 to become the Colored Secretary at Orange, New Jersey. He was succeeded by W. F. Bardeleben who was there through the 1912 fundraising campaign. S. S. Booker followed as Druid Hill's secretary and presided over the opening of the new building in 1919.

[34] Baltimore YMCA, Minutes, Board of Directors, December 5, 1893; June 5, 1894; February 5, 1895; June 6, 1899; and December 4, 1900, UBA.

[35] For information on the sports program of the Colored YMCA/Druid Hill Avenue Branch, see James Roland Coates Jr., "Recreation and Sport in the African-American Community of Baltimore, 1890–1920" (Ph.D. diss., University of Maryland, 1991), 89–118.

[36] By late 1904, a bathroom was fitted up featuring two showers and "complete toilet accommodation." That combined with "20 second handed lockers" sufficed. Baltimore YMCA, Minutes, Board of Directors, June 6, 1899, and September 30, 1904, UBA.

[37] *Survey Commission, YMCA, Baltimore, MD,* 1924, Part II, 26, UBA.

[38] In 1924 the Baltimore YMCA undertook a survey of "the immediate needs of the boys and young men" of Baltimore to ascertain what kind of expansion the Central Branch required. The compilation of much useful and disturbing information about Baltimore's African American community was an important by-product. Problems of housing, health, and recreation in black areas were reported and put "at the disposal of other groups of people who might be influential in having the problems met." John R. Cary, a board member of the Druid Hill YMCA, brought the issue of the high levels of tuberculosis in West Baltimore to the attention of the nascent Urban League, which in turn advocated for a much larger study of the African American community, and ultimately, for the razing of the area known as the "lung block." Baltimore YMCA, *Survey Commission, YMCA, Baltimore, MD,* 1924, *Druid Hill Avenue Branch: The YMCA*

and Negro Youth, February 26, 1944, and *The Interracial Situation and the YMCA,* UBA.

[39] Baltimore YMCA, *Baltimore Men,* June 3, 1915, UBA.

[40] In September 1904, boarding house information was provided to eight young men. Two months later the branch sent four other men to boarding houses. Baltimore YMCA, Minutes, Board of Directors, September & November 1904, UBA.

[41] *Baltimore Afro-American,* September 28, 1912. Baltimore YMCA, Minutes, Committee of Management, Druid Hill Avenue Branch, December 13, 1927, UBA.

[42] A classroom to accommodate working men featured used desks and blackboards bought from "Mrs. Pendleton's school on Charles St. near Read." Students ranged in age from sixteen to fifty-seven years old. The enrollment of working men in night school classes was relatively small in the early years, totaling eighteen in 1904. Baltimore YMCA, *Association Bulletin,* September 1899, 5; and October 1899, and Board of Directors, August 1900 and September 30, 1904. UBA.

[43] Baltimore YMCA, Minutes, Board of Directors, May 31, 1904, UBA.

[44] Baltimore YMCA, *Association Bulletin,* October 1899, UBA; *1901 Annual Report,* 24; and *1906 Annual Report,* 34.

[45] Baltimore YMCA, Minutes, Board of Directors, November 31, 1904, UBA.

[46] Baltimore YMCA, Minutes, Board of Directors, January 7, 1900, UBA.

[47] For more information on Rosenwald's philanthropy, see Judith Sealander, *Private Wealth and Public Life: Foundation Philanthropy and the Reshaping of American Social Policy from the Progressive Era to the New Deal* (Baltimore: The Johns Hopkins University Press, 1997), 69–72. Mjagkij, *Light in the Darkness* 76–77. *Baltimore Afro-American,* November 16, 1912

[48] Ibid.

[49] *Baltimore Afro-American,* November 9, 16, and 30, 1912. The district captains were: T. A. Date; Walter S. Emerson; P. D. G. Pennington; Thomas J. Smith; Dr. Albert O. Reid; Dr. J. C. Robinson; W. T. Greenwood; Samuel E. Young; and Dr. T. S. Hawkins. The original pledge list survives and is quite instructive, UBA.

[50] For more information on the *Afro's* history and advocacy, see Hayward Farrar, *The Baltimore Afro-American, 1892–1950* (Westport, Conn.: Greenwood Press, 1998).

[51] *Baltimore Afro-American,* November 23, 1912.

[52] Ibid.

[53] *Baltimore Afro-American,* November 30, 1912; December 14, 1912; and July 12, 1918.

[54] Ibid., August 23, 1918.

[55] Ibid., December 22, 1917.

[56] Baltimore YMCA, *Baltimore Men,* June 3, 1915, UBA.

[57] *Baltimore Afro-American,* August 30 and September 20, 1918.

[58] For insights into the YMCA's military work, see David Lee Shillinglaw, *An American in the Army and YMCA, 1917–1920* (Chicago: University of Chicago Press, 1971).

[59] In April 1918, 2,261 soldiers visited, 198 stayed overnight, and 3,642 were directed to services like restaurants, barbershops, railroad stations, homes, and churches. *Baltimore Afro-American,* December 29, 1917, and May 24, 1918.

[60] Ibid., February 9, 1918.

[61] S. S. Booker, a graduate of Virginia Union University, class of 1910, and an accomplished athlete and outdoorsman, joined the Druid Hill YMCA as secretary in 1912 after working for YMCAs in Chattanooga and in Indianapolis. *The First Colored Directory of Baltimore City* (Baltimore: R.W. Coleman Publishing Co., 1916), 96.

[62] For this campaign there had been a contest. J. D. Lewis, who brought in 148 members, won first place and a pair of gold cuff links. Desmond Lynch, in second place with eighty-two members, won a gold scarf pin. Benjamin P. Dixon won third place and a leather ticket case. An incentive for joining were dues of $1 for boys and men, which for men doubled to $2 following the close of the contest. *Baltimore Afro-American,* March 1, 1918.

[63] *Baltimore Afro-American,* April 12, 1918, May 10, 1918, and October 11, 1918.

[64] Ibid., May 3, 1918.

[65] Ibid., August 23, 1918.

[66] Ibid., September 20, 1918, and October 11, 1918.

[67] Ibid., January 3, 1919.

[68] Ibid., January 10, 1919.

[69] Ibid., December 27, 1918, and Baltimore YMCA, *Baltimore Men,* January 9, 1919. UBA.

[70] Baltimore YMCA, *Baltimore Men,* January 9, 1919; 1919 *Annual Report,* 13–14, UBA; and *Baltimore Afro-American,* January 10, 1919.

[71] Baltimore YMCA, *1918 Annual Report,* 3–4.

[72] Baltimore YMCA, *Baltimore Men,* January 9, 1919, UBA.

[73] Data was drawn from the Fourteenth Census of the United States, 1920, Manuscript Population Schedules, Baltimore City, Enumeration District 240, Sheet 11B, Ward 14, page 23A. Five of the men were between 28 and 33, another six were between 35 and 39. There were also three each in their forties and fifties and one man who was 76. More than one-quarter were employed as waiters. Three men each worked as elevator operators and chauffeurs. Two men each were employed as clerk, bellboy, laborer, cook, porter, tailor and YMCA staff. Hotels employed more than a third of the borders. Four men worked for private families. Three were employed by restaurants Other industries employing one or two Druid Hill residents were: the post office, an apartment house, railway, music conservatory, schools, shop, factory, construction, a bank, a department store, a bakery, clubs, and the YMCA itself.

[74] Baltimore YMCA, *1921 Annual Report,* 10; *1926 Annual Report,* 7; and *YMCA Survey Commission,* 1924, Part I, 47, UBA.

[75] Of these, 8,198 were public school students between the ages of five and twenty-one, all but 619 in elementary school. An additional 6,900 young men were between 18 to 24. In the 24 to 49-year-old category there were 23,354 men. Baltimore YMCA, *YMCA Survey Commission,* 1924, 18, 39, and 42, UBA.

[76] Baltimore YMCA, *1921 Annual Report,* 10 and *1922 Annual Report,* 14.

[77] Baltimore YMCA, *YMCA Survey,* 1924, Part II, 25, UBA.

[78] A year after its opening, at a cost of $7,500 the Druid Hill YMCA was retrofitted with a swimming pool. William Morriss, the Baltimore YMCA's secretary and a member of the City Public Bath Commission, received credit for seeing the pool to fruition as "a great public service for the community." Baltimore YMCA, *1920 Annual Report,* 8.

[79] Baltimore YMCA, *YMCA Survey,* 1924, Part II, 25–26, UBA.

JOHN R. BREIHAN

Wings of Democracy?
African Americans in Baltimore's
World War II Aviation Industry

ORLD WAR II was an era of rapid and massive social change. It marked the end of the economic depression of the 1930s, and it intensified the long movement of Americans from farms to cities. Sixteen million Americans entered the armed services, trained for new jobs, and moved—literally—around the world. Another fifteen million left their homes to take jobs in war production centers. Besides building the weapons of war, they built new military bases, new factories, and new communities. These population movements changed the face of America.[1]

African Americans expected to benefit from these developments. Black workers had been disproportionately unemployed or underemployed during the depression. Now they hoped to gain access to skilled jobs in the defense plants. Many took the opportunity to move away from southern agricultural communities into the new war production centers. It is true that similar changes had taken place during World War I, only to lead to disappointment during the 1920s. But the World War II mobilization was much larger, and it was to last much longer. Moreover, this war was fought against avowedly racist regimes, and American leaders made explicit references to social justice as a war aim. Many Americans hoped that victories against fascism abroad would inspire more militancy against racism at home.

Jack Breihan has degrees in History from Princeton and Cambridge. Since 1977 he has taught at Loyola College. Besides British politics and administration, his research has included studies of the aviation industry in Baltimore and communities associated with it.

172

Sixty years later, historians have different opinions about to what degree these hopes were fulfilled. For some, World War II was a "turning point" in African American history, a "seedtime of the civil rights movement," an era of dramatic breakthroughs in employment and civil rights.[2] Others are not so sure, seeing only temporary deviations from underlying patterns of racial exclusion and discrimination.[3]

This article will examine these phenomena from the perspective of Baltimore. Wartime mobilization came early to Baltimore, and so lasted longer. In February 1939, nearly three years before Pearl Harbor, the Glenn L. Martin Aircraft Company plant received its first rush orders from the French. Martin began working around the clock, adding to the plant and growing rapidly from three thousand employees to thirteen thousand by the end of the year.[4] The fall of France in June 1940 alarmed the U.S. government, producing floods of new orders, plants, and workers. That year saw British orders go to Bethlehem Steel, Bendix Radio, and Western Electric—and traffic quadruple at the Western Maryland Railway's Port Covington docks. Martin built a second factory as large as the first; Bethlehem Steel a second shipyard at Fairfield.[5] The new shipyards and plants attracted thousands of workers, both black and white, from across the U.S.A. In July 1942 the War Manpower Commission declared Baltimore the nation's first "critical labor supply area," curtailing further government contracts in favor of less congested areas.[6] Labor, housing, recreation, even food were all in short supply in Baltimore for the rest of the war.

Of the ten largest American cities, Baltimore had the highest proportion of black residents in 1940. One hundred sixty-eight thousand black citizens were roughly 20 percent of the city's population. Although subject to many forms of official segregation, black Baltimoreans were justly proud of their public schools, churches, and strong local chapters of the NAACP and Urban League.[7] The war would attract between sixty and ninety thousand more African Americans to Baltimore. Because of local housing segregation, they had no choice but to squeeze into already crowded black residential areas.

Unlike other industrial cities under similar stresses, however, Baltimore experienced little racial violence. Perhaps the city's closest brush with violence came characteristically early, in May of 1942. In February, a white policeman shot and killed a black soldier from Fort Meade in the Pennsylvania Avenue entertainment district. It was this particular officer's second shooting of a black man. After the case against him was dismissed and still another racial incident had taken place at the same spot, two thousand demonstrators gathered in the state capital to protest.[8] Herbert O'Conor, the governor of Maryland, appointed an interracial Commission to Study Problems Affecting the Colored Population that served at least in part to defuse tensions.[9]

So did war work. African Americans held thousands of jobs in Baltimore's war industries, many of them skilled or semiskilled jobs previously denied to black workers. Eventually 17.6 percent of wartime manufacturing jobs were held by African Americans, including a substantial proportion of women. African Americans were also active in civil defense and other volunteer home front activities.

The consequences of wartime changes were mixed. Although most of the new industrial jobs evaporated literally overnight at the end of the war, wartime training and experience led to noticeable improvement in the occupational profile of black workers. In the final analysis, though, the changes to the physical and social landscape of the city were probably more important than the new jobs. Wartime choices regarding the location of factories, roads, and housing produced long lasting effects, decentralizing industry, increasing residential segregation, and beginning the familiar postwar pattern of black urban neighborhoods surrounded by burgeoning white suburbs.

In discussing these developments I will focus primarily on the Glenn L. Martin Aircraft Company. Although Martin employed fewer workers overall than either Bethlehem Steel or the B&O Railroad, it was arguably the most dynamic of the city's war industries. Not only did Martin's wartime expansion come first, but the company's main factories in suburban Middle River, ten miles east of the Baltimore City line, involved more modern technologies than the steel mills, shipyards, or engine shops of older smokestack industries. Finally, building gleaming aluminum wings for the forces of democracy was simply more glamorous than any other war industry. Oral history interviews often make it clear that people came to work at Martin not just for economic reasons but because of the romance of building airplanes. Labor surveys continually pointed to Martin as the chief attraction for "inmigrant" workers coming to Baltimore from across the country.

After initial resistance the company was among the first local defense manufacturers to hire black workers, eventually employing three thousand.

During the war Martin was in fact one of the largest employers of African Americans in Baltimore. I will discuss three principal aspects of this involvement: first the hiring of black war workers, then their conditions of employment, and finally housing.

Before the war it was well-known in Baltimore that the only black worker employed at Martin's suburban factory in Middle River was Glenn Martin's chauffeur. This was also true in aircraft factories in other cities, and indeed across all the defense industries. A survey in 1940 showed that 90 percent of new defense jobs nationwide were barred to black workers, many of whom remained unemployed. The number of African Americans in WPA "relief jobs" actually grew between 1939 and 1942.[10]

Aviation was an early focus of opposition to racial discrimination in defense industries. In July 1940 *The Crisis,* the magazine of the NAACP, ran a cover photograph of an aircraft factory with the words "For Whites Only" superimposed and the caption "Warplanes—Negroes may not build them, repair them, or fly them, but they must pay for them."[11] During 1941 most attacks on discrimination included reference to the aircraft industry and various hostile statements made by aircraft executives.

Given its early start in defense orders and proximity to Washington, D.C., it was not surprising that Martin became a particular target. In the spring of 1941, after an unprofitable meeting with Martin's personnel director, John P. Davis of the National Negro Congress launched a campaign against the company's ban on black workers. A leaflet demanded seven thousand jobs for African Americans, to match their proportion of the Baltimore population.[12] A leaflet challenged the unfairness of Martin's "waxing fat on more than 300 million dollars worth of government defense contracts," including a plant expansion built at government expense, while refusing to hire black citizens. The leaflet urged "mass pressure" on federal officials and nonviolent protest at the Martin plant. The NNC offered to organize transportation for black job applicants to go to Middle River to be rejected in person, looking to "give Glenn L. Martin a chance to turn down 5,000 Negro workers."[13] Nearly three hundred applied.[14]

Meanwhile, the Baltimore Urban League took a different approach. In March 1941 a number of Baltimore organizations sponsored a Conference on the Participation of Negroes in National Defense. Speaking on employment, Furman Templeton, Industrial Secretary of the Baltimore Urban League, identified three key areas: access to worker training, the integration of labor unions, and modification of local Jim Crow laws.[15] In particular, Regulation No. 26 of Baltimore's health code operated as a barrier to African American employment, specifying separate toilet facilities for the two races. Plants with only male and female toilets thus had an easy excuse to bar black workers.[16]

The Urban League began with job training. This was particularly critical for aircraft-industry jobs. Given the industry's appeal, Martin could afford to be choosy, insisting on prior training. With Martin's cooperation, the Baltimore City Public Schools had begun to offer such training in July 1939. In 1940, with federal funds for defense training now available, the city schools enrolled more than nine thousand white men and women in classes at the "National Defense Vocational Training School," School Number 250 on East Baltimore Street.[17] Although the congressional appropriation had a non-discrimination clause, none of these students was black. The excuse was that since no defense jobs were open to African Americans, it did not make sense to train any for them.

The Baltimore Urban League threatened a suit to force the school board to establish job training courses for black citizens.[18] A few courses were offered at the beginning of 1941 at Douglass High School. In midsummer the federally funded "National Defense Vocational-Training School for Colored" opened in School Number 453 at 775 Waesche Street in West Baltimore.[19]

There was also action at the federal level. In late June, A. Philip Randolph's March on Washington movement yielded in response President Franklin Roosevelt's landmark Executive Order 8802, barring racial discrimination in firms holding government contracts. The historians Joe Trotter and Earl Lewis have called this a "turning point in African American history." According do Harvard Sitkoff, another historian, it "secured for Afro-Americans the most important official recognition" of their aspirations since Reconstruction.[20]

Nevertheless, it had no immediate effect in Baltimore. Along with other defense contractors, Martin resisted. The Martin Company pointed out that its federal contracts predated the president's nondiscrimination order—so that there was no immediate obligation to follow it.[21] The Martin personnel office continued to insist that workers referred by the U.S. Employment

National Negro Congress demonstration against Martin's discriminatory hiring.
(Smithsonian Institution.)

Service be white only.[22] Questioned by a congressional committee just a
week after the president's executive order, Glenn Martin explained that the
company's refusal to hire black workers was necessary to keep up production. White workers, he said, were the problem. "The skilled men in the plant
will walk out when the Negroes walk in," Martin declared. "In the interests of
national defense," he continued, "[we are] not going to do anything to disturb
a social problem until someone else has straightened it out."[23]

Local efforts to end discrimination at Martin had more success. Although
the National Negro Congress in 1941 was not a large organization and was
mistrusted by many due to communist influence over it, Martin nevertheless
felt pressure from its campaign. In July Glenn Martin admitted that the company was making a study of methods to be used in employing African
Americans.[24] In September the company actually negotiated with the NNC
about the public announcement of the end of Martin's color bar. In October,
ten black workers were hired—all graduates of the Waesche Street training

school. A press release sent only to the *Baltimore Afro-American* newspaper asserted that the company's new black employees would enjoy the same pay rates and opportunities for advancement as white workers.[25] During the same month, the Martin Company's first women production workers were also hired. In both cases the new policies were publicly linked to labor shortages.

Another press release in January 1942 asserted that nearly all of the initial group had received raises, and one had been promoted to foreman. This was probably Saul Perdue, a vocational education teacher loaned by the Baltimore Department of Education.[26] Workers' ages ranged from eighteen to thirty-eight with 22.5 the average. Black workers were thus somewhat older than white ones—"Boys' Town" was a local nickname for the Martin plant at the end of 1941.[27] By April 1942 Martin Aircraft had 150 African American employees, making Martin the fifth largest industrial employer of black workers in the Baltimore area, after Bethlehem Steel, the Edgewood Arsenal, Maryland Drydock, and Revere Copper and Brass.[28]

Martin's black workforce of 150 would probably have remained at a token level if not for external events. The company continued to succeed in attracting white in-migrant workers in 1942. It was their presence, not their absence, that opened opportunities for local African Americans. More than ninety thousand new residents in 1941 and early 1942 placed severe strains on Baltimore's infrastructure of roads, sewers, and housing. Clark S. Hobbs, editor of the *Baltimore Evening Sun*, had long been interested both in urban planning and in African American affairs. A series of articles beginning in April 1942 explicitly linked the problems of overcrowding with employers' failure to hire local black workers.[29] Hobbs urged them to "tap a new reservoir of local labor which is already housed and serviced (inadequately, to be sure) and requires nothing beyond what is already under construction or planned."

Hobbs's call was answered by the War Manpower Commission (WMC), which began private conversations among local industrialists on how to manage war labor by voluntary means—with the threat of labor conscription if these failed. After the WMC declared Baltimore the nation's first "critical labor supply area" in July 1942, Alexander Liveright was detached from Chairman Paul McNutt's staff to oversee this effort in Baltimore. Meeting with a committee of eight leading labor and business figures (which included a vice president of Martin Aircraft), Liveright devised "the Baltimore Plan." This was widely publicized as a model for effectively managing the nation's manpower.[30] The Baltimore Plan focused first of all on reducing in-migration of workers to Baltimore, thereby easing the local housing short-age, and secondly on reducing "labor piracy" (in which higher pay or better conditions at one defense plant might lure workers to quit their jobs at an-other), thus moderating upward pressure on wages. Hiring new workers from the local black and female populations was thought to be a way of addressing both problems.

The employment of black and female workers at Martin rose sharply after the adoption of the Baltimore Plan in August 1942. In September a labor organizer estimated that one thousand African Americans worked there.[31] In January 1944 the WMC put the proportion of black workers at 5 percent, more than two thousand. Sixty-six percent of the black workers were women, as compared to an overall female employment rate of 35 percent.[32] While Martin's white "Rosie the Riveters" gained more attention, the participation rate of black women in the war effort was thus roughly twice that of whites. By the end of the war, the total number of African American Martin workers had grown to three thousand.[33]

Local leaders proclaimed that the implementation of the Baltimore Plan had effectually removed barriers to black employment. Already in June 1942 the number of African Americans on the relief rolls of Baltimore had hit an all-time low.[34] By September the Commission to Study Problems Affecting the Colored Population declared that the "battle against discrimination has been won, or so largely won that the emphasis must be upon taking advan-tage of the opportunities now being offered for training and placement in more highly skilled jobs."[35] This conclusion was taken up enthusiastically by the *Sun,* which proclaimed the "door is open for Negroes in industry."[36]

Local black organizations seemed to agree. They shifted their focus away from the war factories to more permanent jobs in public utilities, in particular the Chesapeake and Potomac Telephone and Baltimore Transit Companies. These companies' color bars and continuing discrimination at the United States Employment Service office, were the main focus of the Total War Employment Committee organized by Dr. J. E. T. Camper, a promi-nent physician and social leader, early in 1943. A February 1943 rally at the Union Baptist Church attracted twelve hundred, and six hundred marched in parades as part of Total War Employment Week in March 1944.[37] Martin was not mentioned.

In July 1941 Glenn Martin had said that his company was at work planning "a proper and efficient way to use the colored man in our skilled jobs." When the company's first black employees were hired in October, the Martin's definition of a "proper and efficient way" became clear. It was segregation. Black and white employees would work separately, most often in separate buildings. Glenn Martin had already supplied the reason:

> Because Baltimore has segregation. The Negro does not go to the white man's theater, nor does he go to the white man's restaurant or hotel. There are no colored people in the legislature in Maryland. The schools have segregation. We are willing to help with any social reform or change, but we do not feel that we have time to lead in such a reform at this time.[38]

In common with other industries in border and southern states, Martin confined its wartime African American employees almost entirely to a separate factory. Instead of the gleaming new plants in Middle River, black workers were assigned to Martin's Canton Division. This operated out of eighteen wooden buildings in Baltimore City's principal industrial district. Owned by the Canton Company, the structures had been built as warehouses. The Martin Company rented one of them as temporary quarters when it moved to Baltimore in 1929; another lease had been signed in 1939 to build wings panels there for Martin's French bombers.[39]

Canton in 1941 was definitely not an African American district. Most of the adjoining factories had all-white workforces; the surrounding residential neighborhoods were also all-white. Calvin Lee Tolbert, a wartime worker at nearby Crown Cork and Seal, described the district as a place African Americans entered warily, expecting rocks to be thrown at streetcars carrying black passengers.[40]

Photographs show that the Canton buildings were considerably more Spartan than the other Martin plants. There were eight modern cafeterias at Middle River, for example, while at Canton meals were purchased from

Glenn L. Martin's Canton factory. (Glenn L. Martin Aviation Museum.)

mobile canteens and consumed in alcoves off the production floor. The plant was duly equipped with separate black and white toilets in accordance with the Baltimore City health code.

According to James Myers, who was one of Martin's first ten black employees, white workers at Canton who objected to working with blacks were given the chance to transfer to Middle River.[41] Initially the Canton workforce was integrated, but as more and more black workers were hired and white ones assigned elsewhere, it increasingly became a segregated workplace. The same process seems to have been followed at Martin's turret assembly plant on Sinclair Lane.

With its purpose-built warehouses and an adjoining railyard, Canton became the central receiving department for the Martin Company during the war. Nearly a thousand workers were employed in warehouse work. Others assembled wings, landing gear, and gun mounts that were then transferred to Middle River for final installation. Nose sections for the Model 187 "Baltimore" bomber built as a Lend Lease project for the British were probably the most complex of these "subassembly" jobs.

WINGS OF DEMOCRACY?   181

Martin's attempted to be a paternalistic employer, providing a wide range of recreational and social activities for its workers. Martin himself was a keen sponsor of factory baseball and basketball squads. While these competed on an all-white basis in Middle River, a completely separate recreation program for black workers was established at the Druid Hill YMCA. Company photographs show African American workers in company-sponsored archery and volleyball competitions, as well as department dinners and company picnics at local hotels, parks, and beaches open to black customers. A delegation of "colored representatives" sat somewhat uneasily through the celebration of Martin's "E" efficiency award in 1945 in the ballroom of the normally segregated Alhambra Hotel.[42]

Compared to other Baltimore defense plants, Martin seems to have followed a middle course. The Western Electric Point Breeze plant just to the east of Martin's Canton plant initially appeared to be more integrated. Blacks and whites worked side by side. They shared the same toilets—the Baltimore Urban League having succeeded in persuading the city council to change the health code in this regard.[43] In July 1943 some white workers began a protest against the integrated toilets that eventually led to a six-day "hate strike" in December. This ended when the plant was taken over by the U.S. Army. Eventually new segregated toilets and locker rooms were built.[44] Earlier in 1943 two thousand white shipbuilders at the Bethlehem Steel Fairfield yards walked off the job after black workers were admitted to training classes in riveting. The strike was settled only after a seniority system was installed that would exclude black workers from more skilled jobs.[45] At Martin, where black workers routinely did riveting, such turmoil was avoided.

On the other hand, a greater degree of integration was successfully achieved at the Baltimore General Motors plant, which was just north of Martin's Canton Division. In 1942 this was converted to aircraft production under the name Eastern Aircraft. Although slow to hire African American workers (there were only three on the payroll as late as September 1942), Eastern Aircraft eventually had a substantial number of black workers. Photographs of the factory floor show an integrated production force doing much the same kinds of jobs as at Martin.[46]

Eastern Aircraft continued to work under General Motors' contract with the United Auto Workers, CIO. The fact that Eastern's wage rates were higher was a source of continual grievance at Martin and was frequently brought up during a massive unionization drive in 1943. This pitted the Martin Company, which wanted no union at all, against the A.F. of L. International Association of Machinists and the UAW-CIO. Union elections held in Martin's Baltimore facilities in July and September 1943 were rated as the largest "single plant" elections yet monitored by the National Labor Relations Board. Both unions spent heavily on campaigns, directing their rhetoric not only against the company but also against each other.

Although race was not an explicit issue in the election, it almost certainly lurked in the background. The two unions differed sharply. The initiation ritual of the IAM, as specified by the union's constitution, explicitly restricted full membership to whites. Although powerful West Coast aircraft lodges of the IAM had rejected it and enrolled African Americans as full members, the Baltimore organizing committee, financed directly by union headquarters, lacked the confidence to do so. Instead they issued "associate" memberships to black workers.[47]

By contrast, the CIO followed a policy of nondiscrimination. Not only was this on exhibit nearby at Eastern Aircraft, but speakers from the local Industrial Union Councils of the CIO had spoken at the Total War Employment rally in February 1943.[48] When local opposition surfaced to a housing project for black workers in July, the council leaders publicly defended the project, even suggesting that the protests constituted "a conspiracy to intimidate citizens."[49] UAW ads addressed to Martin workers stressed "equal pay" for men and women workers.[50] The UAW complained about cards circulated among employees just before the July union election stating that "If You Want a Negro Boss—Vote for the CIO and Get Him." and "Jimcrow in toilets, cafeteria, and jobs will end if CIO wins."[51]

Vote totals were not broken down by division, but under the circumstances it is difficult to believe that the "Cantoneers" did not vote overwhelmingly for the CIO, perhaps providing a narrow margin of victory, 50 percent to 46.[52] When the Canton plant was closed at the end of the war and thousands of Martin workers were laid off, union seniority rules allowed some African American workers to transfer to jobs at Middle River, finally bringing black workers to the suburban plant in 1945.

The housing of war workers, both black and white, was perhaps the most explosive aspect of the company's—and the city's—race relations policies. As mentioned earlier, the influx of white in-migrant workers in 1942 put serious strains on the physical infrastructure of Baltimore. Martin's workers were a particular problem. Though they crowded into rooming houses, back-yard trailer camps, vacation houses, and even converted chicken coops, Middle River and surrounding rural hamlets were unable to house even a fraction of them. Water and sewer connections were simply inadequate. Middle River's location ten miles beyond the city limits also overloaded existing roads. *Life* magazine ran a photo story on traffic jams at Martin in December 1941.[53] In-migrants frustrated by traffic or housing problems simply left for other cities. Replacement workers then had to be recruited and trained. Martin's turnover topped 8 percent *per month* in early 1942. Surveys showed that housing led the list of causes for departure.[54]

It became necessary to build a "new town" around the plant, even though this diverted materials and effort from other war programs. In 1941 public agencies began to provide new water lines and sewers to Middle River, and two high-speed divided highways connecting it with the city. One of Maryland's first cloverleaf interchanges was built just in front of the Martin plant at the junction of the new Eastern and Martin Boulevards. The Martin Company's real-estate arm constructed two subdivisions of prefabricated bungalows, Stansbury Estates on Wilson Point and Aero Acres along the new dual-lane Martin Boulevard. The federal government brought in 1,700 trailers and put up 1,100 prefabricated houses in Victory Villa in 1942 and a thousand more apartments at Victory Villa Gardens in 1943. Private builders with FHA-guaranteed loans constructed thousands more garden apartments in Riverdale, Mars Estates, Oak Grove, and Burkleigh Manor. The new community was laid out by a team of city planners headed by Hale Walker, who had planned the futuristic Washington suburb of Greenbelt. They provided sites for schools, recreational facilities, and community and shopping centers.[55]

All this construction was made necessary by Martin's preference for in-migrant white labor over local African American workers. Even after the Baltimore Plan was instituted in August 1942, Martin and other local employers continued to attract in-migrants to the area. In the plan, they had agreed "whenever possible to refrain from recruiting or scouting workers outside the Baltimore area except through the facilities of the United States Employ-

Lunch facilities at Canton. (Glenn L. Martin Aviation Museum.)

ment Service."[56] Walter Sondheim, a department-store executive installed by Liveright as head of the United States Employment Service in Maryland, admitted in 1943 that his office never had the manpower to oversee hiring practices. Many employers, Martin included, continued to hire new workers "at the gate," not inquiring seriously as to whether they were recent arrivals in Baltimore or long-time residents. The flood of in-migrants thus continued into 1943. The number registering with U.S.E.S. leapt from 2,600 a month at the beginning of 1942 to as high as 4,500 at the end of the year. A survey in March 1943 estimated that more than 160,000 men, many with families, had arrived in Baltimore since 1940, marking a sharp increase over the figure of ninety thousand estimated by Liveright at the end of 1942.[57]

While white in-migrants were provided with new housing in Middle River, conditions in Baltimore's African American neighborhoods deteriorated. Restrictive covenants prohibited black residence in surrounding districts. All told, Baltimore's black neighborhoods occupied only one and a half square miles—one-fiftieth of the city's area housed one-fifth of its citizens. They occupied older houses originally built for single families but now given over to makeshift conversions into apartment. Poor maintenance was common, and disease rates were alarmingly high.[58] The Baltimore Housing Authority had begun to provide some newer housing during the later 1930s, but at the cost of displacing nearly eight hundred black families who had no choice but to crowd in to the remaining older houses.[59]

The war made matters still worse. Already in February 1941 the rental vacancy rate in Baltimore's African American neighborhoods was only 0.6 percent; a year later it had fallen to zero. A survey by the *Evening Sun* in May 1942 showed an average of eight persons per dwelling unit in black neighborhoods.[60] When the rate of African American in-migration to Baltimore hit 2,500 to 3,000 a month in 1942, matters grew still worse. The morning edition of the *Sun*, worried about the threat of disease from overcrowding, identified housing as the chief challenge to race relations:

> the problem of housing lies at the base of a dozen other undesirable conditions. Until something is done to relieve the terrible overcrowding that affects Negro sections, most discussions of other Negro problems and disabilities is certain to have a hollow ring.[61]

The Governor's Commission on Problems Affecting the Colored Population advised drastic course of action: either turning away black in-migrants who could not prove that they had work or erecting dormitories for them in the public parks.[62]

In the spring of 1943 matters came to a head when federal authorities made $8 million available for new housing for African American war workers. City officials and planners saw this as a chance for permanent housing to ease the crowding in the black ghetto. Their proposal was to build it on a vacant site adjoining Herring Run Park, on the east side of the city, not far from the main war plants. Federal housing authorities agreed. Massive protests, however, soon came from nearby white neighborhoods. Eight hundred angry citizens marched on City Hall to heckle Mayor Theodore McKeldin. Congressman H. Streett Baldwin called the project a "socialistic experiment."[63] Senator Millard Tydings, after a survey of local industrialists, declared that there was a surplus of African American labor in Baltimore, that no more should be imported.[64] City Solicitor F. Murray Benson denied that black in-migrants deserved new housing, charging that they shunned war work in favor of "cruising the streets of this city and terrorizing the population." The Baltimore City Council passed a resolution calling for their approval of any permanent housing site.[65]

All of this blew up during the summer 1943, one of the hottest on record, during which newspapers also carried stories about racial violence on the streets of Detroit and New York, and "hate strikes" in local factories. In July an interracial coalition, declaring that "a tenseness exists in the city, particularly among the Negro population," organized a "Unity for Victory" rally in Druid Hill Park. Housing problems for black residents were the chief problems cited, along with job discrimination and mistreatment by company police.[66] Fifteen thousand people came to hear Paul Robeson sing and Mayor McKeldin and Lester Granger, executive secretary of the National Urban League, plead for improved race relations.[67] Meanwhile the mayor appointed a special Interracial Committee, including social luminaries like Robert Garrett, to study housing sites.

Although this committee also supported the Herring Run site, the project there was eventually abandoned.[68] In October, after both the weather and perhaps tensions had cooled, it was announced that new permanent housing for African Americans would instead be built at Cherry Hill on the extreme southern border of Baltimore, across the harbor from most of the city, on a vacant marshland between the city incinerator and the potters field burial ground.[69] Two other permanent all-black housing projects were built at Turner's Station in Baltimore County, an historically black settlement south of Dundalk. Temporary housing and trailer camps for African American war workers were set up at Fairfield and Fort Holabird.[70]

Martin's record in enlisting African American support in the war effort was clearly mixed. Jo Anne Argersinger has shown how Baltimore authorities resisted central government initiatives during the New Deal; in a similar way Martin delayed implementing wartime non-discrimination regulations handed down from Washington.[71] The company was nevertheless one of the first to drop its color bar, though its segregation of the workplace itself denied black workers at Canton access to a broad range of skilled jobs done by workers at Middle River. The overall proportion of African American workers at Mar-

TABLE 1: AFRICAN AMERICAN MALE WORKERS IN BALTIMORE, 1940–50

Percentage by Occupational Categories	1940	1950
Professional, technical	2.4	2.5
Managers, officials, proprietors	2.8	3.1
Clerical, sales	3.8	6.4
Craftsmen, foremen	5.3	9.1
Operatives	17.4	24.1
Domestic service	3.2	1.2
Other service workers	20.9	16.4
Laborers	42.9	34.9
Other and not specified	1.3	2.3
TOTAL ABSOLUTE NUMBER	39,241	55,469

Source: Census of Population, Maryland, 1940, 1950.

tin—10 percent—was twice the norm for the aircraft industry nationwide.[72] But it was far less than African Americans' share of the Baltimore population—20 percent—or of their participation in local war industries, 17.6 percent.[73]

Martin's failure fully to utilize African American workers probably had an adverse effect on the company's production record. Despite Martin's early start in 1939, the company's deliveries fell seriously behind schedule in 1942 and 1943, causing considerable consternation among top procurement officials.[74] The company blamed much of the problem on shortages of trained personnel. Glenn Martin and his executives complained of disproportionate losses to selective service and a high turnover due to shortages of housing for in-migrant white workers.[75] An earlier and greater reliance on local black workers, particularly women, would have reduced these problems.[76]

As soon as peace returned in 1945, Martin laid off all but thirteen of its three thousand black workers.[77] Seniority rules in the new UAW-CIO contract, however, provided that former employees be called back in preference to new hires. Several hundred wartime African American employees returned to the company. Some worked at Martin for more than forty years, earning incomes far above the average in the black community.[78] This did not mean complete integration. After the Canton Division was closed in 1945 and all operations consolidated in Plant No. 1 at Middle River, racial segregation continued. All African American workers were initially assigned

TABLE 2: AFRICAN AMERICAN FEMALE WORKERS IN BALTIMORE, 1940–50

Percentage by Occupational Categories	1940	1950
Professional, technical	4.1	5.2
Managers, officials, proprietors	.7	1.1
Clerical, sales	1.7	6.7
Craftsmen, foremen	.2	.6
Operatives	8.2	16.2
Domestic service	68.1	44.6
Other service workers	14.9	22.6
Laborers	1.2	1.6
Other and not specified	.9	1.4
TOTAL ABSOLUTE NUMBER	26,893	33,798

Source: Census of Population, Maryland, 1940, 1950.

to work in the basement of one building at Middle River. Separate toilets and a separate sitting at the plant cafeteria were duly provided. New black workers were not particularly welcome. Only gradually after the war did black workers come to work throughout the plant.[79]

Baltimore's civil rights organizations, already strong before the war, helped break down some employment barriers, in particular the city health code requirement of segregated toilets. A comparison of occupational profile of black workers in Baltimore before and after the war reveals some modest gains. The 1940 and 1950 census figures provide a good illustration of the war's effects, since few African Americans were hired for "defense" jobs before 1940, and the 1950 census was taken before the next build-up during the Korean War. Clearly there were more black workers in 1950 than ten years earlier. This was due both to greater prosperity and to in-migration—the black population of Baltimore rose from 168,000 before the war to 225,000 by 1947. Also evident is a shift of about 10 percent between traditional unskilled service and laborers' jobs for men (Table 1). Among women the shift is even greater (Table 2). Women moved away from prewar patterns of dependence on domestic service to more jobs in factories, offices and stores, and non-domestic service. The tables do not, however, show revolutionary change; a majority of black workers remained in the unskilled labor and service job categories.

The longest-lasting effects of Martin's wartime racial policies do not concern production or employment but the physical and social landscape of the city. Here the trend was in the direction of increased segregation. The company's preference for white in-migrant workers and the construction of a new suburb for them proved to be a powerful model for change. "Aero Acres" and the other new communities built near the plant reflected a decade's worth of innovative thinking in architecture and planning that had mostly gone to waste during the Depression. Prefabrication and new building materials provided single-family detached houses that were affordable even for ordinary factory workers. FHA financing also provided attractive and affordable garden apartments. Instead of the old urban grid, houses and apartments were laid out on gently curving streets and dead-end cul-de-sacs that moderated car traffic and provided residents better access to grass and trees. Advance planning also provided shopping and community centers, new schools, and modern, high-speed roads linking the new community to the city. These design features had previously been available only to residents of upper-income suburbs.[80]

They proved enormously popular after the war. Developers with wartime experience in large-scale production of low-cost housing during the war put their skills (and supporting government financing mechanisms) to use all across the country after the war. The Levitt Brothers, who had built wartime housing in Richmond and then built Levittowns in three states, are the most famous, but Baltimore has several local examples like Ralph DiChiaro and Henry Knott, who progressed from wartime housing to postwar suburban development.

Back in the city itself, racial segregation in housing increased during the 1940s. Donald Cowgill's index of dissimilarity between black and white residence by block grew from .847 in 1940 to .910 in 1950. From ranking as the forty-fifth most segregated city in at the beginning of the decade Baltimore "rose" to eighteenth place by 1950.[81] Population density in black neighborhoods, swollen by wartime in-migration, remained high despite physical expansion into Cherry Hill and Turner's Station.[82] Although these new settlements shared some of the planning ideas of the all-white suburbs—curving streets, cul-de-sacs, community buildings, and shopping centers as part of the overall plan, no more suburban sites were made available for such low-density developments. Instead, postwar attempts to provide better housing for Baltimore's African American citizens were located in the inner city and

FROM MOBTOWN TO CHARM CITY

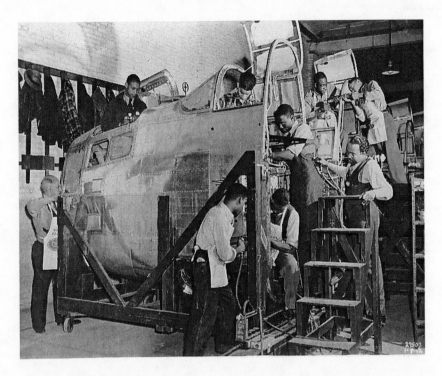

African American crew, with supervisor, at work on the nose assembly of an A-30 "Baltimore" bomber for the RAF. (Glenn L. Martin Aviation Museum.)

at the existing high density levels. This could only be accomplished by building up. Four clusters of high-rise housing projects built in the early 1950s managed temporarily to contain the black population within existing black neighborhoods. Eventually, this attempt to restrict the expansion of black neighborhoods failed. During the 1950s and 1960s African Americans occupied large tracts of formerly "white" housing.[83]

By then white Baltimoreans in greater numbers were moving to affordable suburbs of the sort pioneered in Middle River during World War II. Even here housing segregation increased. Again Middle River can serve as an example. In common with rural areas throughout eastern Maryland, it had contained a significant proportion of black residents before 1940. Two black church congregations trace their history back into the early nineteenth century. Glenn Martin's chauffeur, his only black employee before 1941, lived in Middle River.[84] The new subdivisions and garden apartments, though, were restricted to whites. The single-family houses were sold to their wartime tenants after 1945, with restrictive covenants specifying "white race only."[85] Middle River became known as a "white" suburb, a label it retains a half-century later.

Baltimore's black population emerged from World War II considerably larger, slightly better off economically, but increasingly concentrated and segregated. The war does not seem to have touched off a new militancy. No new organizations or leaders emerged. There were no protests over segregated factories like Martin, or even over massive layoffs of black workers in 1945. The cancellation of the Herring Run housing project in favor of less desirable sites brought complaints but no active protests.[86] Instead of launching the civil rights movement, the war launched some of the urban problems that have proven to be most resistant to it: the high-rise projects of the 1950s and "second ghetto" of the 1960s—as well their seeming opposites, the low-density, mostly white suburbs that extend ever farther from the old city center. Their differences mark the extent to which Baltimore's "wings of democracy" failed to soar.

Notes

I am very grateful to acknowledge financial support given to me for a "community history" project concerning the wartime history of the Martin Company and Middle River. Funds came from the Maryland Historical Trust, Maryland Humanities Council, National Trust for Historic Preservation, and the Baltimore County Office of Planning. Jessie Payne conducted oral history research on this project. Later support came from the Smithsonian Institution, National Air and Space Museum, which granted me a Verville Fellowship in 1996–97.

[1] Bureau of the Census, "Civilian Migration in the United States: December, 1941, to March, 1945," Special Reports, Series P-S, No. 5, September 2, 1945; John Jeffries, *Wartime America* (Chicago: Ivan Dee, 1996), ch. 4.

[2] Louis Ruchames, *Race, Jobs, and Politics: The Story of the FEPC* (New York: Columbia, 1953), 21; Sumner M. Rosen, "The CIO Era, 1935–55," in Julius Jacobson, ed., *The Negro and the American Labor Movement* (Garden City, N.Y.: Anchor, 1968); Richard M. Dalfiume, "The 'Forgotten Years' of the Negro Revolution, *Journal of American History (JAH)*, 55 (1968): 90–106; A. Russell Buchanan, *Black Americans in World War II* (Santa Barbara, Calif.: Clio, 1977), 132–34; Harvard Sitkoff, *A New Deal for Blacks*, Vol. I (New York: Oxford, 1978), 298; Doug McAdam, *Political Process and the Development of Black Insurgency 1930–1970* (Chicago: University of Chicago Press, 1982), 84; John Modell, Marc Goulden, and Sigurdur Magnusson, "World War II in the Lives of Black Americans: Some

Findings and an Interpretation, *JAH*, 75 (1989): 818–48; Merl E. Reed, *Seedtime for the Modern Civil Rights Movement* (Baton Rouge: Louisiana State University Press, 1991), 345–57; Richard W. Thomas, *Life for Us Is What We Make It: Building Black Community in Detroit, 1915–1945* (Bloomington: Indiana University Press, 1992), 313–20; William L. O'Neill, *A Democracy at War* (New York: Free Press, 1993), 238–41; Jeffries, *Wartime America*, 107–19; Joe W. Trotter and Earl Lewis, eds., *African Americans in the Industrial Age* (Boston: Northeastern University Press, 1996), 253.

[3] Richard Polenberg, *War and Society: The United States, 1941–1945* (Philadelphia: Lippincott, 1972), 99–130; John Morton Blum, *V Was for Victory* (New York: Harcourt Brace, 1976), 182–20; Karen Tucker Anderson, "Last Hired, First Fired: Black Women Workers during World War II," *JAH*, 69 (1982): 82–97; Alan Winkler, *Home Front U.S.A.* (Arlington Heights, Ill.: Harlan Davidson), 57–66; Daniel Kryder, "The American State & the Management of Race Conflict in the Workplace & in the Army, 1941–1945," *Polity*, 26 (1994): 601–34; and (revising his earlier view) Harvard Sitkoff, "American Blacks in World War II: Rethinking the Militancy-Watershed Hypothesis," in James Titus, ed., *The Home Front and War in the Twentieth Century* (Colorado Springs: U.S. Air Force Academy, 1984), 147–79.

[4] John R. Breihan, "Between Munich and Pearl Harbor: The Glenn L. Martin Aircraft Company Gears Up for War, 1939–1941," *Maryland Historical Magazine (MdHM)*, 33 (1993): 389–419.

[5] Harold Randall Manakee, comp, *Maryland in World War II* (Baltimore: War Records Division, Maryland Historical Society, 1950–58), vol. 2, passim.

[6] U.S. House of Representatives Select Committee Investigating National Defense Migration, pursuant to H.Res. 113, 77th Congress, 2nd Session, Fifth Interim Report, August 10, 1942, 17–18.

[7] Jo Ann E. Argersinger, *Toward a New Deal in Baltimore* (Chapel Hill: University of North Carolina Press, 1988), 3–7, 15–16; Karen Olson, "Old West Baltimore: Segregation, African American Culture, and the Struggle for Equality," in Elizabeth Fee, Linda Shopes, Linda Zeidman, eds., *The Baltimore Book* (Philadelphia: Temple University Press, 1991), 57–74; Andor Skotnes, "The Black Freedom Movement and the Workers' Movement in Baltimore, 1930–1939" (Ph.D. dissertation, Rutgers University, 1991).

[8] Amy Bentley, "Wages of War: The Shifting Landscape of Race and Gender in World War II Baltimore," *MdHM*, 88 (1993): 425–29.

[9] "Housing, Work, School Aid Is Proposed for Negroes," *Baltimore Sun*, March 23, 1943; "The Report of the Governor's Commission Demands Immediate and Close Attention," *Baltimore Afro-American*, March 27, 1943.

[10] Lester B. Granger, "Negroes and War Production," *Survey Graphic*, 31 (Nov. 1942): 469–70; Robert C. Weaver, *Negro Labor* (New York: Harcourt Brace, 1946), 18–21.

[11] Sitkoff, *New Deal for Blacks*, 300.

[12] Davis to Daniel Siemon, March 15, 1941, National Negro Congress Papers, Reel 26, Library of Congress (LC); "Negro Congress Demands Jobs at Aircraft Plant," *Pittsburgh Courier*, March 22, 1941.

[13] National Negro Congress Papers, Reel 26. LC.

[14] "Martin Plant to Yield on Job Policy," *Baltimore Afro-American*, September 27, 1941.

[15] "Negroes to Make Defense Job Plea," *Baltimore Sun*, March 23, 1941; Findings and Recommendations, Conference on the Participation of Negroes in National Defense, "National Defense Migration Baltimore Hearings, July 1 and 2, 1941" (Washington, USGPO, 1941), 6073–77. This conference was probably modeled on the November 1940 conference with a similar title held at Hampton Institute in Virginia. Ruchames, *Race, Jobs, and Politics*, 13–14.

[16] "National Defense Migration Baltimore Hearings," 6071–72.

[17] Ibid., 5966.

[18] Edward Lewis, president of the BUL, pointed out that this "puts the Negro in a hopeless dilemma: He cannot get a job because he has no training, and he cannot get the training because he could not get a job." Ibid., 6088.

[19] Ibid., 5975–76, 5970. The Murphy Homes housing project was later built on this site.

[20] Trotter and Lewis, 253; Sitkoff, *New Deal for Blacks*, 298.

[21] "War Dept. Balks FDR Order Against Jim Crow," *Daily Worker*, July 7, 1941; "Playing with Defense," *Baltimore Afro-American*, August 26, 1941.

[22] Eleanor Brady, "Well-known No. 8802," *Manpower Review*, 10 (December 1943): 5.

[23] "National Defense Migration Baltimore Hearings," 6022–6025.

[24] Report by T. P. Wright to War Production Board, July 11, 1941, WPB Policy Documentation Files, 313.05, "Aircraft," National Archives (NA); transcript of telephone conversation between Joseph Hartson and [George B.] Murphy, September 5, 1941, Glenn L. Martin Papers, box 11, LC.

[25] Martin Company Press Release #222, Glenn L. Martin Aviation Museum, Middle River, Maryland.

[26] After the war Perdue was principal of the George Washington Carver Negro Vocational High School.

[27] Martin Company Press Release #184, Glenn L. Martin Aviation Museum.

[28] "Negroes and the War Industries," *Baltimore Evening Sun*, April 13, 1942. This article is discussed in Weaver, *Negro Labor*, 22, with the incorrect date of March 13.

[29] "Negroes and the War Industries," *Baltimore Evening Sun*, April 13, 1942; "Report as to Progress," ibid., September 4; "Our Voluntary Manpower Program," ibid., November 20; "Negro Housing" report, Citizens Planning and Housing Association Papers, Series 1, Box 19, Folder 4, Langdale Library, University of Baltimore.

[30] "Baltimore as a Laboratory for Testing Man-Power Plans," *Baltimore Sun*, August 28, 1942; A. A. Liveright, "What's Ahead on Manpower?" *Personnel*, 10 (1942): 578–83; Larston D. Farrar, "Manpower Under a Microscope," *Nation's Business*, 30 (December 1942): 17–19.

[31] Henry McFarland to Frank Fenton, September 30, 1942, International Association of Machinists Papers (IAM Papers), Reel 332, Wisconsin Historical Society, Madison.

[32] War Manpower Commission (WMC), Labor Effectiveness Report on Mar-

tin Company, January 31, 1944, Appx. III.C.6, Records of the WMC, RG211, Entry 271, Box 5. I am indebted to Jacob VanderMeulen for this reference..

[33] Editorial "Our Number 1 Job Bottleneck," *Baltimore Afro-American*, August 25, 1945.

[34] "Negro Labor Getting Jobs in Industry," *Baltimore Sun*, June 21, 1942.

[35] "Significant Report on Progress Against Discrimination," *Baltimore Sun* editorial, September 30; Frank B. Ober, "Summary of the Report," ibid., October 12, 1942. The Martin Company Personnel Director was one of twelve white and six black commission members.

[36] "Door Is Open for Negroes in Industry," *Baltimore Sun*, September 29, 1942.

[37] "Negroes Hold Mass Meeting," *Baltimore Sun*, February 20, 1943; "Jobs for Negroes Urged at Meeting," ibid., March 15, 1944; "C.-P., Transit Co. Officials Rebuff TWE Committee," *Baltimore Afro-American*, March 13; "War Job Body Hires Secretary, Opens Office," ibid., March 20; W. A. Brower, "USES, War Plants Seek, Refuse Workers," ibid., March 27, 1943. See profile of Camper in Fee, Shopes, Zeidman, *Baltimore Book*, 75–76. See also his obituary, "Dr. John Camper, 83, Physician and Activist," *Baltimore Evening Sun,* November 22, 1977.

[38] "National Defense Migration Baltimore Hearings," 6023–6024.

[39] "Beehive Today, Canton Refused Role in Oblivion," *Martin Star*, 2 (October 1943), 15.

[40] Telephone conversation with the author, October 1995. See his oral history interview, Middle River Community History Project tapes, 21 MR96 JP/CT, Maryland Historical Trust, Crownsville.

[41] Middle River Community History Project tape, 4 MR 96 JP/JM.

[42] "Canton" photo file, Glenn L. Martin Aviation Museum.

[43] Edward S. Lewis, BUL, to Lester Granger, January 2, 1942, National Urban League Papers, Series 3, Box 13, LC.

[44] Alexander J. Allen, "Western Electric's Backward Step," *Opportunity: Journal of Negro Life* 22 (Summer 1944): 108–43.

[45] Protest Shipyard Jim Crow," *Baltimore Afro-American*, July 31; "Tensions Eased at Shipyard," ibid., August 7, 1943. Although it was rumored that the federal Fair Employment Practices Committee would hold hearings in Baltimore (see ibid., May 1, 1943), these never took place.

[46] Labor Market Developments Report for Baltimore, September 1942, Records of the U.S. Employment Service, Labor Market Surveys, Maryland, RG 183, box 161, NA; *A History of Eastern Aircraft Division*, 1944, copy in Johns Hopkins University Library.

[47] Henry McFarland to Frank Fenton, September 30, 1942, IAM Papers.

[48] "Negroes Hold Mass Meeting," *Baltimore Sun*, February 20, 1943; see also Michael Carter, "Head of CIO Sees Unionism as Bar to Post-War Race Hate," *Baltimore Afro-American*, March 27, 1943; Rod Ryon, "An Ambiguous Legacy: Baltimore Blacks and the CIO, 1936–41," *Journal of Negro History*, 65 (1980): 18–33.

[49] "Tydings Asks for Census of Negro Labor," "Drury Asked to Discuss Housing Complaint" *Sun*, July 21, 1943.

[50] Although both the IAM and UAW purchased newspaper ads, only the

UAW put one in the *Afro-American* (July 10, 1943); interestingly it stresses the UAW's patriotic no-strike pledge rather than equality issues.

[51] Nicholas Dragon (UAW) to Charlie Mitzel (War Production Board), June 22, 1943, enclosed with H. W. Brown (International President, IAM), to James Casey (WPB), June 30, 1943, Reel 332, IAM Papers; "This Week" column in *Baltimore Afro-American*, July 24, 1943.

[52] "NLRB Okays UAW Group at Martin's," *Sun,* October 20, 1943.

[53] Breihan, "Between Munich and Pearl Harbor," 403–4; *Life,* December 8, 1941.

[54] "2,000 Workers Leave Here Monthly, WMC Says," *Evening Sun,* August 24, 1943; WMC Labor Effectiveness Report, Appx. III.C .a1b, Charts IIIC (a1–a2), RG 211, Entry 217, Box 5, NA.

[55] John R. Breihan, "Glenn Martin and the Air City," *The Meaning of Flight in the 20th Century: National Aerospace Conference Proceedings* (Dayton: Wright State University, 1999), 431–37; John R. Breihan, "Historic and Cultural Resources of Middle River," National Register of Historic Places Multiple Property Documentation Form, Maryland Historical Trust, Crownsville (1996).

[56] Farrar, "Manpower Under a Microscope," 19.

[57] U.S. Office of War Information, "Wartime Problems and Conditions in the City of Baltimore, Maryland" (Washington: OWI, 1943)[copy in Johns Hopkins University Library], 4–7. I am indebted to Amy Bentley for this reference.

[58] Clark S. Hobbs, "Negroes and the Community," *Evening Sun,* November 20, 1935; "City Negroes Crowded Into Small Living Areas," ibid., February 12, 1940.

[59] Clark S. Hobbs, "Plight of the Non-Defense Workers," *Evening Sun,* September 26, 1941; "Park Barracks for Negroes Suggested," ibid., October 2, 1942.

[60] Office of War Information, "Wartime Problems . . . of Baltimore," 15–17; WPA Surveys of Vacancies in Dwelling Units of Baltimore, Maryland, February 10, 1941 and March 19, 1942, "Housing" Vertical File, Envelope 3, Maryland Department, Enoch Pratt Free Library, Baltimore; "Only 1 House Offered Every 15 Negroes Entering Baltimore," *Evening Sun,* October 14, 1944.

[61] "Health Peril Disclosed In Housing Here," *Sun,* September 18, 1942; "Overcrowding—A Perilous Phase of the Defense Boom," *Sun* editorial, October 4, 1941; "Abnormal Difficulties Confront This Commission," ibid., May 19, 1942.

[62] "Park Barracks," *Evening Sun,* October 2, 1942.

[63] "Negro Housing Foes Boo and Cheer Mayor," *Sun,* July 14; "City Council to Face Negro Housing Issue," ibid., July 21, 1943; Bentley, "Wages of War," 425–29.

[64] "Tydings Opposes Housing Project," *Sun,* July 22, 1943; "Tydings Asks for Census of Negro Labor," ibid., July 24.

[65] "Idle In-Migrants Make Trouble, Benson Says," *Evening Sun,* September 2, 1943; "Council Votes City Control of Housing," *Sun,* July 27, 1943.

[66] "Paul Robeson at Rally Here," *Evening Sun* July 31; "Unity Committee Invites Robeson," *Sun,* August 4, 1943.

[67] J. Harvey Kerns, "How Baltimore Eases Its Racial Tensions," *Sun* magazine, February 12, 1944. Perhaps because the turnout was only half the 30,000

expected (*Evening Sun*, August 21, 1943), the rally received surprisingly little publicity.

[68] "Recommendations of Local Baltimore Authorities on Negro Housing Submitted to the Federal Government," July 10, 1943, MS 2010, Box 142, Maryland Historical Society, Baltimore.

[69] This too aroused opposition from the adjoining neighborhood of Brooklyn.

[70] "Urban League Disapproves of Housing Sites," *Sun*, October 25 "FPHA Approves 4 Sites Recommended by HAB in Housing of Negroes," ibid., October 26; "War Homes Sites Dubbed Undesirable," *Baltimore Afro-American*, October 30, 1943; Clark S. Hobbs, "Cherry Hill's Possibilities," *Evening Sun*, April 13, 1944.

[71] Argersinger, *Toward a New Deal in Baltimore,* passim.

[72] Herbert Northrup, *The Negro in the Aerospace Industry* (Philadelphia: University of Pennsylvania, 1968), 19–21.

[73] Manakee, *Maryland in World War II,* 2:542–43.

[74] John R. Breihan, Stan Piet, Roger S. Mason, *Martin Aircraft, 1909–1960* (Santa Ana, Calif.: Narkiewicz/Thompson, 1995). 101–15; Victor C. Tannehill, *The Martin Marauder B-26* (Arvada, Colo.: Boomerang, 1997), 15–19, 36–42, 75–88.

[75] Labor Market Developments Report for Baltimore, September 1942, Records of the U.S. Employment Service, Labor Market Surveys, Maryland, RG 183, Box 161, NA; Glenn Martin to Gen. H. H. Arnold, November 2, 1943, copy in WMC Report, RG 211, Entry 217, Box 5, NA.

[76] William O'Neill also makes this point, *Democracy at War*, 237–41, 431.

[77] "Only 13 Left of 3,000 Former Martin Employees," *Baltimore Afro-American*, September 22, 1945.

[78] Oral history interviews with James Myers, Minerva Gordon, Middle River Community History Project tapes, 4 MR 96 JP/JM, 5 MR 96 JP/MG.

[79] Ibid., plus interview with Andrew Rock, Middle River Community History Project tapes, 16 MR 96 JP/AR, Calvin Lee Tolbert, 21 MR 96 JP/CT.

[80] Donald Albrecht, ed., *World War II and the American Dream: How Wartime Building Changed a Nation* (Cambridge, Mass.: MIT Press, 1995); John R. Breihan, "Aero Acres," in *Air & Space*, 14 (June/July 1999): 36–44.

[81] Donald O. Cowgill, "Trends in Residential Segregation of Nonwhites in American Cities, 1940–1950," *American Sociological Review*, 21 (1956): 43–47. The Taeubers subsequently produced a different "segregation index," which also shows a rise from 90.1 in 1940 to 91.3 a decade later. Karl E. Taeuber and Alma F. Taeuber, *Negroes in Cities* (Chicago: Aldine, 1965), 40.

[82] The Taeubers rank room-crowding in Baltimore second only to Cleveland and St. Louis among big cities. Ibid., 168.

[83] W. Edward Orser, *Blockbusting in Baltimore* (Lexington: University Press of Kentucky, 1994).

[84] Interview with Virginia Preston and Mildred Gardner, Middle River Community History Project tape, 27 MR96–JP/VP–MG.

[85] Aero Acres Civic Improvement Association, *Property Manual,* (Middle River MD, n.d.), 3.

[86] The Hollander Ridge housing project was eventually built on part of the land included in the original Herring Run scheme.

DEBORAH R. WEINER

From New Deal Promise to Postmodern Defeat: Two Baltimore Housing Projects

I N AUGUST 1995, the city of Baltimore threw a neighborhood celebra
tion complete with marching bands and commemorative T-shirts. The
occasion: the demolition of the six high-rises of Lafayette Courts, the
city's largest public housing project. A crowd of some 2,500 witnessed "one
of the largest multistructure implosions in the Western Hemisphere." Bricks
taken from the buildings before the blast were sold as souvenirs. While
some former Lafayette residents in the crowd protested the destruction of
their homes, most seemed to share the official view that the best way to
deal with the project's intractable problems was to tear it down and start all
over again. This strategy was not unique to Baltimore; according to the *New
York Times* the final decade of the 1900s witnessed "a national chain reaction to demolish high-rise public tenements," with Chicago, Newark, Atlanta,
and Philadelphia all participating.[1]

Yet, when it opened for occupancy in 1955, Lafayette Courts represented the latest thinking among public housing officials. To Baltimore's
black population, afflicted by a severe shortage of decent, affordable housing, it promised opportunity for a better life. However, serious problems
soon became apparent in Lafayette and other high rise public housing projects
built across the nation in the 1950s and 1960s. As these problems grew, the
social evils associated with poverty, such as crime, unemployment, welfare

Deborah R. Weiner received a Ph.D. from West Virginia University in 2002. The
Baltimore City Life Museums supported her research on Baltimore public housing as part of its Community Gallery initiative.

dependency, and squalid living conditions seemed to the public to intensify and concentrate in the massive hulking edifices that loomed over city neighborhoods throughout the country. Rather than distinguish among the various kinds of public housing and their varying degrees of success or failure, the media, political figures, and the public imagination seized on high-rise public housing—and by extension the very notion of publicly subsidized housing—as one of the most telling examples of failed liberalism, good intentions gone bad.

What happened to turn public housing from a promise to a widely-perceived failure? This essay addresses this question by studying the history of Lafayette Courts and a neighboring low-rise project, the Clarence Perkins Homes, which opened as one of the nation's earliest public housing projects in 1942. It traces the impact of federal and local government policies on the actual, day-to-day conditions of life at Perkins and Lafayette from their creation through the early 1970s, and also explores the political, social, and economic circumstances that influenced the two projects. It concludes that while misguided housing policies contributed to the breakdown of inner city public housing, the most significant factors were out of the hands of housing officials. Fierce opposition to public housing, present from the very start at local and national levels, shaped housing policy in decisive ways and at key points, while other federal and local urban policies worked to negate the best efforts of public housing advocates and officials. Meanwhile, economic and societal trends overburdened public housing and guaranteed its inability to fulfill its original goals.[2]

A Time of Hope: 1937–1949

In the 1930s, public housing was seen as a solution, not a problem. For the social workers, municipal reformers, and planners involved in the housing reform movement, decent housing was the key to "uplifting" the urban poor—the mostly foreign-born and African American low wage workers whose increasing concentration in the nation's industrial cities had alarmed white middle-class Americans since before the turn of the century. Ever since Progressive-era journalist Jacob Riis declared that "in the tenements all the influences make for evil" in his acclaimed exposé *How the Other Half Lives,* slums had been accused of breeding crime, disease, poverty, and immorality. Destroying overcrowded, dilapidated tenements and creating decent housing would solve a host of urban problems, many believed. According to influential reformer Edith Elmer Wood, "No nation can rise higher than the level of its homes. Whether we approach the subject from the point of view of health, morals, child conservation, industrial efficiency, Americanization, or good citizenship, the housing problem is fundamental."[3]

The title of Wood's most noted work, *The Housing of the Unskilled Wage Earner*, signifies how reformers defined the "urban poor"—as unskilled workers whose low earnings forced them into dangerous and unsanitary slums. Housing reformers hoped to accomplish several goals: to provide these people with decent low-cost housing; to rehabilitate their health and character, which they believed had suffered from the unhealthy slum environment; and to remove the blight of tenement housing from the nation's cities. But housers—as the early public housing pioneers called themselves—disagreed over the relative importance of these aims. Some focused on the effects of bad housing on the poor; they championed the creation of low-rent housing, preferably on vacant land in outlying areas. Others stressed the harm tenement districts caused to larger society; they saw slum clearance as the main objective. While these goals were not mutually exclusive, a "spirited contest" was "waged in housing circles . . . concerning low-rental housing versus slum clearance." Catherine Bauer, a major leader in the movement, saw early on that the division signaled a confusion about the movement's overall mission that could have serious consequences, and urged housers to "make clearer to ourselves what we really do want." The ongoing debate would have important policy implications for decades to come.[4]

The passage of the U.S. Housing Act in 1937, which provided federal funds for local governments to develop and operate low-rent housing, gave America its first full-fledged public housing program. Like all social legislation, the act emerged from a process of compromise among competing and often-hostile interests. Housing advocates used the potent idea of slum clearance to gain support and quell intense opposition. "Decades of anti-slum literature" by writers such as Riis had built a consensus on the evils of urban slums; moreover, city officials, businessmen, and real estate interests could see the potential economic benefits of redeveloping inner city areas. As a result, the act linked public housing to slum clearance by requiring the elimination of one unit of slum housing for every new unit of public housing built. Because the real estate industry strenuously protested that public housing would compete with private enterprise, the act limited the program to very low-income families who could not afford housing on the private market. In tying public housing to the concept of slum clearance and restricting it to the very poor, the act set precedents that would prove to be critical.[5]

After passage of the act, Baltimore public housing supporters fought for the creation of a housing authority which would receive federal funds to operate a local program. "Stubbornly anti-New Deal" Mayor Howard Jackson aligned with local real estate interests to oppose the city's participation, but after a comprehensive campaign by a broad-based housing coalition, the city council created the Housing Authority of Baltimore City (HABC) in December 1937. The coalition's role was highlighted by the National Association of Housing Officials (NAHO), which noted that the city formed the HABC "largely as the result of pressure from labor unions, Negro groups, and social welfare and civic organizations." The coalition also managed to get one African American appointed to the HABC governing board.[6]

Baltimore's new housing officials took as their mandate a 1934 report to the mayor on "blighted or slum areas" which noted, "Such areas are like festering sores, spreading their contagion to all contiguous territory, and a burden upon all other sections:—they must be tolerated no longer than necessary." In full accord with the slum clearance philosophy, the HABC confidently embarked on a "demolition and rehousing program" that, it assured the public, would improve wretched housing conditions while reducing crime, diseases such as syphilis and TB, and excessive costs to taxpayers for police, fire, and other municipal services.[7]

Taking into account such factors as land values and the location of properties already held by the city in tax foreclosures, the HABC selected five sites from among the "extensive regions of blight" identified in the 1934 report, and set about acquiring land from 1938 to 1940. Two of the sites were located just east of downtown. As the "port of entry" for immigrant groups this area contained the largest number of low-income white families in the city. It also contained a racially mixed section and a small but congested black enclave on its northern edge. The HABC decided to place a black project to the north, to be called Frederick Douglass Homes, and a white one to the south, which would be named Clarence Perkins Homes in honor of the HABC's first director, who died before the project was completed.[8]

This official segregation of housing projects followed both local and national patterns. Baltimore had enacted segregation ordinances in the years before World War I, and although these had been declared unconstitutional, real estate practices and white citizens' groups continued to enforce racial separation with the support of city officials. On the federal level, a small New Deal housing program had set a precedent in 1934 with the "neighborhood composition rule," which prevented federally funded projects from altering the racial composition of their neighborhoods. Housing authorities across the country, north and south, institutionalized residential segregation by designating their projects as "white" or "Negro," although some northern authorities built "mixed" projects in integrated neighborhoods. Because the HABC did not build mixed projects, it not only sanctioned segregation but actually increased it: the white-designated Perkins site was in the midst of a 38 percent black census tract in 1940, an unusually high level of integration for Baltimore.[9]

Residents of the future Perkins site expressed ambivalence about the impending destruction of their neighborhood in a 1938 newspaper account. They acknowledged parts of the area were "run down . . . crowded and miserable," but the article left the impression of a bustling, close-knit community where small homes and well-kept gardens vied with cramped and deteriorated housing. "I like it here and I always have," said a postal clerk named Potocki, owner of a home described by the *Sun* as well-painted, neat, and clean. "I'd like to come back again, but I guess it won't be the same neighborhood." Mary Struzinski, daughter of a stevedore, talked about her family's inability to find a larger house that they could afford. "It would be great to live in the new houses. Maybe we'll come back."[10]

Relocating the families it removed from condemned slums proved to be the HABC's greatest challenge in the early years. Since the authority destroyed more housing than it built, most residents of future public housing sites had to be moved to other parts of the city. To address the problem, housing authority officials decided that, in addition to the five slum clearance projects, two projects would be built on vacant land on the city's edge, one for whites and one for blacks. These projects would house some of the displaced slum residents; others would be assisted in relocating to private housing.[11]

This HABC decision no doubt received support from United States Housing Administration chief Nathan Straus, a firm advocate of housing in the "housing versus slum clearance" debate. The USHA encouraged local authorities to acquire cheaper vacant land on city outskirts. According to Straus, purchase of more costly slum sites led to higher project densities while profiting slum landlords. He noted that "all of the power of wealth and political influence was invariably exerted on behalf of purchase of slum sites" while the USHA's vacant land policies "aroused bitter opposition and constantly threatened the housing program with defeat." This issue in fact led to his resignation in 1942. Around the nation, the purchase of vacant land provoked the special ire of real estate groups, who often assisted and even led local site selection battles waged by property owners' associations. The HABC's selection of the two vacant sites prompted an immediate hostile response, including a lawsuit filed over one site (designated for whites) which resulted in "a sweeping opinion supporting the rights of the Authority." According to the HABC, opposition to the other site "was based on the claim that the use of vacant land would compete with private builders, and that negroes were to be placed on the edge of a white section of the City." The HABC moved the "negro" project to another site and managed to get approval of both projects from the city's Board of Estimates.[12]

Demolition at the Perkins site began in August 1940, and construction of the new housing began in October, but another unexpected challenge arose before the project was ready for occupancy—World War II. As defense industry workers poured into cities all over the country, causing tremendous housing shortages, the federal government directed housing authorities to house war workers in the projects they were preparing for occupancy. Income limits were waived, and Perkins opened in May 1942 with a population of newly arrived white war workers rather than low-income white Baltimoreans. The project contained 688 apartments, arranged in a series of three-story brick courtyard buildings.[13]

Public housing was always intended to be more than just bricks and mortar. Housing officials throughout the nation believed part of their duty was to help their tenants overcome whatever debilitating effects their previous slum environment had on their character and their way of life. In promoting social services for tenants, the USHA fused this Progressive notion of "uplift" with a New Deal enthusiasm for citizen participation. "Shelter alone is not enough," said one participant of a national public housing management workshop. Community activities should "offer the opportunity for the adequate use of leisure time through which we may expect improved social adjustments (and) the development of a community spirit." Baltimore officials subscribed to this view, and from the start the HABC enlisted other agencies in providing community services to its tenants. City departments, the Citizens Housing Council (an influential local civic group), the YMCA and YWCA conducted a variety of activities at public housing sites, and all the projects provided community space for special events and programs.[14]

Perkins offered services to its tenants even though its population of war workers did not necessarily come from slum housing. As soon as the project opened, the city's health department placed Baltimore's first Well Baby Clinic there. Mothers brought in twenty-two healthy babies on the first day. "Their diets and health habits will be subjects of conferences between the mothers and the clinic physicians and public health nurses," stated the health department. In fact, until the mid-1950s, most social programs related to housing were operated by the city's health department, indicating the extent to which housing and disease were linked in the minds of city officials. The city's recreation department offered "organized play" for 450 Perkins children each week, and a nursery school opened in late 1942. According to HABC managers, wartime employment for women, "quite usual among the Authority's tenants, has in turn created needs for greatly augmented child care and recreation."[15]

While the HABC invariably painted a rosy picture of its activities in its early years, controversies did occasionally erupt. In November 1942 the Perkins Tenant Council held a mass meeting "to demand more heat and hot water from the Federal Government." Management had limited the tenants to two days of hot water per week, and tenants complained that lack of heat was "causing the walls in many of the apartments to sweat, making the apartments damp and unhealthy to live in." After a meeting with the HABC director, the two-day limit was rescinded, although the heat issue was not fully resolved.[16]

After the war, "in line with the nationwide policy," the HABC embarked on a program "to return the projects to low rent occupancy." At Perkins, 20 percent of the tenants would have to move out because their incomes were too high. They were first given notices of ineligibility, then notices to vacate, on a drawn-out schedule starting in 1947. The HABC did not want to suddenly dump its over-income tenants into a housing market plagued by tremendous shortages at all income levels.[17]

Public housing advocates nationwide looked forward to resuming a construction program after the war to alleviate the massive shortage of low-income dwellings. A comprehensive housing bill was introduced into Congress in 1945, authorizing new public housing construction as one of its many provisions. But public housing legislation, difficult enough to pass during the New Deal 1930s, faced even tougher times in the conservative postwar era. The housers found themselves in a ferocious battle with the real estate industry. The National Association of Real Estate Boards and the National Association of Home Builders fired the first shot in a 1944 letter to Straus's successor: "We ask that no funds or priorities of any kind be used for permanent public housing during the war . . . (that) you refrain from adding to the growing hordes of public payrollers for an unnecessary purpose since private industry can produce better housing at less cost." When a comprehensive housing bill was defeated in 1946, NAHO's *Journal of Housing* noted that "the bill was lost just about 100 percent on the basis of its provision for an extended public housing program. The terms in which that program was attacked displayed an outrageous sense of irresponsibility in the face of the housing ills of this country."[18]

Public housing suffered from a political liability that resulted from the very measure that had allowed it to become politically possible in the first place. The 1937 act had restricted public housing to the very poor in order to appease the real estate industry, yet, as the historian Leonard Freedman has pointed out, "the profound weakness of the poor in the American system of government and politics" made its constituency powerless to shape its policies or advocate on its behalf. Supporters came from the small ranks of city officials, social workers, planners, and the like. Meanwhile, opposition came from many directions. Government ownership of housing smacked of socialism and ran counter to the ideal of home ownership, which was increasingly seen as an important American value in the postwar era. The real estate industry, not assuaged by public housing's position at the bottom of the housing market, lobbied against it in Congress and in highly effective public campaigns, calling it an enemy of free enterprise and a burden to taxpayers.[19]

Public housing supporters fought back with a campaign of their own, again relying heavily on the slum clearance argument. The *Journal of Housing* praised Chicago newspapers for publishing a series of articles with headlines such as "Human Beings Live in These Dirty Hovels" and "Children and Rats Bedfellows in Chicago's Slum Dwellings." The articles "gave unprecedented publicity to the need for better local housing . . . and a better national housing program," offered the *Journal*. Finally, after strong Democratic majorities were elected in 1948, Congress passed the Housing Act of 1949, with the public housing provisions barely squeaking through. Not surprisingly, slum clearance figured prominently. Title I provided funds for the redevelopment of blighted areas, going far beyond the 1937 measure by authorizing local governments to acquire land for a variety of purposes, not just housing. Reformers did achieve a victory with the inclusion of language that for the first time signified a federal government commitment to "the realization as soon as feasible of the goal of a decent home and a suitable living environment for every American family."[20]

By May 1950 the HABC had selected five sites for a new ten-thousand-unit program using funds from the 1949 act. Three were to be on vacant land "in order to provide a reservoir of dwellings for those families that will be displaced in the process of slum clearance." The other two sites were located along Fayette Street and Pratt Street in "one of the worst slum areas of the city"—between Douglass Homes and Perkins Homes, just east of downtown. The Fayette Street site would eventually become Lafayette Courts, an 816-unit development featuring the latest architectural innovation, a mixture of high-rise and low-rise buildings.[21]

Uneasy Years: 1949–1956

Early in 1950 the *Journal of Housing* proclaimed that "the art of architecture is beginning to serve democracy." The *Journal* noted "a new feeling among [architects] under the impetus of the Housing Act of 1949 . . . a sympathetic response to the needs of the families to be housed, a promise of great things to come." The *Journal* opened a debate on public housing design, printing a critique from an anonymous architect who charged that the existing public housing stock was "fundamentally deficient" and that its "monotonous and institutional appearance . . . was considered justified, at the time, for reasons of economy." Responses from several public housing officials, architects, and planners followed, including one from Philip Darling, Director of Development for Baltimore's housing authority, who agreed with many of the critic's ideas but argued that the consideration of cost was too critical to be ignored.[22]

In the 1950s grand visions clashed with rising housing costs and stingy congressional appropriations. These economic and aesthetic factors combined to create the public housing high rise. Darling explained the problem succinctly in 1952: "Slum sites have become so expensive that more dwelling units per acre are needed to absorb site acquisition costs." Rather than increase the density on the ground, HABC planners decided to build up. Elevator buildings would allow "more open space between buildings and increase the area which can be devoted to landscaping and recreational uses." In turning to the high rise, Darling and public housing officials across the nation followed influential Modernist architects such as Walter Gropius, who recommended high rise public housing to prevent "crowded-on-the-ground city districts" and to provide "more light, air, and tranquility, and better view." To Gropius, the high-rise was "a direct embodiment of the needs of our age."[23]

Not all housers reacted positively to the idea of the high-rise. Differences of opinion harkened back to the slum clearance versus low-rent housing debate: "high-risers stress the importance of getting rid of slums *now* . . . low risers talk more about the livability of new housing." While high-risers embraced the notion of supplanting ground-level slums with modern skyscrapers, low-risers argued that elevator buildings were highly unsuitable for children and that vast "open spaces" would prove largely unusable. Catherine Bauer observed that the high cost of slum site acquisition and demolition would force housing authorities to build high-rises at greater densities than most architects thought suitable. Comparing high-rises to the disastrous "dumbbell tenement" reforms of the late nineteenth century, she prophetically asserted,

> A great many historic mistakes have been made by putting the negative goal (of slum clearance) ahead of the positive one. . . . To make the ghettoes narrower, if higher, is indefensible retrogression . . . we are building highly subsidized skyscrapers at greater densities than ever . . . skyscrapers that will ultimately look just as obsolete as the "new law" tenements do today.[24]

Bauer and her allies were fighting a losing battle, partly because of the fierce opposition housing authorities encountered when they tried to acquire vacant land on city peripheries. In 1950 a Baltimore "citizens' neighborhood group" backed by "the home builders and the real estate fraternity" again forced the HABC to forgo a selected outlying site, an abandoned cemetery, even though the cemetery was "a rat infested jungle" with title problems that discouraged private developers. The project was intended for whites, so racial considerations did not play a role. On the other hand, the inner city Fayette and Pratt Street sites passed the city council by a vote of twenty to one.[25]

Despite frequent controversy, the HABC had reason to be proud as it celebrated its fifteenth anniversary in 1952. It had successfully developed some five thousand units of housing under the 1937 act and was in the midst of building ten thousand more. It offered its tenants a range of activities and programs and maintained a strong commitment to "tenant education," as the community services program began to be called in the 1950s. To critics who predicted the projects would revert to slums, the HABC asserted, "testimony to the contrary comes from the lips of many interested citizens, who have seen projects eight, ten, twelve years old, and have found deep satisfaction from the evidences of care and pride that these projects present."[26]

But problems loomed that would prove even more intractable than site battles. In 1951 the *Journal of Housing* printed a debate as to whether "problem families" should be excluded from public housing. New postwar terms such as "personal maladjustment" crept into the discussion, reflecting the growing influence of psychological theory. Social workers began to refer less to the "character" of the poor, which during the first half of the century was thought to respond favorably to improvements in environment, and to focus more on deep-seated psychological causes which they now believed required more systematic intervention. Yet the concept of "problem families" remained socially constructed and ill-defined, covering such diverse phenomena as mental and physical illness, criminal behavior, unemployment, "broken" (single-parent) families, and bad housekeeping practices. In addition, housers often expressed confusion over whom they actually intended to serve—"maladjusted" people in need of social uplift, or "deserving," "working poor" families who needed low-cost housing temporarily, before moving on to a home of their own. The HABC echoed this confusion. In its 1950 *Annual Report* it asserted that "A good many of our tenants use the benefits of public housing to tide them over a time of crisis or low earning power," while later in the report it promoted its tenant education efforts by observing that "a model house or apartment is no cure-all for deeply-entrenched attitudes and habits."[27]

In actuality, two types of tenants were being served: those who needed temporary help, and those who suffered from the effects of chronic poverty. But while tenants who increased their earning power were forced to move out when their incomes got too high, the tenants who could not advance economically stayed on. Some housers warned that for public housing to succeed, a balance between the two would have to be maintained. Instead, government policies and economic trends combined to upset the balance.

The Housing Act of 1954 introduced a new concept: urban renewal. The activities allowed by Title I of the 1949 act were expanded even further, and a new emphasis was placed on comprehensive planning, so that public housing became subsumed under the larger renewal process. The 1954 act required that priority for admission to public housing go to families displaced by urban renewal projects. As a result, "the opportunities were reduced for screening out the most disruptive 'problem families.'" Eventually, as prominent houser Elizabeth Wood later recalled, "If they didn't know what to do with a family they'd send them to a project. So there was a crash input of people on welfare and broken families. The feeling of the 'project people' changed . . . it was no longer a step up." Public housing became merely an urban renewal tool. Its reduced role was reflected in Baltimore in 1956 when the HABC was placed under the control of the new Baltimore Urban Renewal and Housing Agency. Formerly, housing and urban redevelopment had existed as separate but equal departments.[28]

As large federally funded renewal projects such as highway construction got underway, whole neighborhoods disappeared, along with the homes of large numbers of poor and working-class people. While the 1954 act channeled the displaced poor into inner city public housing, Federal Housing Administration loan policies successfully encouraged the working and middle classes to head for the suburbs. The urban poor were becoming increasingly isolated—and they were also becoming increasingly African American. The second great migration of southern blacks into the cities had started with the pull of defense work during World War II and continued through the 1950s as the mechanization of southern agriculture pushed black laborers off the farms. Like other cities, Baltimore experienced "white flight," aided by the "blockbusting" techniques of local realtors who played on the fears of white homeowners in order to stimulate real estate sales. The FHA assisted urban racial isolation by actively promoting restrictive covenants barring blacks from suburbia in its early years and continuing to support such discrimination at least until the early 1960s. Meanwhile, economic trends in the inner cities exacerbated the poverty of those who remained. As early as 1962, Michael Harrington noted that the flight of manufacturing from the central cities left few options for an unskilled labor force, and especially for African Americans whose social and geographic mobility was severely constrained.[29]

Baltimore's black population grew from 17 percent in 1935 to 40 percent by 1965. As the racial composition of the inner city changed, so did the racial composition of public housing. In 1951 blacks made up 54 percent of the city's public housing families; by 1961 they made up 74 percent. According to the HABC, housing and employment discrimination in the private market channeled blacks into public housing and kept them there longer than whites.[30]

In response to the 1954 Supreme Court desegregation ruling, the HABC adopted a desegregation strategy based on a "policy of preference" which allowed applicants to apply to the project of their choice without racial restriction. For Perkins Homes, the new policy would result in a "mixed" development. Anticipating his new clientele, the Perkins manager surveyed the facilities available to blacks in the neighborhood in late 1954. He noted that Perkins bordered "an all Negro and mixed area, as well as a section exclusively white . . . there is considerable doubt as to whether certain facilities such as restaurants, taverns, theatres etc. in the all White area will be available." Desegregation occurred quietly for the most part. By 1960 Perkins was 40 percent black. But the period of integration was brief; throughout the 1960s whites left the project, to be replaced by blacks, and by 1970 Perkins was 88 percent black. Lafayette, planned as an all-black development, officially opened as an integrated project. However, because it was built in a black neighborhood and previously designated for blacks, the HABC's "policy of preference" ensured that only a small handful of whites would apply to live there. Lafayette would open with a population that was virtually all-black, and would remain that way.[31]

Demolition of the Lafayette slum site started in late 1952, and construction of the new project began in August 1953. Following the pattern for high-rise developments suggested by Gropius and others, the project contained a combination of high- and low-rise buildings. Families with school-age children were intended to live in the low-rises and the lower floors of the high-rises. In all, six eleven-story buildings, ten three-story buildings, and seven two-story buildings were erected, containing 816 apartments on 21.5 acres, with a density of forty families per acre, well above the twenty-five to thirty families recommended by housing experts for high-rise developments. (In fact, Nathan Straus believed that densities should be no greater than twenty families to the acre.) The buildings covered less than 18 percent of the land, with the rest given over to parking, streets, and open space.[32]

The novelty of high-rise public housing intrigued the Baltimore press. Articles described Lafayette's design in great detail, usually echoing the HABC's rationale for various features. They duly noted that the high-rises contained cement tot lots on every floor so that small children would not have to travel down to the ground to play, and that the apartments opened onto outdoor corridors in order to achieve a sense of openness. However, the need to enclose these walkways with heavy-duty mesh to prevent children from falling gave "something of the effect of a well-kept prison," according to one reporter. This reporter, observing also that the floors were made of concrete, and bedroom closets were merely recessed alcoves with no doors, termed the buildings "Altitude Without Frills." Most newspaper accounts, however, stressed the similarities with more upscale high-rise developments, particularly referring to the views of the harbor.[33]

Lafayette opened with celebration and hope in April 1955. More than two thousand families applied for apartments, demonstrating that the housing was sorely needed by Baltimore's black population. The first three families to move in arrived from Holabird Homes, a deteriorated temporary housing project for black war workers that had long outlived its intended usage. Mrs. Irene Lee and her eight children, fertilizer company worker Charles and Cora Burton and their five kids, and cement blockmaker Edward Diggs, wife Ruth and six kids all moved into low rise buildings. Mrs. Lee's sentiments were typical of the early residents: "I have been hoping and praying that my family would get the chance to move in. It's everything I've dreamed of for so long." One month later the first family moved into a high-rise: Navy veteran John Greene and his wife had been on the HABC waiting list since 1949.[34]

"Troubled and Troublesome" Years: 1956–1968

Problems with Lafayette Courts began to appear even before it opened. Ceiling cracks developed, delaying the opening day. The ceiling cracks led to chipping paint, causing one of Mrs. Lee's daughters to get lead poisoning, and the family was moved to another Lafayette apartment. In March 1956 an HABC manager reported that children were managing to squeeze trash through the balcony fencing which then fell to the ground below, lobby windows were frequently broken, and teenagers were vandalizing the elevator areas. He recommended that security, which was practically nonexistent at the time, be increased.[35]

Perkins also experienced disturbances in 1956, including one with racial overtones. Nine white teenage boys were "continuously harassing" the black director of the Perkins Recreation Center and "were even threatening bodily harm." At a meeting to address the situation, a resident named Mrs. Gibson remarked that "there was little, if any difficulty at the housing project because of the racial question." Local police and community leaders were inclined to agree that "the racial factor" was not as important as the family background of the boys, many of whom came from troubled homes.[36]

By 1956 juvenile delinquency and "problem families" had become major issues for housing authorities around the nation. Vandalism, harassment, and gang fights occurred with increasing frequency. No longer could public housing officials debate whether or not to accept "problem families"; now the question was what to do about them. Social service programs began to receive greater attention in the *Journal of Housing*. In April 1957, the *Journal* devoted an entire issue to "Troubled and Troublesome Families." As a Newark public housing official wrote, "alarmed by the deterioration of project life, a number of the authority's best tenants began to leave." The HABC annual report for 1956 analyzed the problem in an essay entitled, "The Changing Nature of Baltimore's Public Housing Program," which concluded,

> The net effect of a rising economy, with its accompanying social trends, has been the elimination of many of the more self-sufficient

families among the low income population . . . and the addition of more households dependent on a wide range of assistance. This condition is not local in nature. It is spurring study throughout the country. . . . Instead of serving a cross section of the low income group, the Housing Authority finds itself serving more and more broken, old-age, and single person families, many of whom have serious problems. . . . Even though ["problem families"] constitute no more than five percent of the total . . . [they] are taking an increasingly disproportionate amount of staff time and services.[37]

Of course, juvenile delinquency was not unique to public housing. It had become a concern throughout American society, surfacing in popular culture in movies such as *Blackboard Jungle* and *The Wild One*. But public housing, which had always been subject to conservative attack, now became even more suspect for such social ills. In an article about public housing's "problem families," the *Wall Street Journal* in 1958 complained about "baby production by unmarried females living in tax-supported apartments . . . welfare and police cases, alcoholics, the chronically unemployed, and such."[38]

A sociological study of Lafayette Courts conducted between 1955 and 1958 reflected the growing concerns of reformers and social science experts. The researchers, from the Johns Hopkins University, had hypothesized that residents of "good" housing in Lafayette Courts would enjoy better physical, social, and psychological health than residents of "bad" housing in various neighborhoods throughout Baltimore. They found, however, that "close working experience with the population under study began to throw doubt on the likely pervasiveness of the influence of the housing environment." Residents at the brand new housing project showed only a slight improvement over "slum" residents in some categories and showed an actual decline in others.[39]

Lafayette residents who participated in the study expressed greater satisfaction with their housing, showed more interest in the upkeep of their community, had better relations with their neighbors, and slightly better physical health than residents of private housing. However, they expressed greater concern over "misbehaving" teenagers as well as fights between adults and between children. They suffered from moving away from their relatives and did not yet look on the project as "home." Perhaps most disappointing, improved housing conditions did not lead Lafayette residents to develop "heightened aspirations" for themselves, as the researchers had expected. The authors of the study refrained from drawing any overall conclusion, however, and pronounced the results decidedly "mixed."[40]

Public housing advocates and pioneers grew increasingly restive over trends in the field. Some even began to fear that "the wholesale leveling and rebuilding of city neighborhoods may often create as many social problems as they cure." In an influential 1957 article, Catherine Bauer criticized the paternalism and rigidity of public housing management. The many enemies of public housing had put its officials on the defensive, she asserted, and "the hostility had probably tightened management controls, making 'project' housing more and more institutional." Elizabeth Wood, first director of the Chicago Housing Authority, found the cause of public housing's growing problem in two policies: the increased enforcement of over-income rules and the obligation to serve families displaced by slum clearance. While she accepted the responsibility to house such families and called for a renewed commitment to social services, she stressed that public housing could not survive if "normal" families were forced out by income ineligibility or bad neighbors. She concluded that "so long as public housing is the temporary home of the capable, the honest, the ambitious . . . but it is the permanent home for the damaged, the non-moral, the deceitful—public housing will not produce good neighborhoods."[41]

Conditions in the high rises offered particular incentive for those with financial resources to leave. The difficulty of supervising children, the vast open spaces, and the inordinately high densities created an environment conducive to mayhem. The desperation of some families to move out is reflected in the Lafayette Courts management files as early as 1963, when a widow with four children wrote, "I would like a transfer from 1364 East Fayette to any where else in the city . . . this neighborhood is affecting me and my children physically and mentally."[42]

Constriction of economic opportunity led to an increasing reliance on public assistance for residents in public housing projects throughout the country. Analysts such as William Julius Wilson have revealed how inner city job loss made urban poverty increasingly difficult to escape, confirming Michael Harrington's earlier observations. In his study of Philadelphia public housing, John Bauman traced how urban renewal, industrial mechanization, corporate consolidation, and suburbanization combined in the 1950s to deprive residents of employment and increase their dependence on public aid. The same forces were at work in Baltimore. In 1950, 35 percent of Perkins households relied on public assistance. By 1974, 78 percent of the families at Perkins and 80 percent of the families at Lafayette received public aid.[43]

As Harrington had pointed out, large, impersonal public housing projects only contributed to feelings of hopelessness engendered by the lack of opportunity. Meanwhile, as the poor became more isolated inside public housing, the projects themselves became even more isolated by urban renewal. Despite the authorization of 810,000 units of housing in the 1949 act, Congress annually refused to appropriate money for new projects through most of the 1950s. However, money could be obtained for other types of urban renewal projects, and cities pursued those vigorously, turning former neighborhoods into highways, municipal buildings, or vast wastelands awaiting industrial development.[44]

Lafayette and Perkins were cut off from downtown by the construction of the Jones Falls Expressway in the early 1960s. Between 1960 and 1962, twenty-four acres just east and north of Lafayette were razed to make way for an industrial park that never materialized. By destroying 234 structures, this urban renewal project displaced 133 black and seventy-four white households and also removed commercial and industrial enterprises which had provided local jobs. The area remained vacant until the city built the new main post office in 1970. A "neighborhood" no longer existed around Lafayette Courts.[45]

As the 1960s progressed, vandalism, fights, and harassment at Lafayette and Perkins started to give way to more serious forms of trouble, such as robbery, assault, rape, and murder. Management tried to deal with these issues by imposing order first with social programs and, later, increased security. Perhaps responding to escalating racial tensions, Perkins held "Brotherhood Week." A flyer announcing the program featured black and white hands clasped together. In 1962, the Perkins manager noted some success in "encouraging" single mothers to marry their children's fathers, theorizing that children of unwed mothers were "likely to strike out in resentment and exhibit behavior taking the form of vandalism and rowdyism." As in many housing projects, management believed that the acceptance of middle-class norms—in particular the nuclear family—would make "problem" families "normal." However, as John Bauman and others have observed, efforts at social control may actually have worked against the development of strong families by discouraging reliance on extended kinship networks and other traditional sources of family nurturing. At the same time, welfare departments effectively undercut attempts to promote the nuclear family by imposing the "man in the house" rule, which dictated that only single mothers with children could receive welfare benefits. In interviews, two observers of life at Lafayette Courts emphasized how this rule broke up families and helped create an absence of an adult male presence at the project. From 1960 to 1970, the number of female-headed households at Lafayette increased from 43 percent to 71 percent.[46]

By the mid-1960s, Lafayette and Perkins turned to more direct efforts to control an increase in crime and disorder. Both projects hired a private security firm in 1965. The Lafayette manager reported in 1966 that "a number of watchmen have requested and received transfers due to 'unpleasant working conditions.'" In 1967 tenant groups at both projects became more active in trying to improve project life, aided by Community Action Agencies that appeared on the scene that year. Occasionally the tenant groups clashed with management; the CAA brought a measure of militancy that had previously been absent. The CAA coordinator at one point complained that Perkins manager Joel Newton "made it clear to me that he did not need me to help him 'manage his tenants.'" The management files of both Lafayette and Perkins reveal a significant increase in tension throughout the year, perhaps bearing out the claim of political scientists Bachrach and Baratz that "the new mood of exasperation and impatience among blacks [in Baltimore] was partially a direct result of the 'educational' work of community organizers."[47]

Isolated by race, class, and geography, housing projects such as Lafayette and Perkins were natural places for mass discontent to break out in the highly charged 1960s. As riots hit many other major cities from 1965 to 1967, many Baltimore whites thought their city had been spared. They were wrong. On April 6, 1968, two days after the assassination of Martin Luther King, unrest turned into mass disorder. It started with the smashing of a window on the 500 block of North Gay Street, just north of Lafayette. The riot spread throughout Baltimore's ghettoes. At Flag House Courts, the housing project just to the south of Lafayette, tenants in the high-rises threw bottles at the police and firemen below. On Monday at 2 P.M., a large crowd of whites was seen forming on the east side of Broadway near the Perkins Homes . . . inhabited primarily by Negroes. A group of small Negro children in the homes gestured at the white crowd—mostly boys in their upper teens. . . . There was much taunting and swearing by both groups. As some of the whites entered the projects, a shower of bottles and bricks greeted them.

National Guardsmen arrived and broke up the confrontation.[48]

Years later, people who lived and worked in the area remembered the riot as a major turning point. Dwight Warren grew up in Lafayette Courts but moved in the mid-1960s when his family's earnings became too high. He later returned to the neighborhood to direct a local community center. Warren believed that the riots "made the young black man bitter," and that bitterness never subsided. Neighborhood health clinic administrator Earline Washington and community activist Irona Pope also cited the riots as marking a significant change. To Washington it "seemed like from there it just went down, down, down, down." Some of the few community businesses that had survived urban renewal were damaged in the riots and never reopened. Most whites would no longer enter the area. Lafayette in particular, and Perkins to a lesser extent, became more isolated than ever.[49]

Epilogue: Post-1968

To compound these problems, the Nixon years brought decreased funding for public housing. The 1969 Brooke Amendment stipulated that tenants were to pay no more than 25 percent of their incomes for rent; the federal government was to make up the difference between operating costs and rental income. In 1972 HUD cut this subsidy "substantially," and housing authorities, no longer allowed to increase rents, were left with holes in their budgets. A growing inability to pay for maintenance and services led to rapid property deterioration. The administration's rhetoric did not bode well for the future. HUD Secretary George Romney declared, "I am taking a look at the question of whether I am going to tell twenty cities in this country, 'There are certain areas of your city we are not going to put any more money in because it will be wasted.'" Given the state of public housing, the few advocates left had little strength to fight back.[50]

Throughout the late 1950s and 1960s public housing friends such as

Catherine Bauer and Elizabeth Wood had sounded warnings about misguided policies. Evicting over-income people, building massive high-rises, and promoting slum clearance and urban renewal all served to isolate the poor in huge, impersonal, alienating structures within devastated central cities. However, intense opposition to public housing from the real estate industry, conservative politicians, and citizens groups drove those policies from the very start and played a major role in the result. Meanwhile, economic and societal trends such as the flight of manufacturing from the cities, the development of pockets of poverty amidst rising affluence, the intensification of residential racial segregation, and the suburbanization of America—all assisted by government policy—contributed to the failure of public housing to live up to its promise.

The pioneers of public housing asked too much of it. Decent low-cost housing could not, all by itself, eliminate the evils of poverty. Their grand claims—the claims of the slum clearance movement—contributed to public housing's eventual downfall by raising expectations and encouraging massive alterations in the patterns of our cities. Lee Rainwater, in a mid-1960s study of St. Louis's notorious Pruitt-Igoe housing project, noted that his research team attempted to figure out where the project went wrong but soon "found ourselves pushed to questions at even higher levels." Unlike the Lafayette Courts researchers, he did not shy away from the conclusion that housing policies "have had almost no impact on the poverty problem as such." To Rainwater, the key to poverty was not bad housing but "income inequality," and the solution lay not in improving the housing or habits of the poor, but in increasing their relative income through full employment, higher wages, and other measures. By ignoring the income problem, federal policy only created "a more visible kind of slum, and by its very existence as a *public* program highlights the failure of the federal response to poverty."[51]

Ultimately, the story of public housing reflects the failure of America to adequately confront poverty, racism, and urban decline. Nevertheless, in its first couple decades in Baltimore and across the nation, public housing operated quite well, fulfilling a valuable function often obscured by the rhetoric of reformers, politicians, critics, and the media: providing decent, low-cost housing to people who truly needed it. (Notwithstanding that policymakers constantly added to the numbers of people in need with their slum clearance and urban renewal activities.) To this day, it continues to serve as an alternative for people who have no other. The latest version of "slum clearance," the destruction of the Lafayette high-rises, forced Baltimore officials to relocate hundreds of residents, just as they had had to relocate people to make way for Lafayette. This task could not have been easy, because the same conditions pertained in the 1990s as in the 1930s—an acute shortage of decent and affordable housing.

Meanwhile, the city announced plans to pursue a new housing policy—the creation of low-income townhomes rather than high-rises. But the experience of Perkins Homes suggests that low-rise housing, while not as conspicuous or perhaps as debilitating as life in a high-rise, still isolates the poor and concentrates such phenomena as unemployment and welfare dependency. Moreover, prospects for adequately funding such a program were even bleaker at century's end than they were for the underfunded programs of the past. In 1952, Catherine Bauer warned that unless housing officials learned from past mistakes, high-rises would prove no more successful than the failed Progressive-era "dumbbell tenements." Her advice certainly holds true today. To turn the destruction of Lafayette Courts from a symbol of failure into something positive, policymakers would do well to examine the history of such projects. They will find that housing strategy cannot be conceived in a vacuum.[52]

[1] Charles Cohen, "Destroying a Housing Project, to Save It," *New York Times,* August 21, 1995.

[2] While many scholars have written about national trends in public housing, few local studies have been attempted. One prominent exception is Lee Rainwater's study of Pruitt-Igoe in St. Louis, *Behind Ghetto Walls: Black Families in a Federal Slum* (Chicago: Aldine Publishing Company, 1970). In *The Origins of the Urban Crisis: Race and Inequality in Postwar Detroit* (Princeton: Princeton University Press, 1996), Thomas Sugrue uses Detroit as a case study to argue that "a multiplicity of structural forces" revolving around race, economics, and politics interacted to produce the nation's urban crisis, with public housing as a key arena for conflict (5). Peter Harry Henderson's "Local Deals and the New Deal State: Implementing Federal Public Housing in Baltimore, 1933–1968" (Ph.D. dissertation, Johns Hopkins University, 1994) focuses on the role of local actors in shaping and implementing federal housing policy.

Other local studies include: John F. Bauman, *Public Housing, Race, and Renewal: Urban Planning in Philadelphia, 1920–1974* (Philadelphia: Temple University Press, 1987); Arnold R. Hirsch, *Making the Second Ghetto: Race and Housing in Chicago, 1940–1960* (New York: Cambridge University Press, 1983); Anthony Jackson, *A Place Called Home: A History of Low Cost Housing in Manhattan* (Cambridge: MIT Press, 1976); Douglas S. Massey, "Public Housing and the Concentration of Poverty," *Social Science Quarterly,* 74 (March 1993). For an examination of public housing in popular discourse, see A. Scott Henderson, "'Tarred with the Exceptional Image': Public Housing and Popular Discourse, 1950–1990," *American Studies,* 36 (Spring 1995).

[3] Jacob Riis, *How the Other Half Lives* (1890; repr. New York: Charles Scribner's Sons, 1936), 3; Edith Elmer Wood, *The Housing of the Unskilled Wage Earner: America's Next Problem* (New York: The MacMillan Company, 1919), 1. On the genesis of the housing reform movement, see Roy Lubove, *The Progressives and the Slums: Tenement House Reform in New York City, 1890–1917* (Pittsburgh: University of Pittsburgh Press, 1962).

[4] Mabel L. Walker, *Urban Blight and Slums* (Cambridge: Harvard University Press, 1938), 128; Catherine Bauer, "'Slum Clearance' or 'Housing,'" *Nation* (December 27, 1933): 731. For an exploration of the evolution of thinking among housing reformers, planners, and urban policymakers, see Robert B. Fairbanks, *Housing Reform and the Community Development Strategy in Cincinnati, 1890–1960* (Urbana: University of Illinois Press, 1988).

[5] Lawrence Friedman, *Government and Slum Housing: A Century of Frustration* (Chicago: Rand McNally & Company, 1968), 110; Alexander Von Hoffman, "Slums and Housing: The Fateful Marriage," paper delivered at the Organization of American Historians Conference, April 2, 1995, Washington, D.C.

[6] Jo Ann E. Argersinger, *Toward a New Deal in Baltimore: People and Government in the Great Depression* (Chapel Hill: University of North Carolina Press, 1988), 94–99; Coleman Woodbury, ed., *Housing Yearbook 1940* (Chicago: National Association of Housing Officials, 1940), 63. NAHO was formed in late

1933 by federal, state, and local officials involved in an increasing number of housing activities during the early New Deal years. It provided training to members and advocated for national housing policies. In 1954, it changed its name to the National Association of Housing and Redevelopment Officials (NAHRO), reflecting the ascendancy of the urban renewal approach.

[7] Housing Authority of Baltimore City (HABC), *Baltimore Building Low Rent Homes: First Report, 1939* (Baltimore: HABC, 1940), 10, 14–15.

[8] HABC, *Baltimore Building Low Rent Homes*, 6, 14, 19; "Area To Be Known as Perkins' Homes," *Baltimore Sun*, August 24, 1939.

[9] Sherry Olson, *Baltimore: The Building of an American City* (Baltimore: Johns Hopkins University Press, 1980), 277, 372; Hirsch, *Making the Second Ghetto*, 14; U.S. Census Bureau, *16th Census of the U.S., 1940, Housing: Baltimore Block Statistics* (Washington D.C.: Government Printing Office, 1942).

[10] "Section F's Excited Over Slum Plan," *Baltimore Evening Sun*, June 4, 1938.

[11] Argersinger, *Toward a New Deal in Baltimore*, 103; HABC, *Baltimore Building Low Rent Homes*, 15.

[12] Nathan Straus, *The Seven Myths of Housing* (New York: Alfred A. Knopf, 1944), 53, 61–62; Roger Biles, "Nathan Straus and the Failure of U.S. Public Housing, 1937–1942," *Historian*, 53 (Autumn 1990); Rosalie Genevro, "Site Selection and the New York City Housing Authority, 1934–1939," *Journal of Urban History*, 12 (August 1986); Coleman Woodbury and Edmond Hoben, eds., *Housing Yearbook 1941* (Chicago: NAHO, 1941), 93; HABC, *Baltimore Building Low Rent Homes*, 15. For an analysis of the issue of race in public housing site selection battles, see Sugrue, *Origins of the Urban Crisis*, 57–88.

[13] HABC, *Public Housing in Baltimore, 1940: Second Report* (Baltimore: HABC, 1941), 13; HABC, *Public Housing in Baltimore, 1941–42: Third Report* (Baltimore: HABC, 1943), 7.

[14] Argersinger, *Toward a New Deal in Baltimore*, 106, 112; National Association of Housing Officials, *Managing Low Rent Housing* (Chicago: NAHO, 1939), 125–126; William Theodore Durr, "The Conscience of a City: A History of the Citizens' Planning and Housing Association and Efforts to Improve Housing for the Poor in Baltimore, 1937–1954," Ph.D. dissertation, Johns Hopkins University, 1972; "Prospective Tenants to Get Lessons in Home Furnishing," *Baltimore Sun*, August 31, 1940; HABC, *Report to the Commissioners, 1943*, 6.

[15] Baltimore City Health Department, "City Authority and Health Department Build Together," *Baltimore Health News*, 1942; HABC, *Report to the Commissioners*, 1942, 8; HABC, *Report to the Commissioners, 1943*, 3.

[16] "Turn Up Heat Is Demand of U.S. Tenants," *Baltimore Sun*, November 18, 1942.

[17] HABC, *Annual Report of the Housing Authority of Baltimore City, 1947* (Baltimore: HABC, 1948), 5–7.

[18] "Realtors, Home Builders, U.S. Chamber of Commerce Challenge Administrator Blandford on Public Housing," *Journal of Housing*, 1 (November 1944): 19; "The Failure," *Journal of Housing*, 3 (August 1946): 162.

[19] Leonard Freedman, *Public Housing: The Politics of Poverty* (New York: Holt, Rinehart and Winston, Inc., 1969), x, 9–17.

[20] "Housing Makes Headlines in Chicago," *Journal of Housing,* 2 (1945): 23; Freedman, *Public Housing: The Politics of Poverty,* 1, 17; "Housing Act of 1949 Is Passed by House—Victory in Sight," *Journal of Housing,* 6 (1949): 214.

[21] *HABC Monthly Report,* May 1950, 1.

[22] "The Art of Architecture Is Beginning to Serve Democracy," *Journal of Housing,,* 7 (1950): 42; "The New Issue in Public Housing," *Journal of Housing,* 7 (1950): 202; "A Technician Agrees," *Journal of Housing,* 7 (1950): 304.

[23] Philip Darling, "HABC Considering Use of Elevator Buildings," *HABC Quarterly Review,* January 1952; "High Rise Housing: Does It Have a Place in the Public Housing Program?" *Journal of Housing,* 9 (1952): 46.

[24] "Why the Argument?" *Journal of Housing,* 9 (1952): 227–29.

[25] "Housing Site Problems," *Journal of Housing,* 9 (1952): 48; "Baltimore Cemetery Site Opposed," ibid., 7 (1950): 9; "City News," ibid., 7 (1950): 125; "City News," ibid., 7 (1950): 269; Hans Froelicher, Jr., "Citizen Action," ibid., 8 (1951): 271; *HABC Monthly Report,* October 1949; *HABC Monthly Report,* July 1950.

[26] HABC, "Fifteen Years of Public Housing," unpublished report, 1952.

[27] Bette Jenkins, "Problem Families," *Journal of Housing,* 8 (1951): 283; Sara Hartman, "First 'Problem Family' Step—Get the Facts: This Was Baltimore's Approach," ibid., 14 (1957): 118–19; HABC, *Twelve Questions: Annual Report, 1950* (Baltimore: HABC, 1951), 6, 13.

[28] "Housing Act of 1954," *Journal of Housing,* 11 (1954): 261; Freedman, *Public Housing: The Politics of Poverty,* 110; Elizabeth Wood quoted in Studs Terkel, *Hard Times: An Oral History of the Great Depression* (New York: Pantheon, 1970), 386.

[29] Hirsch, *Making the Second Ghetto,* 10; George Groh, *The Black Migration: The Journey to Urban America* (New York: Weybright and Talley, 1972), 63; Nicholas Lemann, *The Promised Land: The Great Black Migration and How It Changed America* (New York: Alfred A. Knopf, 1991); Amos Hawley and Vincent Rock, *Segregation in Residential Areas: Papers on Racial and Socioeconomic Factors in Choice of Housing* (Washington, D.C.: National Academy of Science, 1973), 118; Michael Harrington, *The Other America* (New York: MacMillan Publishing Company, 1969 [1962]), 10–11, 79. For a recent study of segregation, the real estate industry, and "white flight" in Baltimore, see W. Edward Orser, *Blockbusting in Baltimore: The Edmondson Village Story* (Lexington: University Press of Kentucky, 1994).

[30] Peter Bachrach and Morton S. Baratz, *Power and Poverty: Theory and Practice* (New York: Oxford University Press, 1970), 69; HABC, *The Characteristics of Families in Low Rent Public Housing, 1951* (Baltimore: HABC, 1952), 12; Baltimore Urban Renewal and Housing Agency (BURHA), *Types of Families Living in Baltimore's Low-Rent Projects, 1951–1961* (Baltimore: BURHA, 1962), 3; *HABC Quarterly Review* (Summer 1952): 4, 15.

[31] Ellis Ash, "The Baltimore Story: An Account of the Experience of the HABC in Developing and Applying a Desegregation Policy," unpublished paper, 1955; HABC Project Files, Baltimore City Archives (BCA), Record Group 48, Series 14, Box 41, "Report on Neighborhood Negro Facilities," October 26, 1954; U.S. Census Bureau, *U.S. Census of Housing, 1960, City Blocks: Baltimore, Maryland* (Washington, D.C.: Government Printing Office, 1961); Ibid., *Block Statis-*

tics, *Baltimore, MD Urbanized Area: 1970 Census of Housing* (Washington, D.C.: Government Printing Office, 1971).

[32] "Lafayette Courts," HABC Fact Sheet, May 1955; Straus, *The Seven Myths of Housing,* 68.

[33] Dudley P. Digges, "Altitude Without Frills," *Baltimore Evening Sun,* May 24, 1955; "Ten 12-Story Business Area Dwellings Due," *Baltimore Sun,* February 24, 1952; "Rooms With a View," *Baltimore Sun,* April 3, 1955.

[34] "First Tenants Move Into Lafayette Courts," *Baltimore Afro-American,* April 14, 1955, 17; "First Family to Move Into New Apartment," *Baltimore Evening Sun,* May 20, 1955.

[35] "Lafayette Courts Still Delayed," *Baltimore Afro-American,* March 5, 1955; Irona Pope, interview with the author, Baltimore, July 1994; HABC Project Files, BCA Record Group 48, Series 14, Box 23, "Field Inspection Report," March 6, 1956.

[36] HABC Project Files, BCA Record Group 48, Series 14, Box 41, "Perkins Homes Recreation Center Situation," January 1956.

[37] "Juvenile Delinquency," *Journal of Housing,* 12 (1955): 44; "Troubled and Troublesome Families," ibid., 14 (1957): 117; "Tenant Relations Experiment," ibid., 15 (1958): 13; HABC, *Focus on the Future: 1956 Report* (Baltimore: HABC 1957), 1–3.

[38] Ray Vicker, "Taxpayers' Tenants: 'Problem Families' Hike Public Housing Upkeep, Help Create New Slums," *Wall Street Journal,* April 10, 1958.

[39] Daniel M. Wilner, et al., *The Housing Environment and Family Life: A Longitudinal Study of the Effects of Housing on Morbidity and Mental Health* (Baltimore: Johns Hopkins University Press, 1962), ix. Wilner's method consisted of surveying Lafayette residents and control group residents (who lived in private "slum" housing) with a series of multiple choice questionnaires, and analyzing the results statistically.

[40] Wilner, et al., *Housing Environment and Family Life,* 198–200, 243, 248–50.

[41] Stanley Penn, "Public Housing Friends Complain of Its Failure to Remedy Social Ills," *Wall Street Journal,* January 11, 1963; Catherine Bauer, "The Dreary Deadlock of Public Housing," *Architectural Forum,* 106 (May 1957): 140; Elizabeth Wood, "Public Housing and Mrs. McGee," *Journal of Housing,* 13 (1956): 424–28.

[42] HABC Project Files, RG 48, Series 14, Box 23, BCA.

[43] William Julius Wilson, *The Declining Significance of Race* (Chicago: University of Chicago Press, 1978); John Bauman, et al., "Public Housing, Isolation, and the Urban Underclass: Philadelphia's Richard Allen Homes, 1941–1965," *Journal of Urban History,* 17 (1991): 264; HABC, *The Characteristics of Families in Low Rent Public Housing, 1951,* 75; Baltimore Dept. of Housing and Community Development (HCD), *Statistical Bulletin, 1974.* Statistics on public aid at Perkins and Lafayette were not found for the intervening years.

[44] Harrington, *The Other America,* 149; Freedman, *Public Housing: The Politics of Poverty,* 22.

[45] Baltimore Urban Redevelopment and Housing Agency (BURHA), *Outline*

of *Urban Renewal, Baltimore, 1961;* BURHA, *1966 Highlights,* 23; 1952 Sanborn Map, corrected to 1965; HCD, *1971 Annual Report,* (Baltimore: HCD, 1972), 7.

[46] HABC Project Files, RG 48, Series 14, Box 41, BCA; Bauman, et al., "Public Housing, Isolation, and the Urban Underclass," 282; Dwight Warren, interview with the author, July 1994; Earline Washington, interview with the author, July 1994; BURHA, *Types of Families Living in Baltimore's Low-Rent Projects, 1951–1961;* U.S. Census Bureau, *Block Statistics, Baltimore, MD: 1970 Census of Housing.*

[47] HABC Project Files, RG 48, Series 14, Boxes 21, 23, 41, 42, BCA; Bachrach and Baratz, *Power and Poverty,* 86.

[48] Bachrach and Baratz, *Power and Poverty,* 86; *Baltimore Sun,* April 8, 1968; April 9, 1968.

[49] Irona Pope, Dwight Warren, Earline Washington interviews.

[50] "Senator Edward W. Brooke Explains How New Public Housing Rent Reductions and Operating Subsidies Will Be Funded By HUD," *Journal of Housing,* 29 (1972): 69; HCD, *Baltimore Public Housing* (Baltimore: HCD, 1973), 2; William Lilley and Timothy B. Clark, "Immense Costs, Scandals, Social Ills Plague Low-Income Housing Programs," *National Journal,* July 1, 1972, 1075.

[51] Rainwater, *Behind Ghetto Walls: Black Families in a Federal Slum,* 399, 408–9. Rainwater's method consisted of participant observation and in-depth interviews with public housing residents.

[52] Cohen, "Destroying a Housing Project, to Save It."

KENNETH DURR

The Not-So-Silent Majority: White Working-Class Community

O N JUNE 14, 1976, Gloria Aull told a Senate subcommittee about her neighborhood. Mrs. Aull, fifty-one years old and the third gen eration to live in her family's Southeast Baltimore row house, ex-plained: "Our problems were not with the people of our neighborhood. The source of our dilemma was with government policymakers. . . . We were written off. We were supposed to be the silent majority."[1]

Neither Aull nor her fellow activists in Baltimore's Southeast Community Organization fit the description of "the silent majority." The Southeast Community Organization (SECO) became know nationally as one of the more successful of the grassroots, ethnically based community organizations to spring up in the early 1970s. SECO and groups like it gave white working-class people a voice at a time when many were experiencing mounting economic and social distress and feeling increasingly marginalized by American politics.

The new neighborhood organizations were overtly political—they ac-cumulated and used power to effect social change. But their politics is hard to classify. Some of the social conservatism that marked traditional neighbor-hood protective associations remained. Nevertheless, in its early period, it was avowedly anti-establishment. It empowered otherwise "silent" Baltimoreans and encouraged them to seek change outside of the traditional channels of urban politics.

Although it was centered in white working-class Southeast Baltimore, SECO's base was broad. Middle-class gentrifiers and long-time working-class

Kenneth Durr is a senior historian and director of the History Division at History Associates Incorporated in Rockville, Maryland.

residents, socially conservative Catholics and self-styled radicals mingled in SECO. Working-class activists clashed with its middle-class reformers especially on racial matters. More importantly, conflicting visions of what community activism should be—visions derived from differing urban experiences—finally led many working-class whites to reject SECO.

The trajectory of Baltimore's white working-class organizations during the late 1960s and early 1970s reveals much about white working-class politics. Working whites were above all motivated by deeply ingrained beliefs in democracy and the efficacy of common people. On race, most working whites shared a well-defined position. Experience taught them that "forced" integration, the reigning liberal solution to urban racial inequities, was ineffective, destructive, and most importantly, unfair. Middle-class liberals valued a politics of ideas and ideals, but white working-class politics was grounded in practice—it derived from, and sought to protect, white working-class community.

The incompatibility of these visions on the community level underscores their importance in reshaping American politics. Harbors for a brand of populism that helped drive the nation's conservative political turn in the 1980s, community organizations like SECO link the "white backlash" of the 1960s with contemporary politics. Working-class community activism took up the fragments of New Deal liberalism that survived the upheavals of the 1960s and helped reassemble them into a new form of working-class politics for late twentieth-century America.

Community Organizations in Baltimore

Beginning in the 1880s, Baltimore's early neighborhood associations fought declining property values and pried increased services from city hall. By 1900 there were over thirty such organizations, mostly in middle-class neighborhoods.[2] Some of these groups came together in 1911 to found the Baltimore City-Wide Congress.

Through the 1920s, the City-Wide Congress sought to protect middle-class neighborhoods from racial turnover and backed city ordinances excluding blacks from white areas.[3] A successor organization, the Allied Civic Improvement and Protective Association, advocated "holding up to public scorn" those who sold "white" real estate to blacks.[4] World War II boosted Baltimore's already large black population, and African Americans' search for housing put increased pressure on white areas. After the war a host of neighborhood protective associations took up the fight against racial changes.[5]

Baltimoreans organized around issues besides race, however. A controversial 1953 zoning law sparked a flurry of organizing. Homeowners established thirty-six neighborhood improvement organizations over the next four years, doubling the number of existing groups.[6] In the mid- to late 1940s, several community councils appeared in working-class South Baltimore. Southeast area groups, largely insulated from black expansion, emphasized social and educational programs more than racial exclusion. The community councils though, remained essentially conservative organizations with limited goals, guided by a handful of mostly middle-class leaders who worked within, rather than around, Baltimore's political system.[7]

For two decades after World War II, Southeast Baltimore, centered on Eastern Avenue and, encompassing the communities of Little Italy, Fell's Point, Canton, and Highlandtown, remained the most stable of the city's working-class residential areas. Home to Baltimore's highest proportions of foreign stock, working-class families, the area's abundant and varied industries provided a stable employment base.[8] Mostly Catholic residents nurtured cohesive parish-based neighborhoods that escaped the blockbusting and racial turnover that recast other working-class neighborhoods.[9] It took powerful outside forces to rouse Southeast Baltimore from its quietude.

The East-West Expressway

The first plans for an expressway linking east and west Baltimore (thus the name "East-West Expressway") were laid in the 1940s. These stalled due to financial problems, but the 1956 Interstate Highway Act, with its promise of 90 percent federal funding, gave new life to the project.[10] By the early 1960s, city planners had settled on a route that cut through working-class South Baltimore and spanned the harbor. Citizens' groups had opposed highway plans since the 1940s, but this one drew the first sustained resistance.

In early 1962 a crowd of thirteen hundred, described by the *Baltimore Sun* as "East Baltimore steelworkers and west Baltimore housewives," confronted city planners at an East Baltimore high school. Much of the opposition was voiced in traditional economic terms: a spokesman for three East Baltimore improvement associations insisted, "our property is good tax property, not slum property." A local city councilman, however, defined the conflict in class terms, contrasting middle-class highway supporters from suburban Baltimore county with working-class urban dwellers. City residents, he said "are the people who ought to be heard. . . . Not those who live in the county."[11]

Although the issue slipped out of the headlines, it gained momentum. In early 1965, one councilman warned the mayor that opposition to the expressway was deep, growing, and would soon "awaken the city."[12] Later that year, the first condemnation ordinance cleared the city council. Inside the condemnation lines, real estate began to deteriorate, and once vital neighborhoods were gutted. In Canton's St. Casimir Parish, two hundred Polish families living within sight of the church packed to leave.[13] Tensions building for twenty-five years within Baltimore's working-class neighborhoods began to find release, touching off a remarkable efflorescence of neighborhood activism that crested in the 1970s. Blue-collar Southeast Baltimore was not alone in fighting Baltimore's expressway plans. Residents of white, upscale Bolton Hill, black middle- and working-class Rosemont, and tightly-knit, white, ethnic Locust Point all fought the road.[14] But in Southeast Baltimore, fighting the road was a beginning, not an end.

Protesting the Road

It took time for working-class anger to turn to action. The first major organization to oppose the Road was started by newly arrived middle-class gentrifiers, not long-time blue-collar residents. They founded the Society for the Preservation of Federal Hill, Montgomery Street, and Fells Point (hereafter called "the Society") in early 1967. The group's first leader, a suburbanite, had recently invested in six properties in Fells Point, Baltimore's eighteenth-century shipping and shipbuilding center. At first the Society just wanted the route moved north into a blue-collar residential area away from the historic waterfront.[15] The Society was clearly more interested in safeguarding members' investments than in preserving urban neighborhoods. Its goal was to create "the showplace of our city."[16]

The Society had deep pockets and generated a great deal of quick publicity, but it just as quickly alienated blue-collar locals. In May 1967, more than five hundred residents packed into a standing-room-only meeting of the Society. Over half were against the Society and "hooted down" its members' speeches. Local city councilmen assured residents that "the society are not interested in you people." After only twenty minutes, about three hundred people followed when a man known as "Rocky" called for a walkout. "Let's let the silk stockings hold their own meeting," he said. Many in attendance did not oppose the highway. Instead they had already decided to cut their losses and get out.[17]

Others were not as ready to abandon their homes and neighborhoods. Among these was Gloria Aull. Aull lived in a Canton row house that her German grandmother had bought for five dollars down at the turn of the century. Through volunteer church work she met Barbara Mikulski.[18] Mikulski, like Aull, was a third generation East Baltimorean, the granddaughter of Polish immigrants and the daughter of a local grocer. A college-educated social worker living in Highlandtown, Mikulski shared Aull's outrage against the highway.[19] In early 1969 they joined with Jack Gleason, a new resident of Fells Point and the new president of the Society, to form the Southeast Committee Against the Road (SCAR).[20] SCAR began mobilizing the residents of Southeast Baltimore through educational campaigns, regular press releases and the Catholic church.[21]

The issue of the Road held two major weaknesses. First, for those determined to sell out and move the highway opponents were a problem, not a solution. One group, from a Lithuanian Southeast Baltimore neighborhood, complained to the secretary of transportation that with property declining in the condemnation corridor the greatest injustice was hesitating to build. No longer able to sell their houses on the open market, they concluded that their "only hope has been the expressway." The "expressway dissidents" they complained, were too often outsiders. Those who did live in the condemnation area and wanted to remain, they said, "hardly constitute a neighborhood."[22]

Another problem was residents' apathy. Many living within a few blocks of the condemnation line, activists observed, considered it "someone else's problem."[23] Moreover, because of its protracted nature, the highway fight engendered little feeling of accomplishment. Therefore, although the Road was the catalyst, issues that affected more Southeast Baltimoreans and could be resolved quickly were key in helping mobilize people.[24] SCAR activists helped defeat a zoning ordinance that would have opened much of the area to industry. They also blocked the closing of a local branch library. Its focus and its membership base expanding, SCAR, according to activists, "became the planning committee for SECO."

SECO was not officially founded for another year, but by early 1970 the name was commonly used. By fall 1970, the group had hired an organizer, Catholic activist Joseph McNeeley.[25] During the planning stages both the issues and the tactics that propelled SECO's rise became apparent. It was during this time that activists discovered that the city had essentially "written off" Southeast Baltimore. With the exception of the Road, no capital improvements were projected for the area over the next twenty years.[26] The main objective that SCAR bequeathed to SECO was the reversal of urban policies which, in Gloria Aull's words, showed "insensitivity to, and bias against the older neighborhoods of our cities."[27] But in the battle against the highway, Baltimoreans saw their main adversary not in the federal government, which was responsible for funding, but in the city government, which was responsible for routing.

This diagnosis suggested tactics that were a major departure for Baltimore's working whites. Blue-collar Baltimoreans were not used to "making noise" and crusading on issues. Usually they quietly appealed to local politicians for employment or city services. The politicians' helpfulness, in turn, depended on their ability to turn out the vote. The system was supported by a network of political clubs that were strongest in Baltimore's ethnic and working-class wards.[28] But with few exceptions, city politicians supported the mayor and the business community in favor of the Road. "Machine" politics effectively sidetracked anti-Road initiatives.

Southeast Baltimore's activists turned instead to an Alinskyite model of community organization. They sought to build power bases independent of, and often in conflict with, pre-existing political structures.[29] The "neighborhood populism" unleashed by SECO appealed to those who had long resented the machine system. "Why should we go hat in hand to the b'hoys in the political organizations, begging for handouts?" asked one Southeast Baltimore activist.[30]

SECO: The Southast Community Organizes

In the early 1970s, America's ethnics rediscovered their roots. One of the leading proponents of the "new ethnicity" was SECO's Barbara Mikulski. After giving up social work, Mikulski earned a masters degree and joined the

The new neighborhood politics and the old: Barbara Mikulski and city councilman Dominic "Mimi" DiPietro in the early 1970s. (*Baltimore News-American* Collection, Special Collections, University of Maryland College Park Libraries.)

faculty of the Community College of Baltimore. Unknown outside of Southeast Baltimore, Mikulski became nationally famous after appearing at a meeting of the Urban Task Force of the United States Catholic Conference in June 1970.[31]

Mikulski delivered a stinging rebuke to "phony white liberals, pseudo black militants and patronizing bureaucrats" on behalf of ethnic Americans long "politically courted and legally extorted by both government and private enterprise." Her statement, printed in full by the *New York Times* and much excerpted elsewhere, was the rallying cry for what was soon dubbed "ethnic power."[32]

Mikulski's unapologetic championing of immigrant roots, a heritage downplayed by a generation that felt obliged to "Americanize," instilled pride in Southeast Baltimore residents who long felt patronized by Baltimore's establishment. City council president Walter Orlinsky lauded Mikulski's "clear voice." "She made Polish as beautiful as black," he said.[33] Mikulski's ability to put long-held resentments into words was crucial, but Orlinsky's analogy suggests that the ethnic resurgence that powered SECO owed much to the Civil Rights movement. Gloria Aull agreed that it encouraged white Baltimoreans to "look back with pride" on their ethnic heritage.[34]

SECO's April 1971 founding congress, attended by one thousand representatives of some ninety community organizations, revealed some key strengths and weaknesses. A source of strength was the support of working-class institutions like the churches and the labor unions. Working-class Baltimore's generation of experience with industrial unionism served SECO well. "Our people know what it means to be organized," Mikulski said, suggesting that organization on the job led naturally to organization in the community.[35] In its search for a convener who could unite the disparate groups, SECO called on a former president of United Steelworkers' Local 2610 to chair the congress.[36]

But SECO, the avowedly blue-collar, ethnic organization, elected as its first president a man who was neither: Jack Gleason, the most active of the Fells Point gentrifiers.[37] Gleason's vantage point was that of Baltimore's urban middle class rather than the ethnic working class. Each group had used different means to fight the road and their experiences led them to separate conclusions. The residents of Fells Point ultimately kept the Road out by manipulating the system—they got their neighborhood listed in the federal government's register of historic places. Southeast Baltimore's working-class residents, on the other hand, opposed the system head on. They applied unrelenting pressure, backed by community mobilization, on city planners. Having finally realized that city "politics as usual" was a dead end, SECO's working-class members, like its Alinsky-trained organizers, chose confrontation over accommodation.

There was strong opposition to SECO from without. The founding congress, noted the *Sun*, touched off a debate over "whether [SECO] genuinely represents community interests." Some opposition came from politicians and community leaders who felt threatened. Some politicians, citing Mikulski's aspiration to elected office, dismissed it as an attempt by upstarts to build a constituency.[38] On the other hand, some, like Baltimore mayor William Donald Schaefer thought SECO to have been "dangerously anti-establishment" and part of an "underground national movement."[39] Many were disturbed by

SECO's refusal to play politics as usual. Dominic "Mimi" DiPietro, city councilman from Little Italy, supported the Road. He was irritated by what he called SECO's "damned 'goodguys' image." "All they did was fight concrete," he complained.[40] Perhaps most insulting to DiPietro, who could still turn out Little Italy's vote on demand, was SECO's failure to treat politicians with the proper respect. In the Democratic clubs, DiPietro said, the president "rules with an iron hand," and strangers are not "shoved around," "cussed at," or "insulted."[41] "The neighborhood organizations," he lamented, speaking from experience, "they treat you like dirt."[42]

One improvement association president charged SECO with magnifying community problems only to exploit them. Others charged the organization with over-emphasizing Southeast Baltimore's ethnicity in order to "create sides," a practice one critic called "akin to racism."[43] The groups that opposed SECO were long-time, conservative community organizations; usually run by local businessmen and mostly pro-Road. But in a community that revolved around industry they were on firm ground when they opposed as "unrealistic" an early SECO effort to pass an ordinance removing heavy trucks from neighborhood streets. They were also justified in questioning the rediscovery of ethnicity that SECO utilized. SECO's championing of ethnicity in the political sphere must have seemed opportunistic to some. For Southeast Baltimore residents, ethnicity had long been a private, rather than public resource.

SECO's reputation as a working-class organization must be judged by its reception among "average" working-class people as well as its activists. And there was a great deal of blue-collar mistrust. Local residents were most troubled by SECO's reliance on paid organizers. "Around Canton, the SECO staff was all thought to be from Washington," said one local politician.[44] A city councilman recalled rumors that SECO was a communist front. "The organizers were dressed in a foreign uniform of jeans and flannel shirts." The older residents, he said, "saw SECO as radicals coming into their neighborhood."[45] It is revealing that locals seemed to loathe Washington and the Communist Party equally.

But SECO's biggest problem was with race. The *Sun* noted that "at times SECO has been charged with being too ethnic and bypassing the blacks in their area."[46] SECO was not an all-ethnic organization, but it was nearly all-white. This may seem curious given that one of the most notable things about Mikulski's 1970 speech was its call for "an alliance of white and black" as well as "white collar and blue collar."[47] But SECO reflected Mikulski's view of race relations more than it first appears.

Mikulski rejected the dominant liberal vision of integration as panacea. She argued instead for the primacy of the neighborhood. If a neighborhood is integrated, she believed, then its neighborhood organization should be. If not, she told an interviewer, "groups should get together separately, and then, where there are common causes, join together."[48] Mikulski pointed out that SCAR had worked closely with black anti-Road groups. Betty Deacon, another SECO activist, said SECO's members "support the black people in their efforts to have their voices heard in their communities."[49] Rejecting integration in favor of building coalitions between strong but separate racial communities clearly appealed to ethnics who put a high value on whiteness.

The resurgence of "ethnic power" that drove SECO was a legitimate outgrowth of the "rights revolution" of the 1960s. It was not, as some Baltimore black activists charged, "simply undercover racism."[50] It is not surprising though, that Mikulski, as a product of a Catholic community ill-disposed to moralizing, adopted a practical yet principled, view of race relations. This seems to have disturbed liberals who hoped to avoid the contradictions between community preservation and racial exclusion by saying nothing at all. In 1976, Robert Kuttner wrote that "on the race issue, SECO treads a necessarily narrow line."[51] By the time he wrote, SECO's leaders may have felt they had made a misstep or two over the issue of busing.

School Desegregation in Baltimore

Baltimore was still a southern segregationist city when the Supreme Court issued the *Brown* decision in 1954. Most of its white residents probably opposed desegregation. Even liberal bulwarks like the *Sun* expressed only "cautious approval."[52] Nevertheless, Baltimore's schools were among the first in the nation to integrate. Districting had been abolished two years earlier, allowing students to attend any school assigned to his or her race. In the summer of 1954, the school board dropped the racial qualification.[53] Relatively few black students entered all-white schools. But in working-class South Baltimore, when black children did enroll in "neighborhood" schools, parents turned out in protest. In the fall of 1954, a group of mothers began picketing elementary schools in the area. More turmoil came at South

The diverse membership of SECO's truck route task force at work in Southeast Baltimore. (*Baltimore News-American* Collection, Special Collections, University of Maryland College Park Libraries.)

Baltimore's Southern High School, where student pickets and local adults—often voicing their protests in southern segregationist terms—precipitated several days of unrest.[54] All of Baltimore's civic organizations and community leaders condemned the protests.[55]

Unlike South and Southwest Baltimore, Southeast Baltimore escaped the territorial conflicts that came when blacks began breaking out of the overcrowded inner city in the late 1940s and 1950s. Also, with a much higher concentration of Catholics than elsewhere, Southeast Baltimore was not as dependent on public schools. Nevertheless, most Baltimore Catholics still attended public schools, and parochial school enrollments were declining by the early 1960s.[56]

In the decade after 1954, Baltimore's black population rose, its white population fell, and inner city schools became increasingly overcrowded. The school board reimposed districting, implemented double shifts, and used busing to alleviate the situation. Results were meager, however, and the NAACP pushed for the further desegregation of Baltimore's schools. In the spring of 1963, the board agreed to transfer students from crowded black schools to white schools that fall.[57]

In early September, two hundred parents of children in Highlandtown schools slated to receive transfers of black children held a mass meeting. While one parent stated forthrightly that black students "don't belong here," most attacked the board's seeming callousness. One local city councilman opined that residents were "objecting to the transportation and to the methods of integration" above all.[58] In 1963 the Baltimore schools took a step away from voluntary desegregation. In 1971 the Supreme Court issued a decision that pushed it further.

In April 1971, the *Swann v. Mecklenberg* decision declared that busing could be used to integrate schools that remained segregated because of residential segregation.[59] This was precisely the situation in Baltimore. During the 1960s the number of segregated schools in the city continued to climb. By 1970, of the 215 schools in the system, seventy were all-black and twelve were all-white.[60] In early 1974 the civil rights office of the Department of Health Education and Welfare (HEW) instructed Baltimore school officials to draw up a desegregation plan. The board complied, devising a system in which white and black schools would be "paired," and their student populations redistributed.[61]

The chief proponent of the plan dismissed the concerns of parents as "merely emotional" and confidently predicted "they will get over it." But on April 4, 1974, 1,200 parents packed into the Patterson High School auditorium in Southeast Baltimore to protest "forced busing." In populist tones, a city councilman condemned the schemes of "liberal social planners in Washington" and "left-wing do-gooders" who push busing while sending their children to private schools. He warned the crowd that the city's plan to "pair" black and white schools was "just another code word for busing." SECO's Betty Deacon, was more direct. "That [pairing] won't work over here. It would mean busing and I'm against busing."[62]

Busing and the Southeast Coalition

In 1974, Betty Deacon was thirty years old and living with her husband and two children in a formstone-covered row house in Highlandtown that she had bought from her grandmother. Her mother lived across the street; her in-laws around the corner.[63] In 1971 she got active in the United Neighborhood Improvement Association because "the neighborhood was going down and nobody was doing anything about it."[64] Her group became part of SECO at its founding congress and she rose quickly, soon heading up SECO's Truck Route Task Force.[65] By 1972 Deacon was SECO's "education leader in South Baltimore." When a son was diagnosed with dyslexia she organized tutoring programs at his school. With the help of a small corporate grant, Deacon's group took over and reorganized the local PTA and pressured the city into replacing two of Higlandtown's aging school buildings. These successes added to SECO's prestige.[66]

In its 1974 guidelines on desegregation, the federal government directed Baltimore to set up a city-wide Desegregation Task Force, and Deacon became SECO's representative. A few years earlier, Deacon claimed, she would have "very idealistically" backed busing. But her experience on the task force changed her mind. "I became realistic in my views," she said. Deacon was convinced that although many blacks did not want their children bused, they supported it "to get hold of power in the city." She also perceived that Southeast Baltimore "was being ridiculed" for its opposition to busing and "that it needed a spokesman to articulate the feelings of the people."[67] As she abandoned what she considered an unquestioning idealism and adopted an approach more grounded in the realities of urban life, Deacon became a confident proponent of the "community first" approach to race relations enunciated by Mikulski. Her insistence that blue-collar Southeast Baltimore be granted respect overcame her fear of being labeled a "white racist," but SECO had a harder time with the issue.

In the spring of 1974, school officials grappled with desegregation plans while Baltimore parents grew increasingly vocal in opposition. At an April 26 meeting, five hundred mostly white parents urged the school board to resist the HEW directive that they labeled "federal blackmail." Instead they urged the board to "let the communities run the schools."[68] Meanwhile, Betty Deacon was assembling a group called the Southeast Desegregation Coalition. Some members were her long-time supporters, but busing drew much additional support. "East Baltimore housewives," previously uninvolved in community affairs, "suddenly identified with this emotional issue," said SECO. Deacon and Stan Holt, SECO's lead organizer, worked out a strategy that sidestepped race. They decided to argue that the black elementary schools designated for local children were inferior. Black children were welcome at local schools, but the coalition opposed busing white children out.[69]

Anti-busing's new recruits invigorated SECO as well. One hundred and seventy different organizations, nearly twice the eighty-seven SECO member organizations, came to the fourth annual congress. SECO officials unequivocally attributed the turnout to "strong anti-busing sentiment." Acting on what the *Sun* called "an overwhelming mandate," the congress passed a firm antibusing resolution.[70] The "We're Staying" resolution pronounced neighborhood schools "a way of life" and laid out the Desegregation Coalition's plan to combat busing. "Pre-registration days" were announced for each Southeast area school. Parents, acting outside of school system channels were encouraged to pre-register their children at the school of their choice.[71]

On the night of May 28, the school board unveiled what was to be its final desegregation plan. Southeast Baltimore learned that Patterson High School was designated a "magnet school" for courses in the construction trades. The board's action stoked smoldering class resentment. Citizens felt that the board had unilaterally "tracked" Southeast Baltimore children away from academics by making their neighborhood school a trade school. The board had taken Southeast Baltimore's working-class status for granted. SECO's office was flooded with indignant calls. At Patterson High, 95 percent of the 1,200 students assigned to the second shift walked out, initiating six days of protest.[72] On May 30, 750 students, most of them from Patterson High, protested at City Hall. The next day, the crowd reached two thousand.[73] On Sunday night, June 2, Southeast Baltimore residents rallied in Patterson Park, vowing to fight the magnet plan. The next morning two thousand high school students blocked traffic outside of City Hall for an hour.[74]

At a June 4 public hearing, the board gave in. Patterson High would remain a comprehensive high school. Still, Patterson's principal complained, "1,095 junior high students have been permitted to select Patterson and now you're saying they cannot go." Most in attendance ultimately blamed HEW, and two children displayed a banner asking, "What Happened to Democracy?"[75] The next night the board officially adopted a much-diluted plan. Barbara Mikulski, now representing the first district on the city council, took the opportunity to accuse HEW of discriminating against urban working-class whites, demanding to know why it did not order suburban school districts to comply.[76]

Mikulski was not the only Baltimore politician to oppose busing. In the highway fight, councilmen either backed the Road or opposed only plans affecting their districts. But busing was an easy issue and the politicians made hay. When school opened in the fall, the Desegregation Coalition moved into stage two of its plan, holding "sit-ins" at local elementary schools. Parents, grandparents, and neighbors accompanied children to the schools at

Parents and Patterson High school students take to the streets in late May 1974.
(*Baltimore News-American* Collection, Special Collections, University of Maryland
College Park Libraries.)

which they had "pre-registered." In Canton, local politicians "adopted" children whose parents could not attend. Most conspicuous was Mimi DiPietro,
one of SECO's leading detractors.[77]

During the first week of school, parents across Baltimore organized.
One of the larger groups linked several North Baltimore communities, among
them white, working-class Hampden. On September 9, a thousand parents
met in a Hampden high school and decided on a boycott. A Southwest
Baltimore group joined them. The Southeast Desegregation Coalition though,
rejected the boycott, which proved to be only marginally successful, in favor
of the sit-ins that Deacon considered "our most effective weapon at this
point."[78]

The school board released statistics refuting claims that blacks opposed
busing. Black students, it seemed, were complying with the plan far more
than whites. Charges of white racism, tacitly encouraged by the board, grew

louder. Betty Deacon moved to deflect criticism away from Southeast Baltimore. At a press conference in Canton, she denounced "fringe groups" bent on creating racial confrontations. She insisted that busing was not an issue of race, but one of class. "Black and white working class communities seem to be constantly set upon by demagogues of the right and left," she said.[79]

In late September, the board further modified its plan, enabling more elementary students to attend local schools. The board also began granting transfer requests, most of which had been made by Southeast Baltimoreans.[80] Deacon called the board's move "a victory."[81] By October 1, most Southeast Baltimore elementary school children were officially enrolled in schools of their choice.[82]

The Desegregation Coalition's victory heightened Betty Deacon's profile such that her group, not SECO, was garnering headlines. The coalition requested, and got, a meeting with Baltimore's Archbishop Borders. Members recounted their efforts, and Deacon laid out plans to fight busing in secondary schools. The archbishop praised the coalition for its "broad base of participation" and suggested that it assist groups in other areas. In an embarrassing turn, Elaine Lowrey, speaking for SECO, could do little but point out that SECO's and the church's aims were the same.[83]

At the coalition's suggestion, the school board assembled the Southeast Secondary Education Task Force to study the problem of secondary schools. But this drew new attacks from black politicians, who charged that the task force under-represented blacks. The task force had more whites, Deacon countered, "because there are more whites in Southeast Baltimore." "Dunbar [a black neighborhood] is a different community and they're not going to plan my child's future."[84] Deacon, like Mikulski, emphasized that whites and blacks should work within their own communities first, and also warned that each group had a right to decide what constituted "common ground."

But SECO and the coalition had just about run out of common ground. The coalition's success boosted its members' confidence in community activism. But SECO was moving away from activism and toward "community development." In late 1973, thanks to the efforts of Jack Gleason, the Ford Foundation gave SECO a $100,000 grant to finance planning of projects for improving health, housing, and transportation in East Baltimore.[85] The turn toward community development led SECO to work in concert with, rather than against, local government.

By 1974, SECO had a staff of fifteen and a budget of $200,000. In the eyes of many Southeast Baltimoreans, it had become part of the establishment it had once fought. Early that year, several neighborhood improvement associations seceded from the organization that was becoming "too powerful and too uncontrollable."[86] In April an influential member angrily urged the SECO senate to remember that it was "created by the people, for the people," and warned that among a growing number of groups "there are rumbles of pulling out of SECO for good."[87]

The busing controversy appears to have nettled SECO officials, who sought to project a less militant, less blue-collar, and more professional image. One coalition member said SECO had opposed their efforts from the start on the grounds that the coalition was "being racial."[88] Deacon was aware that her role in Baltimore's anti-busing movement "created some tension" within SECO.[89] In December 1974, in advance of founding Southeast Development Incorporated, a platform for this program, SECO's senate decided to resolve the conflict between community activism and economic development by firing Stan Holt, the Alinsky-trained organizer who had helped Deacon launch the Southeast Desegregation Coalition.

Deacon charged that a "liberal clique" had taken over and led a fifth of SECO's constituent groups out of the meeting. In an adjoining room they formed a steering committee for a new group. Her explanation of the split was simple. "It's a class thing," she said. "We are working-class people, and most of the concern is in the neighborhood. . . . They are middle-class professionals who don't have to worry about these things."[90] Others called it "another case of big money winning out over the little people, the big money being Elaine Lowrey [and] the elite executive board of SECO."[91] In early January, SECO fired more neighborhood organizers and announced the formation of the Southeast Development Corporation.[92]

Deacon's group, now comprising forty organizations, took in five of SECO's fired organizers and became Neighborhoods United. The new group intended, in the words of one participant, to keep power "where it belongs—in the neighborhoods."[93] Through the rest of 1975, SECO, afraid that "taking a stand on an issue might an invite an attack by Neighborhoods United" that it would not be able to withstand, assumed a low profile and nurtured its neighborhood contacts the best it could.[94]

Failure, Success and Working-Class Organizations

SECO has sometimes been depicted as a working-class organization or a grassroots ethnic movement. Certainly in its formative period it gained attention and strength by burnishing both these images. On balance, however, SECO is much more complicated. Baltimore city leaders agreed that the organization moved from radicalism toward acting as a partner of city government.[95] Some applauded this development; others did not. SECO's ambitious agenda relied on community resources accumulated through the activities of SCAR and the early SECO campaigns. But SECO's directors realized that more intractable problems required financial resources and government support unavailable to a "radical" group. With growing financial backing and new-found capital at city hall, SECO's directors forgot how important the grassroots were. The late 1974 split reminded them. But in moving from ethnic power to foundation grant power SECO ceded its claim to the powerful populist arguments that it had so skillfully wielded previously.

Betty Deacon and the anti-busers took up the very language that SECO was discarding and used it to great effect. By 1974, the Southeast Coalition, not SECO, was much more the grassroots working-class organization. But Neighborhoods United, begun amid pro-democratic, populist fanfare, lacked a unifying issue and could not weld together its constituent groups.[96] By late 1974, Joseph McNeeley, SECO's first organizer, had exchanged his flannel shirt for a briefcase to study law. He and SECO vice president Elaine Lowrey had married and together were spearheading a formal economic development program intended to curb SECO's neighborhood-based efforts and centralize its decision making in a small planning board.[97] By 1978, Deacon had made an unsuccessful run for the city council and managed a gubernatorial campaign.[98] If her roots were in the community, her heart, like Mikulski's, was in politics.

To an impressive degree, women figured heavily in both controversies. Betty Deacon once ventured that she got her greatest support from women "because they were around a lot more." She was convinced, however, that "women naturally become more involved in community issues faster than men."[99] Although the first explanation is too flip and the last too vague, both contain a kernel of truth. With some exceptions, the most prominent male activists in SECO and the Desegregation Coalition were paid organizers and clergymen—men who were indeed "around a lot more." Women drew more sustenance from the neighborhood and were willing to work harder to protect it.[100] Furthermore, women were more likely to be excluded from pre-existing channels of power. In the neighborhood, if not at work, working-class women in Baltimore were more apt, out of choice and necessity, to seek new means of change.

Historians and policy makers are just beginning to consider that the "integration above all" approach toward social justice championed by "Great Society" liberals and the mainstream Civil Rights movement in the 1960s may have carried serious liabilities. From a moral standpoint, of course, it is hard, if not impossible to argue against it. But from a practical standpoint, integration alone did not accomplish what its proponents hoped it would. In 1970, while integration was still the regnant philosophy, Mikulski called for an interracial alliance, but one in which both races drew strength from their distinctive neighborhoods, be they integrated or homogeneous. It can be argued that this institutionalized pre-existing patterns of residential discrimination and attempted to construct social justice on a foundation undermined by racism. But that argument assumes that the construction of a true foundation was possible given the history of American urban development. Liberals tended to view complex questions in terms of moral absolutes. More conservative Catholic working people were less likely to embrace abstract ideas and more likely to respect history and tradition in framing solutions. More concretely, working-class Catholics had long focused on nurturing and protecting a social vision sharply constrained within "parish boundaries." They continued to do so even after Church leaders encouraged them to take a broader view and to accept integration.[101]

This study suggests that if "the silent majority" was not silent, neither was it capable of maintaining a sustained, powerful voice. Working-class Baltimoreans had learned to mistrust those who made noise: liberal politicians, civil rights advocates, and student protesters. Only under exceptional circumstances would they do likewise. The Road roused Southeast Baltimore where, in the words of one politician, "let's not make waves" was a motto and controversy was anathema.[102] Busing further energized the community, and like the Road fight, it spawned a more ambitious organization. But SECO grew away from its working-class base to take nourishment in the exalted atmosphere of foundation grants and government partnership. Neighborhoods United relied on its roots, withered, and died.

SECO did deal a decisive blow to Baltimore's already moribund machine politics. But in a real sense, the impulse that drove Baltimore's working-class organizations ensured that they remain small. Just as blue-collar Baltimoreans finally rejected political machines, so they rejected large organizations that by nature relied on politics to unify their members. As Betty Deacon recognized, blue-collar Baltimoreans are most interested in the neighborhood. Contrary to her wishes though, most found small neighborhood groups or no organizations at all to suffice. Even Gloria Aull had to admit: "I've never been successful in organizing my own block."[103]

The working-class movements against the road and busing both floated on a tide of populist sentiment. But it is important to note that the target of this sentiment, which pits "the people" against a large, powerful adversary, changed subtly. In the highway fight, the enemy was usually city planners. Some opponents blamed the federal government, but their charges rarely stuck. In contrast, although anti-busers protested to school board officials, their criticisms were ultimately leveled at HEW. In the highway fight local politicians and officials were divided. On busing they were not—all could pass the buck to Washington. At one point Mayor Schaefer did just that, telling Southeast Baltimore parents to stop pressuring him and concentrate on HEW.[104]

Although Baltimoreans criticized HEW's intractability, they ultimately got concessions because the school board was able to compromise. Baltimore was no Boston. There was no Judge Garrity to prescribe and enforce compliance with a single plan. Ultimately, HEW never accepted any of Baltimore's plans and Congress put the brakes on busing before HEW could enforce it there. But blue-collar Baltimoreans learned what they considered to be important lessons about the callousness of government bureaucrats. Gloria Aull later felt that simply having to "rattle chains" to get recognition was troubling. "It kind of changes everybody's vision of the American dream, of democracy and everybody being equal and everybody having a fair share and being able to be heard," she said.[105]

This realization led white working people down different political paths. Gloria Aull and Barbara Mikulski both wound up in Washington, the former for a day's testimony, and the latter for a career. Some blue-collar Baltimoreans became Reagan Democrats in 1980, and even more did so in 1984 when the city's white working-class precincts voted Republican. Busing, even more than the Road, convinced Baltimore's working whites that the underlying causes of some of their problems were national, and the solutions had to be national as well. In the years to come, blue-collar Baltimoreans were not necessarily "silent." But as for politics, white working-class Baltimoreans stuck increasingly to the ballot box to express themselves.

Notes

[1] U.S. Congress, Senate, Committee on Banking, Housing and Urban Affairs, June 14, 1976, *Neighborhood Preservation: The Cause of Neighborhood Decline and the Impact, Positive or Negative, of Existing Programs Policies and Laws on Existing Neighborhoods* (Washington, D.C.: Government Printing Office, 1976), 72.

[2] Joseph L. Arnold, "The Neighborhood and City Hall: The Origin of Neighborhood Associations in Baltimore, 1880–1911," *Journal of Urban History,* 6 (November 1979): 3–30.

[3] Arnold, "The Neighborhood and City Hall," 21–23.

[4] *Baltimore Evening Sun,* May 27, 1947.

[5] Baltimore's black population rose from 19 percent of the city's total to 24 percent during the 1940s. By 1960, 35 percent of the city's residents were black. *U.S. Census of Population: 1950, Census Tract Statistics Baltimore Maryland and Adjacent Area* (Washington, D.C.: Government Printing Office, 1952), 7. *U.S. Census of Population and Housing: 1960, Census Tracts Baltimore, Md. Standard Metropolitan Statistical Area* (Washington, D.C.: Government Printing Office, 1962), 15.

[6] "History of the Greenmount Improvement Association," 1960, RG 9, Series 24, Box 328, Baltimore City Archives.

[7] Robert Fisher, *Let the People Decide: Neighborhood Organizing in America* (Boston: Twayne Publishers, 1984), 72.

[8] In 1966, East Baltimore, from the Fallsway to Clinton Street, was 4 percent native Italian and 11 percent native Polish. Ninety-three percent of residents were hourly workers and 50 percent owned their own homes. Highlandtown, from Clinton Street to the city line, was home to native Poles, Czechs, Germans and Italians all in proportions below 5 percent. Ninety percent of residents were hourly workers and 65 percent owned their own homes. Major employers were Western Electric, General Motors, Lever Brothers, Bethlehem Steel, and Martin. See Baltimore Chamber of Commerce, *Data Profiles: East Baltimore,* 1966, 4–6, and *Data Profiles: Highlandtown,* 1966, 4–6. The 1960 census, from which information on national origins is drawn, inevitably understates an area's actual "ethnicity" since it only counts people of native birth or those of "foreign or mixed parentage."

[9] In 1960 the Catholic population of East Baltimore, defined as encompassing Fells Point, Canton, and Highlandtown, was 55 percent of the total. In Baltimore as a whole, 19 percent of residents were Catholic. Archdiocese of Balti-

more, Rev. Robert G. Howes, "Baltimore Urban Parish Study," 1967, 12–14; For blockbusting postwar Baltimore see W. Edward Orser, *Blockbusting in Baltimore: The Edmondson Village Story* (Lexington: University Press of Kentucky, 1994).

[10] Douglas H. Hauber, "The Baltimore Expressway Controversy: A Study of the Political Decision-Making Process," Johns Hopkins University Center for Metropolitan Planning and Research, 1974, 4–7.

[11] *Baltimore Sun*, January 31, 1962.

[12] Thomas Ward to McKeldin, March 31, 1965, RG 9, Series 25, Box 417, Baltimore City Archives.

[13] *Baltimore Sun,* June 4, 1973.

[14] Robert J. Brugger, *Maryland: A Middle Temperament, 1634–1980* (Baltimore: Johns Hopkins University Press, 1988), 661–62.

[15] *Baltimore Evening Sun,* February 27, 1967.

[16] Society for the Preservation of Federal Hill, Fells Point, and Montgomery Street fliers, May 19, 1967, and May 15, 1967, in "Society for the Preservation of Federal Hill, Fells Point and Montgomery Street," Vertical Files, Maryland Room, Enoch Pratt Free Library.

[17] *Baltimore Sun*, May 24, 1967.

[18] *Baltimore Sun Magazine,* November 13, 1977.

[19] Jane P. Sweeney, "Barbara M. Mikulski: Representing the Neighborhood," in *Women in Contemporary U.S. Politics*, Frank P. LeVeness and Jane P. Sweeney eds. (London: Lynne Rienner Pubs., 1987), 105–6.

[20] Lee Trulove, "SECO History," September 1977, SECO Records, Series 1, Box 2, University of Baltimore Archives, 24.

[21] Ibid. 25.

[22] Virginia Bird to John A. Volpe, July 16, 1970, RG 406 (Records of the Federal Highway Administration) Entry 1B, Box 74, National Archives and Records Administration.

[23] Trulove, "SECO History," 24.

[24] Ibid., 30–31.

[25] "McNeeley was member of the Catholic Church's Marianist Order, which made community building part of its primary mission. Truelove, "SECO History," 32–33.

[26] *New York Times Magazine*, May 9, 1976, 21.

[27] U.S. Congress, *Neighborhood Preservation*, 72.

[28] "The Decline and Fall of Baltimore's Machine Politics," in Thomas Byrne Edsall, *Power and Money: Writing About Politics, 1971–1987* (New York: W. W. Norton & Co., 1988), 82–90.

[29] One of the first and most publicized of the new community groups was Gary's Calumet Community Congress. See Richard J. Krickus, "Organizing Neighborhoods: Gary and Newark," in Irving Howe, ed., *The World of the Blue-Collar Worker* (New York: Quadrangle Books, 1972), 72–88; On Alinsky and his influence in the "new" community organizing see Harry Boyte, *The Backyard Revolution: Understanding the New Citizen Movement* (Philadelphia: Temple University Press, 1980), 49–57.

[30] *Baltimore Evening Sun*, May 3, 1971.

[31] *Baltimore Magazine*, December 1970, 8.

[32] *New York Times*, June 17, 1970.

[33] Walter Orlinsky quoted in Trulove, "SECO History," 94.

[34] *Baltimore News-American*, May 11, 1973.

[35] *Baltimore Magazine*, December 10, 1970.

[36] *East Baltimore Guide*, April 22, 1971.

[37] Trulove, "SECO History," 38–39.

[38] *Baltimore Evening Sun*, April 18, 1971.

[39] Trulove, "SECO History," 93.

[40] Ibid., 101.

[41] Mimi DiPietro Oral History, Interview by Rosewin Sweeney, Baltimore Neighborhood Heritage Project, University of Baltimore Archives, 15.

[42] Edsall, *Power and Money*, 87.

[43] *East Baltimore Guide*, April 22, 1971.

[44] American Joe Medusiewski quoted in Trulove, "SECO History," 100.

[45] Donald Hammen quoted in Trulove "SECO History,", 102.

[46] *Baltimore Evening Sun*, May 31, 1971.

[47] *New York Times*, June 17, 1970.

[48] *Baltimore Magazine*, December 1970, 56.

[49] "Letter to Editor," from Betty Deacon, *Sun,* April 20, 1971.

[50] *News-American*, November 13, 1977.

[51] *New York Times Magazine*, May 9, 1976, 30.

[52] Elinor Pancoast, *The Report on Desegregation in the Baltimore City Schools* (Maryland Commission on Interracial Problems and Relations The Baltimore Commission on Human Relations, 1956), 26.

[53] George H. Callcott, *Maryland and America: 1940 to 1980* (Baltimore: Johns Hopkins University Press, 1985), 244.

[54] Pancoast, *Report on Desegregation in the Baltimore City Schools*, 55–79. On the language of the protestors see Kenneth Durr, "When Southern Politics Came North: The Roots of White Working-Class Conservatism in Baltimore, 1940–1964," *Labor History* (Summer 1996): 309–331.

[55] *Baltimore Sun*, October 3, 1954.

[56] "Baltimore Urban Parish Study," 14.

[57] "Major Win for NAACP in Baltimore Schools," NAACP Press Release, NAACP Papers, Group III, Box A 102, Library of Congress Manuscripts.

[58] *Baltimore Evening Sun*, September 9, 1963.

[59] George R. Metcalf, *From Little Rock to Boston: The History of School Desegregation* (Westport, Conn.: Greenwood Press, 1983), 106–7.

[60] *Baltimore Sun*, November 18, 1970.

[61] Ibid., March 3, 1974.

[62] *East Baltimore Guide*, April 11, 1974.

[63] *Baltimore Evening Sun*, June 10, 1974.

[64] Maureen Fahey, "Block by Block: Women in Community Organizing," *Women: A Journal of Liberation,* 6 (1978): 24–28. See page 24.

[65] Trulove, "SECO History," 43.

[66] Ibid., 47–49.

[67] *Baltimore Evening Sun*, June 10, 1974.

[68] Ibid., April 26, 1971.

[69] Trulove, "SECO History," 65.

[70] *Baltimore Evening Sun*, May 6, 1974.

[71] "SECO Resolution 14," May 4, 1974, SECO Records, Series II, Box 1, University of Baltimore Archives.

[72] *Baltimore Evening Sun*, May 30, 1974.

[73] Ibid., May 31, 1974.

[74] Ibid., June 3, 1974.

[75] Ibid., June 4, 1974.

[76] Ibid., June 5, 1974.

[77] Ibid., September 5, 1974.

[78] Ibid., September 10, 1974.

[79] *East Baltimore Guide*, September 12, 1974.

[80] *Baltimore Evening Sun*, September 21, 1974.

[81] Ibid., September 20 and 21, 1974.

[82] Trulove, "SECO History," 66.

[83] *East Baltimore Guide*, September 26, 1974.

[84] Ibid., November 28, 1974.

[85] *Baltimore Sun*, November 20, 1973.

[86] *Baltimore Evening Sun*, March 18, 1974.

[87] "Statement to SECO Senate" by Matilda Koval, April 23, 1974, SECO Papers, Series IV, Box 1.

[88] *East Baltimore Guide*, February 6, 1975.

[89] *Baltimore Evening Sun*, December 18, 1974.

[90] *Baltimore Sun*, December 18, 1974.

[91] *East Baltimore Guide*, December 26, 1974.

[92] Ibid., January 16, 1975.

[93] *East Baltimore Guide*, January 16, 1975.

[94] Trulove, "SECO History," 71–72.

[95] Ibid., 92.

[96] On Neighborhoods United's demise see James V. Cunningham and Milton Kotler, *Building Neighborhood Organizations* (Notre Dame, Ind.: University of Notre Dame Press, 1983), 76.

[97] *East Baltimore Guide*, December 26, 1974.

[98] Fahey, "Block by Block," 28.

[99] Ibid., 24.

[100] One study finds activist women's "emotional attachment to their neighborhood" to be a an important factor in explaining their activism. See Kathleen McCourt, *Working-Class Women and Grass-Roots Politics* (Bloomington: Indiana University Press, 1977), 220. Another notes that women had a greater stake than men in the neighborhood movements because they were more circumscribed to the neighborhood than men. See Thomas Sugrue, "The Origins of the Urban Crisis: Race, Industrial Decline and Housing in Detroit, 1940–1960" (Ph.D. Diss. Harvard University, 1992), 264.

[101] John T. McGreevy, *Parish Boundaries: The Catholic Encounter with Race in the Twentieth-Century Urban North* (Chicago: University of Chicago Press,

1996) and Eileen M. McMahon, *What Parish Are You From?: A Chicago Irish Community and Race Relations* (Lexington: University of Kentucky Press, 1995).

[102] Donald Hammen in Trulove, "SECO History," 102.

[103] Linda G. Rich et al., *Neighborhood: A State of Mind* (Baltimore: Johns Hopkins University Press, 1981), 133.

[104] *Baltimore Evening Sun*, September 12, 1974.

[105] Rich, *Neighborhood: A State of Mind*, 132.

EDWARD BERKOWITZ

Baltimore's Public Schools in a Time of Transition

O N THE 3800 BLOCK OF Juniper Road, no one cares about the fate of the Baltimore city schools for the simple reason that not one of the families sends its children to them. The families choose expensive private schools, such as Friends or Bryn Mawr, over free public schools. This choice has important consequences for the city of Baltimore. None of the people on the block is a stakeholder in the public school system, depriving the schools of influential advocates who might intercede in the political and budgetary processes to argue for increased school spending. Instead, the residents of Juniper Road complain bitterly about high tax rates. Most of these residents are on the edge of white flight. They eye surrounding Baltimore County as a place with both lower taxes and better schools. What deters these people from moving is not a commitment to urban life so much as the fear that they will not be able to sell their houses. Potential buyers know that they will not only have to pay high city taxes but also very high tuition bills for their children. The cost of tuition discourages many people with children from moving to Baltimore.

As historians, we know that education was once one of the prized services that distinguished cities such as Baltimore from rural areas. But little more than two decades ago demographic realities combined with public policies to produce a crisis from which the schools have never recovered. The events of 1974, in particular, tarnished the reputation of a school system that had once been among the nation's best.

David Weglein served as superintendent of Baltimore's schools from 1925 to 1946, a length of tenure that would be simply impossible in the

Edward Berkowitz teaches at George Washington University and writes on the history of social welfare policy.

modern era. He presided over a growing school system in a placid atmosphere. The year after his arrival the city opened a record number of schools, a situation that Weglein described as "epoch making." Weglein himself strove to put the Baltimore school curriculum in line with progressive principles and, in general, "to improve the efficiency of classroom instruction." It went without comment that throughout Weglein's tenure the city schools remained solidly segregated and honored traditional conventions with regard to gender. In the junior high schools, newly configured to include grades seven through nine, boys learned mechanical drawing and woodwork, and girls received lessons in cookery and housekeeping.[1]

These conventions were the norm and went unremarked, yet in a school system that enjoyed wide participation from a broad array of the city's citizens, not everyone defended the principle of racial segregation, particularly in the years following the Second World War. In the early 1950s prominent members of the school board such as Walter Sondheim, a businessman who would later play a major role in Baltimore's renaissance, did what they could to end segregation in the city schools. Despite the reality of racial segregation, students in Baltimore's public schools absorbed the era's optimistic rhetoric about cultural pluralism and ethnic assimilation.

One could sense this optimism in their writings. Just before the 1954 Supreme Court decision in *Brown v. Board of Education,* a group of students drawn from senior high schools across Baltimore participated in a special social studies project—they wrote a book about Baltimore. Published under the revealing title *Baltimore: City of Promise,* the book reflected the liberal sentiments of the era. Students from all-black, academically oriented Douglass High School wrote that "diversity of population and race is actually one of [democracy's] strong sustaining factors." The students explained that "where Negroes enjoy equal opportunities there are no real differences in mental ability between the two groups." Indeed, racial prejudice was "not only inconsistent with the principles of religion but is also inimical to democracy itself." The nation's racial and religious groups were like the "choirs of instruments in a symphony orchestra," all playing harmoniously.

The same book matter-of-factly noted that nearly all of the city's churches were segregated.[2] The students chosen to write on education pointed with pride to the development of City, Poly, Douglass, and Western high schools; they also reported that of the city's nine high schools, seven were white and two were "colored." Although the students chose not to highlight it, an alert reader could discover that segregation extended to the remotest regions of the school system. Even the schools for the physically handicapped featured the William S. Baer School for white children and the Francis W. Wood School for colored children.[3]

As one might expect from a system with a relative tolerance for the idea, if not the practice, of integration, the Baltimore schools took the *Brown* decision with relative good grace. The school board moved quickly to eliminate race as a consideration in assigning students to particular schools. "It was something we knew we had to do, so we just did it," said Sondheim.[4] Drawing on what might be described as the shadow legacy of tolerance, the superintendent pointed to the fact that Baltimore's schools already had considerable experience in integrated education. He cited such things as interracial staff workshops, visits between white and black schools, integrated adult education programs, and the fact that black students had been admitted to Poly in 1952 (on the rationale that nothing comparable to Poly's technical education existed for black students). Civil rights leaders, Roy Wilkins of the NAACP among them, applauded the Baltimore schools as a model for other cities to follow.[5] Primed by the city's business and professional elite, Baltimore became one of those "border" school systems that complied with *Brown* with a minimum of fuss.[6] In 1961 the U.S. Civil Rights Commission noted that Baltimore was the nation's only southern city to have complied with *Brown*.[7]

Letting Go

However laudable the decision to open all of the city schools to blacks may have been, it failed to end the problem of racial segregation. In 1963 fifty-three of the city's 189 schools still had all-white faculties, and sixty-seven schools had faculties that were all-black.[8]

Complicating the problem of integration, difficult in itself, was the fact that independent of the *Brown* decision the city and its school system soon reached a number of critical racial tipping points. In 1955, the year after *Brown,* 60 percent of the students were white, but by September 1960 more blacks than whites attended Baltimore's schools. Accompanying this shift in population were major changes in the racial composition of individual schools. Clifton Park Junior High School had only thirty-four black students just after desegregation and only twelve white students by the middle of the 1960s.[9]

Other demographic changes adversely affected the schools. During the 1970s, for example, the city lost 13 percent of its population, mostly to the suburbs. Blacks became a majority of the city population in the mid-1970s and a majority of the city's voters in 1980. At the same time, the disparity between the white and black student populations continued to grow. By 1974, 70 percent of the public school students in Baltimore were black; by 1980 the figure was close to 80 percent. Baltimore had become a black city with a declining population and, beginning in September 1970, declining enrollment in a heavily black school system.[10]

Public policies also affected the schools. In particular, two events of the 1960s provided the impetus for the confrontations of the 1970s. The first of these, passage of a comprehensive civil rights law, occurred in 1964. The thrust of the law was to ban racial discrimination in hiring and firing workers, but the law also contained a little noticed title that prohibited racial discrimination in activities that were supported by the federal government.[11] The second event occurred a year later, when Congress passed an aid to education law that supplied local school districts with federal financial support. Proposed in the late 1940s as a means to supplement teacher salaries and build new schools, the measure emerged in 1965 as a way of aiding children who lived in conditions of poverty.[12]

These laws emerged after long legislative struggles that had little to do with Baltimore, though both appeared to work to Baltimore's advantage. Title I of the aid to education law, which based the allocation of money on the number of poor children in a particular district, proved to be a particular boon to the city. Federal funds, which had begun to reach the public schools by 1966, became an important part of the city's school budget. By the 1971–72 school year, Baltimore received 11 percent of its school budget from federal funds. Forty-two percent of those funds came from Title I of the Elementary and Secondary Education Act of 1965; the next largest category was the federal school lunch program.[13]

City and federal authorities disagreed on how to spend the federal funds. Although the bulk of the funds were explicitly intended to expand the city's educational offerings and provide what the educators called "compensatory" education, the money actually became a basic part of the city's operating budget. Aware of this fact, federal legislators passed amendments that attempted to insure that federal funds "supplement, not supplant" local funds. In fact, how the funds were used was difficult to audit.[14] Baltimore continued to spend them as general aid to education, even when the federal government tried to force the city to use them only for the activities authorized by Congress. In 1978 for example, federal auditors claimed that $14.6 million in federal funds were misspent on such things as hiring library staff and paying for personnel in the district's business office.[15]

The growth of federal funds constituted just one of the changes in financing that affected the Baltimore city school system during the 1960s and 1970s and increased its dependency on external sources. As the local property tax base declined, as it naturally did in a city with a declining population and a rising poverty rate, local revenues ceased to be the major means of funding the schools. Between 1970 and 1975, at the same time that the city was becoming more dependent on federal aid, state revenues bypassed local taxes as a source of school operating funds.[16] That meant that the city was responsible to both the state and federal governments for the conduct of its schools at a time when the reputation of those schools had begun to decline.

In the 1970s the Baltimore city schools began to attract unwelcome notice from critics who charged they were unsafe and ineffective, criticisms not unrelated to the fact that Baltimore was becoming a black city. The *Baltimore Sun,* an important molder of public opinion that had once carried uplifting stories about the schools' accomplishments, began running stories on racial conflict in classrooms and hallways. The effect was to heighten middle-class fears, primarily among whites, that the schools were in serious decline.

The decade began with an outbreak of violence. Eastern High School, located across from Memorial Stadium on 33rd Street, was one of the schools that had gone from all-white to perhaps four-fifths black by 1970. The racial composition of the faculty had failed to change as fast as that of the student body, with the result that nearly 80 percent of the teachers were white. On February 12, 1970, a disturbance occurred after a white teacher used a racial epithet in addressing one of the black students at the all-female school. Police arrived, arrested eleven girls, and charged them with disorderly conduct. Some observers claimed that the police used mace in

Baltimore schools responded well to the Supreme Court decision in *Brown v. Board of Education* but did not immediately desegregate. Here, the all-white student body at Baltimore City College photographed in 1953. (Maryland Historical Society.)

making the arrests. The "melée" that resulted soon spread into the streets and reached the student body of nearby (all-male) City College High School. Authorities closed both Eastern and City for the day.[17]

The situation soon escalated. Students at Eastern and City responded to the arrests with a boycott of classes the next day. Administrators decided to station security guards in Eastern High School. The next week more than one hundred black students staged a sit-in at Baltimore Polytechnic's cafeteria. Police arrested them. At Forest Park High School some of the students, angered by the incidents at Eastern, "ran through the hall smashing furniture and breaking windows." Before the police could quell that disturbance, students "ripped out the school's telephone lines."[18] Later that same day students demonstrated at City Hall and at school headquarters.

Nor did those incidents end the violence. In April a fight occurred in front of William H. Lemmel Junior High School. Police had been called after receiving reports that teenagers armed with sticks had threatened teachers. As the police attempted to disperse the crowd that had gathered in front of the school, some of the teenagers began to throw rocks. Two policemen sustained injuries, and six patrol cars were damaged. In the same month fires that authorities believed to have been deliberately set broke out at Forest Park and Douglass. Mayor Thomas D'Alesandro worried that such incidents might lead voters to reject the school bond issue. Other political leaders, including William Donald Schaefer, demanded that more police, equipped with dogs, be brought into the schools to protect against arsonists.[19]

Profoundly local in nature, the disturbances in the Baltimore public schools also formed part of a more general national pattern. The spring of 1970 marked the height of clashes between students and school authorities in all sections of the country and at all levels of education. Just as classes were suspended at Forest Park and Eastern, so too were they cancelled at Princeton and Harvard. But considered strictly as a local matter, the disturbances reflected a revolt of the majority black student body against the still largely white power structure. Well aware that the mayor and the superintendent of schools were white, the students sensed that city institutions, in particular the schools and the police force, lacked racial sensitivity. Well-publicized national incidents gave them cues for highlighting racial grievances in discussions with local authorities.

Meanwhile, Baltimore's political leaders were in conflict over its response. They realized they had to appeal to black voters if they expected to survive in Baltimore politics but also knew only too well that they had to hold on to their white power base if they were to be re-elected. Although there were more white voters than black at the time, it took little imagination to see that the electorate would soon be majority black.

Whatever the reasons for the racial outbreaks, they served to raise barriers between whites and blacks. More ominously, they fed the steady decline in white enrollment. Black enrollment continued to increase—at a very modest rate—until September 1974.[20]

Schaefer Bound

If 1970 was bad, 1974 was much worse. Two events that occurred almost simultaneously that year had a catastrophic effect on the Baltimore public schools. In a volatile era that witnessed the resignation of a president

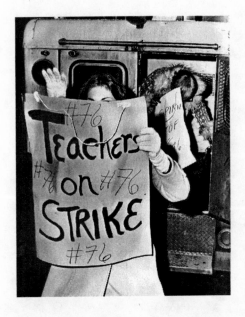

Striking teachers emerge from a police patrol wagon after being arrested, February 22, 1974. (*Baltimore News-American* staff photograph, University of Maryland, College Park.)

and an oil shock that plunged the nation into a severe recession, the Baltimore city schools experienced a teachers' strike and a major confrontation over desegregation.

Roland N. Patterson, Baltimore's first black superintendent of schools, arrived from Seattle to begin his tenure late in 1971. By January 1974 he felt secure enough to buy a $65,000 house in a northwest Baltimore neighborhood, despite persistent rumors that Schaefer, who had become mayor in 1971, would fire him. The mayor maintained that he had no intentions of letting Patterson go.[21]

Then on Monday, February 4, 1974, the Public School Teachers Association (PSTA) announced that its members had gone on strike against the city schools. Although the circuit court issued an injunction against the strike, the teachers decided to ignore it. City authorities optimistically announced that 90 percent of the teachers were working and that the schools remained open. Reporters challenged these assertions. By the second day of the strike, the city admitted that only 29 percent of the students had attended classes. At some schools the rate of absenteeism was so high that school authorities questioned the decision to keep the schools open. On the third day of the strike, school attendance fell to 16 percent, and most

Baltimore teachers union members really in front of City Hall, February 28, 1974. (Photograph by Paul Whyte, *Baltimore News-American,* University of Maryland, College Park.)

schools closed early. Less than a quarter of the staff showed up for work. The teachers had succeeded in shutting down the system.[22]

The background of the strike resembled that of many public sector labor disputes.[23] The teachers had been working without a contract for the 1973–74 school year. In November 1973 the state superintendent of schools declared that negotiations had reached an impasse. Teachers hoped to obtain a package of fringe benefits and salary raises that represented an 11 percent increase over the previous contract, although Mayor Schaefer repeatedly emphasized that such a contract was beyond the realm of financial possibility. In response, teachers carried out their threat to strike, complaining not only about their low salaries but also about poor working conditions and crowded classrooms. Many noted the differential between their pay and that of their colleagues in surrounding Baltimore County. "Everybody around us makes more money," said Sabra Kone, a school librarian.

"The city is a rough place to teach." Jean E. Stegman, head of the English department at Eastern High School, claimed that she could earn $4,000 more if she taught in Baltimore County.[24]

The strike occurred in the middle of a winter in which the public was consumed by news about Watergate and fears about growing gas shortages. Even though the energy crisis added to the cost of running the city schools, Patterson vowed to keep them open. He realized that the level of instruction was less than satisfactory during the strike but added, "we're operating as good a program as we're capable of under the circumstances." Patterson sympathized with the teachers. "For two and a half years," he said, "I have said that the school system is underfinanced." He noted that the lack of supplies and overcrowded conditions added to teachers' frustrations. Still, the schools had to remain open for a reason totally unrelated to the pattern of labor relations. Were the schools to close, the city might not recover money from the state and federal governments.[25]

Two weeks into the strike, the city made another offer that, at the suggestion of the PSTA, the teachers rejected. Karl Boone, president of the association, announced that "we want to close down every school in Baltimore city." Tensions mounted as principals, school security officers, and city police escorted teachers and students past the picket lines. Five teachers were arrested for blocking the entrance to Northwestern High School. At Lake Clifton, where thirty-one of their number were arrested, teachers locked arms and sang, "We Shall Overcome." Six Walbrook High teachers had their tires slashed, and one faculty member who refused to join the strike woke up one morning to discover the word "scab" painted on the windshield of his car.[26]

Sensing that the public's sympathies lay with the strikers, Mayor Schaefer hesitated to criticize the teachers, but as the strike continued, he and the members of his administration appealed to the middle class for support. They stressed the relationship between the teachers' contract and the tax rate. To accede to the teachers' demands would mean that other unions would seek similar raises, and the result would be a large increase in the tax rate. That would put the city at a greater disadvantage compared to the county, hasten the departure of more whites, lower the tax base still further, and lead to more white flight and even higher tax rates. The city therefore had to hold the line. City labor commissioner Robert S. Hillman compared Baltimore's high tax rate to those in surrounding counties. "Increased wages could mean even higher taxes," he warned. Schaefer thought the tax rate might rise from $5.83 to $6.78. "People are beginning to see the financial crunch we're in."

Schaefer simultaneously appealed to the teachers and to the city's middle-class citizens. He wanted the teachers to return to work and to recognize that the city faced nearly insurmountable problems caused by what he described in a letter to the teachers as "socio-economic conditions" that would take "many years of hard work and dedication to reverse." He pointed out that the city contained about a fifth of the state's population but nearly two-thirds of its welfare caseload. "What am I going to do?" he asked a *Sun* reporter while holding up a copy of the budget and wondering aloud which of its items could be cut. Baltimoreans, he argued, would not countenance a property tax increase. "Boy, they'd holler bloody-murder. And they'd move out of the city. . . . You can have the rich, and you can have the poor, but it's the middle class who keep the city together."[27] If he gave in to the teachers, Schaefer feared, the middle class would flee in greater numbers. Here, for perhaps the first time, the costs of middle-class white alienation from the school system became apparent. The interests of the teachers and of the school system were diverging from those of the largely white middle class.

Schaefer found a sympathetic ear in the *Sun,* which ran an editorial portraying the school strike as an urban disgrace, a sign that the city was in disarray. The strike undermined the quality of city life and compromised Baltimore's future at the precise moment when long gas lines were playing havoc with the routines of most city inhabitants. At the end of February the *Sun* plaintively noted that the "school year is running out."[28]

By that time, after the circuit court had imposed fines of $16,000 a day on Karl Boone and the teachers' union, the impasse in the strike had begun to ease. On the last day of the month, William J. Usery Jr., director of the Federal Mediation and Conciliation Service, entered the negotiations. Attendance in city schools had slumped to 8 percent, and only a handful of teachers were coming to work. Among those staying away was the tenth-grade son of Superintendent Roland Patterson.

Early in March teachers reached a tentative agreement with the city that featured a 6 percent wage increase. The leadership of the Public School

Teachers Association declared an end to the strike on Monday, March 4, despite the fact that teachers had rejected the contract by a margin of seventy-four votes. On March 5 teachers and students returned to work. "It's almost as if the last month hadn't occurred," said one principal.[29] Super-intendent Patterson, using the sort of psychological rhetoric common in the field of education, talked about the "high level of anxiety" and "frustration" the year had produced. He hoped to cope with the "dysfunctional behav-ior" by training thirty-six regional staff development specialists in "change agentry."

Patterson's Rip Van Winkle-esque observation glossed over the fact that much had changed. Nor were the problems amenable to solution through the super-intendent's psychobabble about "change agentry." Rancor over the strike undermined the position of the PSTA to bargain on behalf of the teachers, many of whom felt betrayed by a union that had led them into a strike that won little in return for the hardship of going four weeks without pay. Some politicians reflected the public's anger toward teachers and the schools. John T. Gallagher, a delegate to the state legislature from Balti-more, introduced a measure to abolish the city school board and to put the management of the city's schools firmly in the hands of the mayor and city council. That sparked the anger of the four black members of the city school board, who saw in Gallagher's bill an attack on a system that, with a black superintendent and a majority-black student population, was increas-ingly regarded as a black institution. "This is about as racist and blatant as you can get," said James M. Griffin, the board's vice president. Larry S. Gibson, another black school board member, saw the bill as part of a "con-certed conspiracy."[30]

Indeed, the entire episode of the school strike could be read as a betrayal of the city's blacks by the entrenched white political leadership. The city hesitated to spend more money on the school system for fear of making Baltimore, already on the verge of a black majority, even more black. Preservation of the property tax rate in an effort to maintain a good business climate triumphed over a proper concern for the education of the city's school children. In this view, the strike only highlighted the need to replace the city's white leaders with a new group of black leaders, as indeed happened in 1987 when, due in large part to the political skills of Larry Gibson, Kurt L. Schmoke was elected mayor.

Even Schaefer seemed to sense that these politicians were right: The schools belonged to the blacks and should be regarded as an object of black patronage. This perception reinforced Schaefer's inclination to maintain his distance from the schools. As political scientist Marion Orr observed, Schaefer regarded the schools as a "political land mine" and left their administration "to trusted associates on the school board and black administrators who owed their appointment to the city."[31] The mayor attempted to take the schools out of the spotlight and to highlight the urban renaissance instead.

The trouble was that completion of the renaissance inevitably required the rebirth of the city schools. The 1974 strike, true to the fears of Schaefer and his administration, only hastened the process of white flight and brought further deterioration to the schools. As Mike Bowler rather gently stated in his short history of the Baltimore school system, "thousands of whites left the schools in 1974 and 1975."[32]

Patterson's Complaint

Catastrophic as the strike was, it marked only the first of the school system's two major crises in 1974. The second crisis involved a federal mandate that Baltimore produce a desegregation plan, a mandate which further exposed racial tensions within the system and highlighted the intractability of its problems.

After the *Brown* decision, the city had settled into a durable pattern of racial separation based on the earlier system of total segregation. Most elementary school students went to schools close to their homes, leading to a high degree of racial separation. Although the system permitted more flexibility at the upper levels, the enrollment patterns continued to reflect the housing patterns of what was essentially a highly segregated city. Baltimore's department of education did what it could to change the situation by creating a series of magnet high schools intended to draw students from all over the city, but these fell short of altering the prevailing pattern.

The courts eventually caught up with Baltimore. After the *Brown* decision, nothing much was expected except that the city maintain an enrollment policy that did not overtly discriminate against blacks. As years passed, the courts began to examine results rather than possibilities. Pressing the sociological if not the legal reasoning of *Brown,* the courts asked whether any school remained all black or all white. Over time they modified this inquiry and began to question whether the racial balance in individual schools reflected that of the school system at large. If in Baltimore a ratio of seven black to three white students prevailed, the courts expected individual schools not to deviate very far from that ratio.[33]

At the time of *Brown,* invoking the courts' displeasure held very few consequences. In the 1970s failure to desegregate carried penalties that resulted from federal policies of the 1960s. Since Baltimore's schools received substantial federal funds as a result of the Elementary and Secondary Education Act of 1965, they came under the domain of Title VI of the Civil Rights Act of 1964, which prohibited discrimination in entities that received federal funds. The penalty could reach as far as a withdrawal of federal money, a disastrous possibility in the financially pinched atmosphere of 1974. Baltimore's schools had to please federal officials or suffer a 10 percent budget cut; that might in turn evoke the displeasure of state officials and lead to still more cuts. Laws that had brought what seemed to be unambiguous benefit to Baltimore in the 1960s had different connotations a decade later.

The Nixon administration had little sympathy for court intervention into the affairs of local school districts, but could exert little influence over the courts, which increasingly saw themselves as chancellors of equity at a time when the legislative branch could no longer easily effect social change through expansive legislation.[34] Moreover, important parts of the federal bureaucracy, such as the Office of Civil Rights in the Department of Health, Education, and Welfare, believed strongly in upholding court decisions and implementing Title VI of the Civil Rights Act. Lawyers in these offices exercised considerable autonomy, whatever the policies of the administration. Furthermore, the Nixon administration owed little or nothing to cities such as Baltimore, and the rage and social dislocation that might accompany a desegregation order could in fact work to the administration's advantage.

With these mixed motivations, Peter E. Holmes, the young lawyer who headed HEW's Office of Civil Rights, wrote to Superintendent Roland Patterson in April 1973. Holmes informed Patterson of the Supreme Court's recent decision in the case of *Adams v. Richardson,* which required HEW to communicate with Baltimore and other local school districts and put "them on notice to rebut or explain the substantial racial disproportion" in

Baltimore's schools. Holmes ordered Patterson to come up with data on the racial balance in each of the system's schools. He also reminded Patterson of the 1971 decision in *Swann v. Charlotte Mecklenberg*, which warranted "a presumption against schools that are substantially disproportionate in their racial composition."[35]

Patterson did his best to stall. In a June 1973 reply to Holmes, he tried to present the Baltimore situation in the best possible light—he blamed racial segregation on demography. "Shifting population trends . . . thwart [the city's] best efforts," he wrote. Patterson worried that since the city seemed "to be moving toward an almost totally black system, the School Board and staff have grave feelings that mandatory movements of pupils will hasten the progress of the flight of whites from the city, thereby increasing the socio-economic problems that now beset the city." Instead of working on school integration directly, the school system was concentrating on measures that "will halt the relentless pattern of population change from white to black." As proof of the changes, Patterson pointed to the case of City College High School, which was all-white in 1953 and 97 percent nonwhite in 1972.[36]

Federal officials did not reach a decision on Baltimore until the winter of 1974. Then, in the middle of the school strike and the energy crisis, Holmes wrote to Patterson that, "On the basis of the data available . . . I have concluded that further desegregation of the Baltimore City Schools is necessary and desirable." Holmes noted that most of the schools that had been segregated prior to Brown remained racially identifiable, that the city's policy of open enrollment had not been effective, and that the teaching staff remained segregated. In the brusque manner of federal regulators, Holmes gave Patterson only thirty days to come up with a desegregation plan.[37]

On February 16, 1974, on what might have been the single worst day in the history of the Baltimore city schools, news reached the public that the federal government had ordered the city to remove the last vestiges of its segregated school system.[38] The story failed to create an immediate stir because the city was still coping with the school strike and with long gas lines. In addition the kidnapping of Patty Hearst, in what appeared to be a last echo of the Sixties, also diverted the public's attention. Nonetheless, the city somehow had to respond to the deadline the federal government had imposed.

Parents and young children protest before Baltimore City school headquarters, May 31, 1974. (*Baltimore News-American* staff photograph, University of Maryland, College Park.)

Patterson used the strike as a pretext to gain time. He told Holmes, "the welfare of 186,000 school children is dependent upon a settlement of the labor problems which have resulted in the strikes." Holmes extended the deadline but only slightly. The city had until the end of April to come up with a plan.

On February 21, Patterson had a dialogue with the Board of School Commissioners, as the school board was formally known, that underscored the need for the city to act on the matter of desegregation. Patterson did not want to submit a desegregation plan, arguing that the city had already maximized the integration of its schools. Further moves would only lead to a decline in the city's tax base and an increase in social alienation. The energy crisis also mitigated against taking action. "How can we possibly talk about putting additional buses on the street," he asked, "when we drive past the long lines of automobiles waiting at service stations?"

If Patterson, the city's first black superintendent, took a line that might have come from President Nixon, the school commissioners were quick to remind him that he did not have the luxury of ignoring the federal order. The simple reason was that the city received more than $16 million from the federal government. As board member Larry Gibson put it, the city could not afford to lose those funds. He added that the law required integration and the city risked having its school system taken over by the courts. For all those reasons, the school board directed Patterson to prepare a desegregation plan and to organize a community-based desegregation task force.[39]

As Patterson had predicted, desegregation became a highly controversial matter in the spring of 1974. The superintendent continued to hope that students in junior and senior high schools would be allowed to attend the schools of their choice. But he did not explain how such an open enrollment policy would alter the racial composition of the fourteen all- or nearly all-white schools in the system, including Patterson High School, located near the white ethnic neighborhoods of East Baltimore and 92 percent white. Federal authorities who addressed the desegregation task force noted that "massive busing" would not be required.[40]

"Busing," a term that was almost always used derogatively, served as the shorthand symbol for the desegregation effort. Busing implied that children would be moved from one section of the city to another, that they would leave the comfortable confines of their own community and confront the alien culture of another. Whites in particular felt threatened. A thousand people, nearly all of them white, packed a desegregation task force meeting and shouted their opposition to busing elementary school students. "I will not stand for busing. I will take my children out of public school," said Louella Welch. "You've got to go against this busing," warned another parent, "because if you don't you are going to lose your kids and they are going to get hurt." Still another said that she was raised in the city, "but if my elementary school children are bused out of my neighborhood by force my husband and I will sell our house and move to Baltimore County." Among the sympathetic white politicians in attendance was Councilwoman Barbara Mikulski.[41]

Embroiled in controversy over such heated issues as the forced busing of elementary school children, the desegregation task force could not agree on a single plan to recommend to the school board. The board begged the federal authorities for more time. Not until May 29, 1974, did the board unveil its plan, which involved a complicated arrangement to pair certain schools at the elementary level and to extend the magnet arrangement for senior high schools. The board noted that it operated under political constraints such as those imposed by Mayor Schaefer, who insisted that elementary students not be bused to schools that were more than a mile from their homes.[42]

Even the board's relatively mild plan met with considerable resistance. Students from Mergenthaler Vocational School picketed in front of city hall, protesting the proposed merger of their school with Carver Vocational School. Mergenthaler had a roughly equal balance of white and black students; Carver contained only blacks. "Hell no, we won't go," chanted the Mergenthaler students. The next day students from Patterson High took up the same chant, picketing city hall and protesting the plan to turn Patterson into a magnet school. Although the students complained about busing, the fact was that most of them already used buses to get to Patterson. Throughout the system, nearly a third of the students used public transportation to get to school. Still, the threat of change blended with the usual end-of-the-year restlessness to create a series of marches on city hall and school administration headquarters. The academic year, already marred by the strike, ended with students missing still more class time to protest against the desegregation plan.[43]

In the face of these protests, the school board retreated from its initial plan. It voted against making Patterson a magnet school, in part because of pressure from politicians like city comptroller Hyman Pressman. "The federal government has put a gun to our head and the Patterson plan would pull the trigger," argued Pressman, who then urged the city not to submit any desegregation plan. On June 4, 1974, in a bitterly divisive meeting, the school board reduced from twenty-seven to fourteen the number of elementary schools that were to be paired in order to improve racial balance.

They also adopted a plan that would limit the number of junior high school students who would be moved from one area of the city to another and approved what the *Sun* described as a "vaguely worded senior high school plan." Larry Gibson labelled the new plan "a farce" that federal authorities would surely reject. Mrs. M. Richmond Faring, a white member of the board who represented the interests of largely white South Baltimore, invited HEW either to accept the plan or to "drop dead."[44]

The fight over school desegregation marked the unsatisfactory end of an unsatisfying academic year. Nearly everyone knew that more trouble lay ahead. If HEW rejected the plan, Mayor Schaefer would sue; if HEW approved the plan, the NAACP would sue. Most observers thought it unlikely that HEW would accept the plan and hoped the disarray within the Nixon administration would delay HEW from taking action.[45]

Patterson lasted only another year as superintendent. He and Mayor Schaefer had a showdown meeting on Labor Day, 1974. As the two talked, pickets demonstrated outside protesting the "feeder" plan for junior high schools that, according to Mike Bowler, "put an end to the concept that junior and senior high school students could attend the school of their choice."[46] The meeting erupted into a shouting match with the result that Patterson lost the mayor's confidence. The following summer Patterson was gone.

The History Lesson

Events of 1970 and 1974 illustrated aspects of the Baltimore school system's transformation from white to black. Disturbances in 1970 showed the high degree of racial tension within the schools at a time when most of the students were black and most of the teachers white. The disruptions sent a signal to middle-class residents that they could not expect the schools to perform the same way in the 1970s as they had in the previous decades. If education was truly "the nexus of generational change," the "dynamic mechanism by which economic level is passed on from one generation to the next," as policymakers believed it was in the 1960s, then it was important for middle-class parents to find high quality schools for their children.[47] The Baltimore schools appeared to be failing that test.

The 1974 strike indicated that teachers shared the frustrations of middle-class parents. Although teachers were supposed to act as agents of change in an increasingly complex world, the city failed to comprehend the diffi-

Demonstrators move up Calvert Street to school headquarters on May 31, 1974, their mood ranging "from militant to jubilant" according to the *News-American*. *(Baltimore News-American* staff photograph, University of Maryland, College Park.)

culty of their task. It appeared to them that the city was unwilling to spend the necessary money to fund quality schools. The city, for its part, was trapped by the economic stringency of the era. More money for education meant higher taxes, which translated into more middle-class flight, which would mean still less money for education. The only solution was to appeal to outside authorities in Washington and Annapolis to come to the city's aid.

The desegregation order demonstrated that all external aid came with strings. If the city received federal help, it had to comply with federal mandates, including the elimination of segregated schools. Although city authorities sympathized with this goal in the abstract, they saw desegregation as another variation on a zero-sum game. Correcting segregation at one place, like Patterson High School, meant disrupting the racial balance at another. The more the city tinkered with mechanisms to produce racial integration—a concept that could only mean racially proportionate schools in a school system that was 70 percent black—the more it risked losing its white, middle-class residents. If those residents left the city or withdrew their children from the schools, the situation could only worsen. It seemed therefore that the city faced a tragic dilemma—accepting federal funds in the short term appeared to mean imperiling the city's future.

The 1970s, a decade of slow economic growth, was a period of much harder choices than the preceding twenty years. In the 1970s, unlike the 1960s, the federal government imposed mandates on localities without providing the financial means for the localities to fulfill those mandates. In the 1970s, unlike the 1950s, the federal government acted against the wishes of local leaders with regard to racial integration. The *Brown* decision provided the impetus for the city to take steps that many people already favored; the court decisions of the 1970s forced the city to take steps with which many people disagreed. In the 1950s the court was the vehicle of progressive change; in the 1970s it was widely regarded as insensitive to local conditions.

The three incidents described here are only snapshots in the process of long-term social change. In a historiographic sense, they show the impossibility of writing the social history of Baltimore and its schools without reference to federal policies. In this case, writing history from the bottom up requires a close knowledge of history from the top down.

In a more local sense, these incidents illustrate some of the reasons that the residents of the 3800 block of Juniper Road view the Baltimore city school system with indifference and occasional disdain. Once a source of great civic pride, the schools no longer unite the city.

Notes

This chapter was originally published in the *Maryland Historical Magazine,* 92 (1997): 413–32.

[1] "The Three 'R's—Plus," in *Speaking of Baltimore,* a pamphlet published in the 1930s by radio station WBAL, n.d., 41.

[2] "We the People," *Baltimore: City of Promise,* Produced by Senior High School Pupils of the Baltimore Public Schools (Baltimore: Department of Education, 1953), 42, 46, 47, 53.

[3] "Progress in Education and Recreation," *Baltimore: City of Promise,* 182–203.

[4] Quoted in Mike Bowler, *The Lessons of Change: Baltimore Schools in the Modern Era* (Baltimore: Fund for Educational Excellence, 1991), 5.

[5] See "Informational Materials for Desegregation Task Force," March 1974, privately obtained. This mimeographed publication was given to the members of the desegregation task force in 1974. I am grateful to Professor Howell Baum for providing me with a copy. (Hereafter referred to as desegregation materials.)

[6] See, for example, Diane Ravitch, *The Troubled Crusade: American Education, 1945–1980* (New York: Basic Books, 1983).

[7] Bowler, *Lessons of Change,* 7.

[8] Ibid.

[9] Ibid., 5–6.

[10] Kenneth K. Wong, *City Choices: Education and Housing* (Albany, N.Y.: SUNY Press, 1990), 55; Marion Orr, "Urban Politics and School Reform: The Case of Baltimore," Paper presented January 1995 at the National Conference of Black Political Scientists, Hampton, Va., 5 ; Bowler, *Lessons of Change,* 43.

[11] See the various articles in Hugh Davis Graham, ed., *Civil Rights in the United States* (University Park: Pennsylvania State University Press, 1994) and *The Civil Rights Era: Origins and Development of National Policy, 1960–1972* (New York: Oxford University Press, 1990).

[12] Ravitch, *Troubled Crusade;* Julie Roy Jeffrey, *Education for Children of the Poor* (Columbus: Ohio State University Press, 1978); Hugh Davis Graham, *The Uncertain Triumph* (Chapel Hill: University of North Carolina Press, 1984); Edward D. Berkowitz, *Mr. Social Security: The Life of Wilbur J. Cohen* (Lawrence: University Press of Kansas, 1995).

[13] Wong, *City Choices,* 59–60.

[14] See Jerome T. Murphy, "The Education Bureaucracies Implement Novel Policy: The Politics of Title I of ESEA, 1965–1972," in Allan P. Sindler, ed., *Policy and Politics in America: Six Case Studies* (Boston: Little, Brown and Co., 1973), 160–200.

[15] Wong, *City Choices,* 78.

[16] Bowler, *Lessons of Change,* 42.

[17] "Racial Disorders Afflict Schools," *Baltimore Sun,* March 18, 1970; Alvin P. Sanhoff, "School Cool-It Plan May Be Too Late," *Sun,* March 22, 1970.

[18] "School Fire Blamed on Arson," *Sun,* April 7, 1970.

[19] Stephen J. Lynton, "Mayor Fears Arson's Effect," *Sun,* April 10, 1970; 2 Policemen Injured at School," *Sun,* April 15, 1970; "School Fire Blamed on Arson," *Sun,* April 7, 1970.

[20] Mike Bowler, "One-race Schools on Rise," *Sun,* March 3, 1974.

[21] Mike Bowler, "Patterson Buys Home Amid Leaving Talk," *Sun,* January 23, 1974.

[22] "Union to Defy School-Strike Injunction," *Sun,* February 5, 1974; Mike Bowler, "71% of Students Absent; Hearings Set on Injunction," *Sun,* February 6, 1974; "School Attendance 16%; Talks Break Off Again," *Sun,* February 7, 1974.

[23] See Paul Johnston, *Success While Others Fail: Social Movement Unionism and the Public Workplace* (Ithaca, N.Y.: ILR Press, 1994).

[24] "School Teachers Dissatisfied with More than Their Salary," *Sun,* February 8, 1974.

[25] Mike Bowler, "Schools to Stay Open, Patterson Vows," *Sun,* February 14, 1974.

[26] Bowler, "Teachers Reject City's Pay Offer by 5-1 Margin," *Sun,* February 20, 1974; Bowler, "City Police Escort Teachers, Pupils Past Picket Lines on Strike's 17th Day," *Sun,* February 21, 1974; Bowler, "Schaefer and Court Delay Action Against Teachers; 3 Strikers Arrested," *Sun,* February 22, 1974; Bowler, "Police Arrest 31 School Pickets," *Sun,* February 23, 1974.

[27] Bowler, "Teachers Reject City's Pay Offer by 5-1 Margin"; "Schaefer Puts

Plea Directly to City Teachers," *Sun,* February 24, 1974; Tracie Rozhon, "Schaefer Asks: What am I to Do?," *Sun,* February 25, 1974.

[28] "Fourth Week of School Crisis," editorial, *Sun,* February 28, 1974.

[29] George J. Hiltner and Mike Bowler, "High-level School Talks Under Way; Fines Imposed on Boone, Teacher Union," *Sun,* February 28, 1974; Bowler, "Top Federal Mediator Enters Teachers' Strike," *Sun,* March 2, 1974; Bowler, "Teachers Reach Agreement with City," *Sun,* March 4, 1974; "PSTA Declares School Strike Is Over Despite Teachers' Rejection of Accord," *Sun,* Tuesday, March 5, 1974; Bowler, "Teachers Strike Ends with Quiet Return to Classes," *Sun,* March 6, 1974.

[30] School Bill Called Racially Inspired," *Sun,* March 15, 1974.

[31] Orr, "Urban Politics and School Reform," 11.

[32] Bowler, *Lessons of Change,* 14.

[33] Ravitch, *The Troubled Crusade,* 145–81.

[34] See, for example, William C. Berman, *America's Right Turn: From Nixon to Bush* (Baltimore: Johns Hopkins University Press, 1994).

[35] Peter E. Holmes to Roland Patterson, April 17, 1953, in desegregation materials.

[36] Roland Patterson to Peter F. Holmes, June 4, 1973, desegregation materials.

[37] Holmes to Patterson, February 5, 1974, desegregation materials.

[38] Frederick B. Hill, "U.S. Orders End to Dual System in City's Schools, *Sun,* February 16, 1974.

[39] Minutes of the Board of School Commissioners, February 21, 1974, Coldstream Park Elementary School, in desegregation materials.

[40] "Patterson Asks Coexistence of HEW Rule, Open Enrollment," *Sun,* March 16, 1974; Michael Weisskopf, "Busing Not Needed in City, HEW Says," *Sun,* March 24, 1974.

[41] Tom Linthicum, "1,000 Parents, Students Pack Patterson High to Protest Busing," *Sun,* April 4, 1974.

[42] Antero Pietila, "Board Proposed Paired Schools, No New Busing," *Sun,* May 29, 1974.

[43] "75 Mervo Students Protest Against Joining Carver," ibid.; Antero Pietila, "Students Protest New Plan, *Sun,* May 30, 1974; Theodore W. Hendricks, "Students Cut Class to March," *Sun,* May 31, 1974.

[44] Antero Pietila, "School Administration Backs Off on Proposal to Change Curriculum at Patterson, 4 Others," *Sun,* June 4, 1974; Pietila, "School Board Votes Diluted Racial Plan," *Sun,* June 5, 1974.

[45] "School Court Fight Due," *Sun,* June 6, 1974.

[46] Bowler, *Lessons of Change,* 14.

[47] James N. Morgan et al., *Income and Welfare in the United States* (New York: McGraw Hill and Co., 1962), 9–11.

"Making Diversity Work: 250 Years of Baltimore History"

November 15–16, 1996, University of Baltimore–Coppin State College

Friday, November 15, 1996 – University of Baltimore
Noon–2:00 PM — "Diversity, Politics, and History" Roundtable
    Live Radio Broadcast with Marc Steiner on WJHU

Session I

A. *"Working in Baltimore, Making Baltimore Work, 1780–1860"*
Dennis Zembala, Baltimore Museum of Industry, Commentator
Amy S. Greenberg, Penn State University, "Volunteer Fire Companies and Community Formation in Baltimore, 1780–1858"
Richard Chew III, College of William and Mary, "Between Slavery and Freedom: Artisans, Slavery and the Formation of Baltimore's Working Class, 1790–1820"
Seth Edward Rockman, University of California, Davis, "The School of Industry: Welfare Reform, circa 1805"

B. *"Making/Breaking Public Policy: Highways and Housing, 1942–75"*
Michael McCarthy, University of Baltimore, Commentator
Deborah R. Weiner, West Virginia University, "Two Baltimore Housing Projects: From New Deal Promise to Postmodern Defeat"
Rhonda Y. Williams, University of Pennsylvania, "The Search for Resident Power: Inside Baltimore's Public Housing in the 1960s"
Susan West Montgomery, George Washington University, "Baltimore's Abbreviated Interstate System: The Consequence of Opposition, Legislation and Federal Intervention"

C. *"Changing Schools in Industrial and Post-Industrial Baltimore"*

Jo Ann E. Argersinger, University of Maryland Baltimore County, Commentator

Robert S. Wolff ,University of Connecticut, Storrs, "Searching for Order: Transformations in Baltimore Schooling, 1865–1920"

Edward D. Berkowitz, George Washington University, "Baltimore's Public Schools in a Time of Transition, the 1970s"

Evening Reception at Baltimore City Life Museum

Program— Cindy Kelly, "Outdoor Sculpture in Baltimore"

Saturday, November 16, 1996 – Coppin State College

Session II

A. *Neither Slave nor Free: African-Americans in Baltimore, 1820–1860*

Bettye Gardner, Coppin State College, Commentator

Christopher W. Phillips, John Carroll College, "'A Conjurer's Morsel': Colonization, Emigration, and Free Blacks in Antebellum Baltimore"

Patrick May, Coppin State College, "The Residential Distribution of Free Blacks in Antebellum Baltimore: Research and Issues"

B. *Helping Oneself, Helping Others: Blacks, Whites, and Social Justice in Baltimore, 1880–1930*

Howard Gillette, George Washington University, Commentator

Robert R. Schoeberlein, Maryland Historical Society, "To Benefit the Human Family: Benevolence Toward African-Americans in Post–Civil War Baltimore"

Hayward Farrar, Virginia Tech, "A Place to Work: The Baltimore *Afro-American*'s Crusade Against Racism in Employment, 1892–1950"

Lillian Howard Potter, Hollins College, "Political Cooperation, Economic Competition: Relationships Between Jewish and Black Communities in Baltimore, Maryland, 1930–1940"

C. *Building Baltimore: Housing, Spaces and Alleys*

Garrett Power, University of Maryland Law School, Commentator

Mary Ellen Hayward, Maryland Historical Society, "The Rowhouse: Baltimore's Basic Building Block"

Mark Cameron, Morgan State University, "Monuments of Urbanity: The Development of Baltimore's Residential Squares"

Eric L. Holcomb, Commission for Historical and Architectural Preservation, "The Suburbanization of Walbrook: A Development and Architectural History"

Roderick N. Ryon, Towson State University, "From Homogeneity to Diversity: Residential Architecture in Baltimore's Outer City"

11:45–12:45 PM Ethnic Baltimore Luncheon

Keynote Address: Michael Olesker, Baltimore Sun, "Beyond Nostalgia"

Session III

A. *Seccession, Strife, and Liberation: Baltimore in the Civil War*

Jean Baker, Goucher College, Commentator

Frank Towers, Clarion University, "Labor Conflict and the Seccession Crisis in Baltimore"

Roger A. Davidson, Jr., Howard University, "Brown-Water, Black-Men: Afro-Baltimoreans in the Potomac Flotilla, 1861–1865"

B. *Making War at Home: Baltimore Experiences World War II*

Linda Shopes, Pennsylvania Historical and Museum Commission, Commentator

Cynthia Neverdon-Morton, Coppin State College, "Conflict and Resolution in Baltimore's Work Places"

John R. Breihan, Loyola College, "Wings for Democracy? African-Americans in Baltimore's World War II Aviation Industry"

People and Places in Time: Baltimore's Changing Landscapes

September 24–25, 1999

Friday – September 24, 1999 – University of Baltimore

Concurrent Workshops

I. *Greetings from Baltimore: The Creation of the Baltimore City Heritage Area*
Kathleen Kotarba, Commission for Historical & Architectural Planning
Eric Holcomb, Commission for Historical & Architectural Planning

II. *Using Local History Locally – Part I*
Patrick May, Coppin State College
Michael Ratcliffe, U.S. Census Bureau
Jennifer Ford, Maryland History Day
Keith Dix, Maryland History Day

11:45AM–12:15 PM Welcome
Calvin Burnett, President, Coppin State College
H. Mebane Turner, President, University of Baltimore

Lunch
12:30–1:15 PM Welcome
Kathleen Kotarba, Commission for Historical & Architectural Planning
    Bill Pencek, Baltimore Heritage, Inc.
Fred Shoken, "Unbuilt Baltimore"

1:30–3:00 PM Session A

1. *Immigrants & Philanthropy in Late 19th Century Baltimore*
Carol Hoffecker, University of Delaware, Commentator
Matthew White, B&O Railroad Museum, "People of Lawrence House"
Robert Wolff, Central Connecticut State University, "A Home for Girls of
     Good Character: Samuel Ready School"

2. *Beneath the Horizon: Slums and Alley Houses*
Bernie Herman, University of Delaware, Commentator
Mary Ellen Hayward, The Alley House Project, "The Alleys of Baltimore"
Garrett Power, University of Maryland Law School, "In Search of Slums"

3. *The Impact of Artists and Their Organizations on the Baltimore
     Urban Landscape: A Roundtable*
Linda Shopes, PA Historical & Museum Commission, Moderator
Daniel Schiavone, Independent Scholar
Linda Day Clark, Coppin State College
Leslie King Hammond, Maryland Institute of Art
Mike Guiliano, Journalist
George Ciscle, Maryland Institute of Art

3:15–4:45PM   Session B

4. *Baltimore in the Early Republic: Property & Civil Society*
Jeffrey Sawyer, University of Baltimore, Commentator
Joshua Civin, Oxford University, "Blurring the Boundaries Between
     Civil Society an the State"
Christopher Curtis, Emory University, "Barron vs. The Mayor and City
     Council of Baltimore"

5. *Going Beyond the Baltimore City Line*

Peter Levy, York College of Pennsylvania, Commentator

Louis Diggs, Independent Scholar, "African American Life in Baltimore County"

Thomas Jacklin, University of Baltimore, "Lessons from Light Rail"

6. *Destruction and Vacancy*

Howard Gillette, Rutgers University, Camden, Commentator

Steve Allan, Baltimore Heritage, Inc., "Detroit Destroyed, Baltimore Pending".

Miriam Schoenbaum, Johns Hopkins University, "Vacant and Underused Land in Baltimore City"

5:00–7:00 PM – Reception — Maryland Historical Society

Welcome — Dennis Fiori, Director

Saturday, September 25, 1999 – University of Baltimore

9:00–11:45 AM – Session C

7. *Mobtown and the Gallows*

Beatriz Hardy, National History Day, Commentator

Richard Chew, College of William and Mary, "Panic, Depression and Rioting: The Origins of Mob Town in the Baltimore Riots of 1812"

8. *Seeking Community*

Jack Breihan, Loyola College, Commentator

Cindi Ptak, Union Square Association, "Putting H.L.Mencken Back on the Cultural Map"

Phillip Merrill, Nanny Jack Company, "Colored Directories and the Search for Community, 1913–1946"

9. *Making Visible an Invisible History: A Roundtable on Gay and Lesbian Landscapes*
J. Dudley Clendinen, Author, Moderator
David Bergman, Towson University
Ann Gordon, Civil Rights Organizer
Paulette Young, Gay & Lesbian Community Center
Louis Hughes, Independent Researcher

10:45AM – Session D

10. *Inner City Challenges*
Edward Orser, UMBC, Commentator
Jessica Elfenbein, University of Baltimore, "Druid Hill YMCA: 1885–1925"
Samuel Roberts, Princeton University, "The Baltimore Public Community's Attitudes Toward the Problem of Tuberculosis Among African Americans, 1880–1920"

11. *Glory & Jubilee: Unrealized Promise in Race Relations*
Bettye Gardner, Coppin State College, Commentator
Richard Fuke, Wilfrid Laurier University, "Race and Public Policy in Baltimore, 1864–1870"
Helena Hicks, Independent Scholar, "Black Entrepreneurs in Early Baltimore"

12. *Selling the Public on Public History: A Roundtable*
Dean Krimmel, University of Maryland School of Nursing, Moderator
Helen Jean Burns, Editor & Writer
Louis Fields, Black Heritage Tours
Joanne Martin, Executive Director, Great Blacks in Wax

12:30–1:45PM— Lunch

Welcome — Barbara Wells Sarudy, Maryland Humanities Council

Joe Arnold, UMBC, "Writing a History of Baltimore: Thinking Big About a
Big City"

2:00–4:30 PM – Concurrent Workshops

I. *Using Local History Locally – Part II*

Thomas L. Hollowak, University of Baltimore

Dean Krimmel, University of Maryland School of Nursing

II. *Preserving Baltimore's Commercial District: The Struggle over the
Westside Plan*

Bill Pencek, Baltimore Heritage, Inc., Moderator

Sharon Grinnell, Baltimore Development Corporation

Chris Lynch, University of Maryland Medical Services

Tyler Gearhart, Preservation Maryland

Index

Note: Page numbers in italics indicate illustrations.

reforms enacted, 104–105
support for secession, 108
Brown, John, 96, 112, 113
Brown v. Board of Education, 251–252, 262
Brune, Frederick W., 96, 102, 118
Brune, John, 111
Buchanan administration, 115
Buchanan, James, 78
Burkleigh Manor, 184
Burr, Aaron, 64
Burton, Charles, 212
Burton, Cora, 212
Busy Alley, 36
Butler Alley, 55
Butler, Benjamin, 108–109
Butler Guards, 131

Calhoun, John C., 71
Camden Station, 53, 54, 55, 107
Cameron, Simon, 99
Camillus (N.Y.), 85
Camper, J. E. T., 179–180
Canton, 42, 227, 228, 229, 239, 240
Canton Company, 180
capital punishment, 67
public opinion, 70, 77, 81, 82–85
Carolinas, 11
Caroline Street, 40, 54
Carroll, Anna Ella, 120
Carroll County (Md.), 12
Westminster, 12
Carver Vocational School, 267
Catholic Mirror, 116
caulker riots, 96, 100
caulker strike, 129–130, 142
Cecelia Furnace, 42
Central YMCA, 156, 158, 166, 167n.10
and Colored YMCA, 151–152, 153, 154, 155
and Druid Hill Avenue YMCA, 157, 159, 164
Chapel Street, 36
Charity Organization Society (COS), 152, 159
Charles Street, 73

Charleston (S.C.), 93
Cherry Hill (Baltimore, Md.), 187, 190
Chesapeake and Potomac Telephone Company, 179
Chesapeake Bay, 7
Chicago Housing Authority (Chicago, Ill.), 214
Chicago (Ill.), 5, 160, 163, 198, 206
cholera, 49, 50, 51
epidemic of 1832, 50
epidemic of 1866, 50, 134, 145
Churchill Street, 36
Cincinnati (Oh.), 163
Citizens Housing Council, 204
City College High School, 255, 264
City Council (Baltimore, Md.), 187
City High School, 251
City Reform Association, 94, 96, 98–99, 100, 111, 112, 114, 116, 118, 119
Baltimore Bills, 101
Brown, George William, 96, 102, 103, 104–106, 108, 109
Kane, George P., 100, 101–102, 108
leaders jailed, 109
Civil Rights Act of 1964, 263
Civil War, 9, 14, 15, 42, 44, 52, 55, 118
Civil War veterans, African American, 130–131, 141
Clarence Perkins Homes, 198, 202, 203, 204–205, 206, 210–211, 215, 216, 217, 219
class
and public life, 64–66, 94
and support for secession, 109–110
class boundaries, and volunteer fire companies, 23, 25–26, 28–29, 31n.26
Clifton Park Junior High School, 252–253
Cockeysville (Md.), 108
Coleridge-Taylor, Samuel, 159
Colored YMCA, 149, 150, 151, 153, 154, 156–157, 167n.18. *see also*

employment of women, 178, 179
Fairfield, 173
Middle River (Md.), 174, 175, 180,
 181, 182, 183, 184, 185, 187
segregation of African Americans,
 180, 187, 188–190
Sinclair Lane, 181
unionization, 182–183
Glover Street, 44
Goines, P. A., 157, 168n.33
Goodwin, Lyle, 74
Grace Presbyterian Church, 157
Granger, Lester, 187
Great Britain, 173
Great Lakes, 5
Great Migration, 154
Greater Baltimore Committee, 5
Greek Revival, 34, 37, 40. *see also*
 architecture
Greenbelt, 184
Greene, John, 212
Greenwood, W. T., 151
Griffin, James M., 261
Griffith, Thomas, 47
Gropius, Walter, 207, 211
ground rents, 35–36
Guilford Avenue, 151

Hackett, George A., 139
Hall, R., 151
Hall, Thomas, 116, 117
Halttunen, Karen, 67
Hamburg Street, 37
Hanover Switch riot, 130, 141, 142
Happy Alley (Durham Street), 36
Happy Days (Mencken), 33
Hare, Joseph Thompson, 67
Harford County (Md.), 12, 78
 Belair, 12
Harlem (New York City, N.Y.), 154
Harlem Park, 40
Harpers Ferry, 108, 113
Harrington, Michael, 210, 215
Harris, J. Morrison, 118
Harvard University, 256
Haynes, Sylvanus, 85

Heaps, - (widow), 79
Heaps, John, 67, 68, 69, 71, 72, 82
Henshaw, J. P. K., 73
Herring Run Park, 186, 187, 192
Hess Court, 55
Hibernian Society, 102
Hicks, Thomas, 95, 103, 108, 120
Highlandtown, 227, 229, 235–236,
 237
Hillman, Robert S., 259–260
Hinks, Charles, 101
Hobbs, Clark S., 178
Hoffman, Henry, 108
Hoffman Street, 157
Holabird Homes, 212
Holloway, Charles T., 25
Holmes, Peter E., 263–265
Holt, Stan, 237, 241
Honey Alley (Hughes Street), 36, 54,
 56
horse cars, 9
House of Reformation and Instruc-
 tion for Colored Children, *145*, 152
Housing Act of 1949, 206, 215
Housing Act of 1954, 209
Housing Authority of Baltimore City
 (HABC), 201–203, 204–205, 206,
 208, 209, 210, 211, 212, 213
housing covenants, 10, 185, 192, 210
Housing of the Unskilled Wage Earner
 (Wood), 200
How the Other Half Lives (Riis), 48,
 199
Howard, Charles, 101, 114, 115
Howard County (Md.), Columbia, 12
Howard family, 112
Howard, John Eager, 36, 40
Howard, McHenry, 114
Howard, William, 115
Hughes Court, 55
Hughes, James W., 161
Hughes Street, 36, 54, 56
Hull, Amos, 70–71, 74, 76, 78, 81, 85
 defense of M. N. B. Hull, 75
Hull, Morris Norton Bartholomew
 arrest, 66, 69

FROM MOBTOWN TO CHARM CITY

need for, 199–200
opposition to, 201, 203, 205–206,
218
segregation, 202
and slum clearance, 200, 201, 206,
207
tenants, types of, 208–209
and urban renewal, 209–210, 214,
215
public opinion
and politics, 65
and printed materials, 65
Public School Teachers Association
(PSTA), 257, 259, 260, 260–261

Quaker Friends Association in Aid of
Freedmen, 132

race
and alley houses, 38, 39
housing covenants, 10, 185, 192,
210
labor relations, 96, 100, 129–130
and poverty, 48–49, 56, 62n.50
segregation ordinances, 10, 44
substandard living conditions, 55–
56, 185–186
suburban migration, 10
racial segregation, 8
racial separatism, 8
Rainwater, Lee, 218–219
Raisin, Isaac Freeman, 56
Randolph, A. Philip, 176
Raymond, Daniel, 84, 86
Redmon Court, 55
Reese, David, 75, 76, 79
Register Street, 39
Reiserstown (Md.), 12
Remarks on Capital Punishment
(Williams), 84–85
Republican Party, 56, 57, 97, 99, 115,
139–140, 141, 142
Revere Copper and Brass, 178
Richmond, Mary, 159
Richmond (Va.), 152, 190
Riis, Jacob, 48, 199

riot of April 15, 1861, 107
riot of April 19, 1861, 92, 94, 107,
109, 112, 113, 114, 115
demographics, 109–110
riot of February 23, 1861, 106
Riverdale, 184
Robeson, Paul, 187
Roland Park, 12
Romney, George, 218
Roosevelt, Franklin D., 176
Rosemont, 228
Rosenwald, Julius, 159, 163
Rush, Benjamin, 85
Russians, 52

Saum, Jacob, 34
Saville, Thomas, 105–106
Schaefer, William Donald, 232, 244,
256, 257, 258, 259, 260, 262, 267,
268
Schley, William, 103, 104
Schmoke, Kurt L., 13, 261
school system
busing, 236–242, *265*, 266–268
demographics, 253
desegregation of, 234–236, 262,
267–269, 270
funding, 253–254
integration of, 10
student unrest, 254–256
teachers strike, *257–258*, 259–262
Scots-Irish, 7
Scott, T. Parkin, 111, 116
Sears Roebuck, 159
secession, 92–93, 103, 108, 111
secession, support for, and African
Americans, 110, 116–117
SECO. *see* Southeast Community
Organization
Second Migration (1890-1920), 7
sectionalism, 93, 94, 104, 107, 114,
117, 118
Sedition Act, and public discourse,
65
segregation, 180–182

financial support for, 20
and fire insurance, 17
generational boundaries, 26,
  32n.30
growth of, 16
Independent Fire Company, 17,
  19
Liberty Fire Company, 20, 21, 22
libraries, 16
Mechanical Fire Company, 15, 20,
  26, 28
New Market Fire Company, 20, 26
Pioneer Hook and Ladder
  Company, 25, 26, 28
social activities, 21–22
Union Fire Company, 18
Vigilant Fire Company, *25*
Watchman Fire Company, 17
voting rights
  and property, 65
  and working class, 64–65
Vulcan Alley, 36

Waesche Street, 176, 178
Waggon Alley, 36
Walbrook High School, 259
Walker, Charles T., 154
Walker, Hale, 184
Wall Street Journal, 213
Wallace, Lew, 133
Wallis, Severn Teackle, 111, 117
War Manpower Commission (WMC),
  173, 178, 179
Ware, John, 137–138
Ware, John Fathergill Waterhouse,
  142, 143
Warner & Hanna, *35*, 36
Warren, Dwight, 217
Washington (D.C.), 108, 159, 160,
  163, 175, 187
Washington, Earline, 217
Washington Street, 42
Watchman Fire Company, 17
Wayman, Alexander, 150, *151*, 161
Weglein, David, 250–251
Welch, Louella, 266

Welcome Alley, 36
welfare agencies, 10
Well Baby Clinic, 204
Wesolowski, Bronislaw, 45
West Baltimore, 149
  African Americans in, 44, 149
  Waesche Street, 176, 178
West Biddle Street, 153, 156
West Indies, wheat, 4
West Virginia, 159
Westerm Maryland Railway, Port
  Covington, 173
Western Electric, 173
  Point Breeze, 182
Western High School, 251
Westminster (Md.), 12
Wethered, Samuel, 112
wheat, 4, 5
Whelpley, John, 68
Whig Party, 93, 97, 100, 102, 104
Whisky Alley, 36
white flight, 10
White, Milton N., 151
white supremacy, 8
Whitesborough (N.Y.), 71
Wild Ones, The, 213
Wilkins, Roy, 252
William H. Lemmel Junior High
  School, 255–256
William S. Baer School, 252
Williams, George, 78
Williams, M., 151
Williams, W. Edward, 156–157
Williams, William, 77, 84
Wilmington (Del.), 68
Wilson, William Julius, 215
Winans, Ross, 111
Winder, William, 74
Wolfe Street, 40
women, exclusion, 82
Women's Guild of the Fells Point
  Mission, 17
Wood, Edith Elmer, 200
Wood, Elizabeth, 209, 214, 218
Wood, Gordon, 18
Woods' City Directory, 134

working class
African Americans, 39–40
and alley houses, 34, 38, 39–40, 42
social activities, 22–23
and support for secession, 110
and working class, 64–65
World War II, 5, 6, 172, 191, 192, 227
WPA, 175
Wyatt, W. E., 73, 74

yellow fever, 49, 50

epidemic of 1797, 49
YMCA of Maryland, 152
YMCA (Young Men's Christian
Association), 25, 149, 204
exclusivity of, 150
Young Men's Christian Association.
see YMCA
Young Women's Christian Associa-
tion. *see* YWCA
YWCA (Young Women's Christian
Association), 204